Sarbanes-Oxley
Guide for Finance and Information Technology Professionals

Sarbanes-Oxley
Guide for Finance and Information Technology Professionals

SANJAY ANAND

WILEY

John Wiley & Sons, Inc.

SOCKET (Sarbanes-Oxley Compliant Key Enterprise Technology) is trademarked by the Sarbanes-Oxley Group.

Library of Congress
Cataloging in Publication Division
101 Independence Avenue, S.E.
Washington, DC 20540-4320

Library of Congress
CIP 20540-4320
9140 East Hampton Drive
Capitol Heights, MD 20743

Library of Congress Cataloging-in-Publication Data
Anand, Sanjay.
 Sarbanes-Oxley guide for finance and information technology professionals / Sanjay Anand.
  p. cm.
 Includes index.
 ISBN-13: 978-0-471-78553-8 (cloth)
 ISBN-10: 0-471-78553-9 (cloth)
 1. United States . Sarbanes-Oxley Act of 2002. 2. Corporations—Accounting—Law and legislation—United States. 3. Disclosure of information—Law and legislation—United States. 4. Financial statements—Law and legislation—United States. I. Title.

KF1446.A945 2006
346.73 06648—dc22   2005031928

Printed in the United States of America

10 9 8 7 6 5 4 3 2

This guide is dedicated to my family and to the innocents who have endured the harsh consequence of corporate fraud.

Contents

Preface

(For updates and worksheets, visit www.SarbanesOxleyGuide.com.)

This book is a comprehensive, authoritative guide to getting your organization compliant with Sarbanes-Oxley. It provides a foundation and an advanced reference for finance and information technology (IT) executives, professionals, and consultants who are involved in or are looking to get involved in Sarbanes-Oxley–related compliance projects. Among other things, the book addresses:

- Key aspects and components of the Sarbanes-Oxley Act.
- A methodology to achieve Sarbanes-Oxley compliancy for your company.
- The road map to compliance, including checklists, worksheets, and project plans.
- The business and technology implications and resource requirements for compliance.
- The future of Sarbanes-Oxley and its impact on corporate America and the world.

The book includes practical, actionable advice that all finance and IT professionals must have at their fingertips as they pursue, or consider pursuing, a journey of Sarbanes-Oxley compliance. Because of the enormity of the Act itself, this book is by no means all-encompassing. Nevertheless, it is a comprehensive guide and an extremely valuable reference book for Sarbanes-Oxley compliance for your organization.

Since the world of Sarbanes-Oxley is not static, and neither is the body of knowledge associated with it, please visit *www.Sarbanes OxleyGuide.com* for recent updates and new worksheets as they are posted to the website.

Acknowledgements

Producing a comprehensive guide like this one requires a team effort. I am grateful to my team at the Sarbanes-Oxley Group and elsewhere, listed here in alphabetical order by last name, for assisting me with the creation of this book:

Paul J. Boller, CPA, CISA, CIA, CFSA, in Switzerland
—for constructive feedback and edits.

Madeleine Ferris, CMA, CSOX, at FEI in Calgary, Canada
—for contributing to the appendices.

Vikas V. Gupta, PhD, at Inkorus in Bombay, India
—for helping to create the SOCKET Framework.

David Kimball, CMA, near Boston, Massachusetts
—for providing process-related content.

John LaCagnina, PMP, CSOX, at KPMG in New York
—for the project management aspects.

Dianna Podmoroff, CHRP, in Vancouver, Canada
—for the finance and human resource context.

Robert Schwind, CSOX, at GKBN in Albany, New York
—for security and related IT aspects.

Joann Skiba, Director, ISACA, in Chicago, Illinois
—for COBIT-related reprint permissions.

William Suda, AICPA in Jersey City, New Jersey
—for COSO-related reprinted permissions.

Jennifer Tran, CSOX, at Oracle in Teaneck, New Jersey
—for providing the enterprise context.

John Wiley & Sons, Inc.'s staff across the United States
—for editorial and publishing expertise.

Thanks also to our families, who allowed us to spend many nights and weekends working on this guide so that we could bring it to you.

Introduction

The Enron fiasco forever changed investor and public reliance on self-regulation measures for accounting and financial reporting. Not since the stock market crash of 1929 and the Great Depression in the 1930s has so much attention been paid to federal securities laws and financial and reporting methodology for public companies. The result has been a staggering shock to the financial and information systems of public companies, as executives and their boards scramble to make sense of, and comply with, the new regulations.

The Sarbanes-Oxley Act of 2002 (PUBLIC LAW 107–204—JULY 30, 2002 - 116 STAT. 745) was enacted after the Enron and World-Com debacles, in response to the resulting dramatic loss of faith in the governance of public companies. As a remedial measure, this Act significantly affects the day-to-day functions of all top-level management and executives of public companies, particularly the CEO, the CFO, and top information officers.

The Act created a five-member Public Company Accounting Oversight Board (PCAOB), which has the authority to set and enforce auditing, attestation, quality control, and ethics (including independence) standards for public companies. The Act gives the PCAOB the right to impose disciplinary and remedial sanctions for violations of the board's rules, securities laws, and professional auditing standards. The Securities and Exchange Commission (SEC) has adopted many of the Sarbanes-Oxley provisions, and the breadth and depth of these changes ensure that CEOs, CFOs, and CIOs must pay close attention to the systems the corporation has set for reporting and auditing of all financial information and securities transactions.

The main goal of the Sarbanes-Oxley Act is to protect investors and increase their confidence in public companies. Specific measures of the Act require that a company's CEO and CFO each certify quarterly and annually that:

He or she reviewed the report being filed.

To his or her knowledge, the report does not contain any untrue statements or omit any material facts.

The financial statements and other financial information fairly present, in all material respects, the financial position, results of operations, and cash flows.

He or she is responsible for, and has designed, established, and maintained, disclosure controls and procedures (DC&P), as well as evaluated and reported on the effectiveness of those controls and procedures within 90 days of the report filing date.

Effectively, this means that on a daily basis, the certifying officers need to ensure that systems are set up and monitored sufficiently to satisfy themselves that all disclosure procedures and controls are operating effectively. In its comment on the Act, the SEC stated:

> *An overall purpose of internal control over financial reporting is to foster the preparation of reliable financial statements. Reliable financial statements must be materially accurate. Therefore, a central purpose of the assessment of internal control over financial reporting is to identify material weaknesses that have, as indicated by their very definition, more than a remote likelihood of leading to a material misstatement in the financial statements. While identifying control deficiencies and significant deficiencies represents an important component of management's assessment, the overall focus of internal control reporting should be on those items that could result in material errors in the financial statements.[1]*

Although the Sarbanes-Oxley Act has not established specific rules and standards for reporting on internal controls and procedures for financial reporting, it is the responsibility of the CEO, CFO, and CIO to establish these guidelines and manage them diligently to remain in compliance with the Act. Ultimately, this Act guarantees that a corporation's commitment to transparent and ethical reporting methodology is as important as its commitment to its bottom line; and government, investors, and the public are looking to top executives to make this happen.

EVENTS LEADING UP TO THE ACT

The last major crisis that prompted a serious overhaul of the accounting and financial reporting standards for public companies came after the stock market crash of 1929. The crash resulted in vast investor losses and the subsequent financial depression. The federal government's response was to establish the Securities and Exchange Commission by the Securities Act of 1933 and the Securities Exchange Act of 1934. The SEC was given statutory authority to set accounting standards and oversight over the activities of auditors. The role of establishing auditing standards was left to the accounting profession.

The accounting profession formed a series of committees that, between 1938 and 1959, issued 51 authoritative pronouncements that formed the basis of what is now known as generally accepted accounting principles (GAAP). Today, the Financial Accounting Standards Board (FASB) sets the ground rules for measuring, reporting, and disclosing information in financial statements of nongovernmental entities. These accounting standards cover a wide range of topics: everything from broad concepts, such as revenue and income recognition, to more specific rules, such as how to report information about the company's different businesses. The SEC officially recognizes the FASB's accounting standards as authoritative.

REGULATION OVERHAUL

For the past 60 years, the U.S. accounting profession's system of self-regulation—including peer review, a Public Oversight Board (POB), Quality Control Inquiry Committee (QCIC), Professional Ethics Division, and Continuing Professional Education (CPE)—has helped create one of the most respected financial markets in the world. Then the plight of Enron spurred a public debate over the effectiveness and ethics of the financial accounting, reporting, and auditing processes.

On December 2, 2001, less than a month after it admitted to accounting errors and irregularities that had inflated earnings by almost $600 million since 1994, Enron Corporation filed for bankruptcy protection. With $62.8 billion in assets, it became the largest bankruptcy in U.S. history.

The day Enron filed for bankruptcy, its stock closed at 72 cents, down more than $75 from a year earlier. Many employees lost their life savings, and tens of thousands of investors lost billions. Shortly after this, WorldCom, crippled by $41 billion in debt and a recent disclosure that it had hidden $3.9 billion in expenses, filed for bankruptcy protection with $107 billion in assets, thus taking over the title of the largest bankruptcy ever filed in the United States.

GOVERNMENT REACTION

On July 30, 2002, President George W. Bush signed into law the Sarbanes-Oxley Act of 2002; the most dramatic change to federal securities laws since the 1930s. The Act dramatically redesigns federal regulations regarding corporate governance and reporting obligations of public companies. It also significantly tightens accountability standards for directors and top executives, including the CEO, CFO, CIO, auditors, securities analysts, and legal counsel.

The Act is organized into 11 titles dealing with auditor independence, corporate responsibility, enhanced financial disclosures, conflicts of interest and corporate accountability, among other things (see Exhibit I.1).

Key Components of the Act

Sections 301 through 308, dealing with corporate responsibility, and Sections 401 to 409, dealing with enhanced financial disclosures, are the most compelling sections and the ones that have received the most attention and analysis. Section 302, pertaining to disclosure controls and procedures, and Section 404, pertaining to internal controls and procedures for financial reporting, are the two sections that are most relevant and have received the most scrutiny.

Section 302 mandates that with each quarterly filing, the CEO and CFO must each certify that they have evaluated the accuracy and effectiveness of the corporation's internal controls. In addition, they must disclose all significant deficiencies, material weaknesses, and acts of fraud. Section 906 also requires certification of the financial reports in a separate document. Section 404 requires an annual eval-

EXHIBIT I.1   Components of the Sarbanes-Oxley Act

Components	Sections
Title I Public Company Accounting Oversight	101–109
Title II Auditor Independence	201–209
Title III Corporate Responsibility	301 –308
Title IV Enhanced Financial Disclosures	401–409
Title V Analyst Conflicts of Interest	501
Title VI Commission Resources and Authority	601–604
Title VII Studies and Reports	701–705
Title VIII Corporate and Criminal Fraud Accountability	801–807
Title IX White-Collar Crime Penalty Enhancements	901–906
Title X Corporate Tax Returns	1001
Title XI Corporate Fraud and Accountability	1101–1107

uation of internal controls and procedures of financial reporting and auditing. Under these provisions, a company must document its internal control mechanisms that have a direct impact on its financial reporting, evaluate them for compliance, and disclose any gaps and deficiencies. For further control, an independent auditor must issue a written report that attests to management's certification on the effectiveness of the corporation's internal financial and audit controls, its procedures, and its financial reporting.

For the first time in history, failure to comply with the certification and disclosure requirements can and will result in personal criminal liability (steep fines and/or imprisonment) for the executives involved. According to the new legislation, "corporate negligence is equally sanctionable as deliberate malfeasance."

It is clear that familiarity with the compliance requirements of the Sarbanes-Oxley Act is critical from both a corporate and personal standpoint. Although the entire Act is too large for this book to cover every regulation in detail, there are some key regulations implement-

:ritical sections of Sarbanes-Oxley that executives and man-
ke need to be aware of:

- **Section 101: Public Company Accounting Oversight Board (PCAOB) Membership.** The board shall consist of five full-time members (two CPAs and three non-CPAs) who are all financially literate. No member of the board may be receiving payment or sharing in the profit of any public accounting firm other than retirement benefits or other fixed payments. The chair may not have practiced as a CPA within the previous five years.
- **Section 103: PCAOB's Duties.** The board is responsible for:
  - Setting the budget and managing its operations.
  - Establishing "auditing, quality control, ethics, independence, and other standards relating to the preparation of audit reports for issuers."
  - Registering and inspecting accounting firms.
  - Investigating irregularities and imposing appropriate sanctions.
  - Enforcing compliance with the Act and other laws or standards relating to the preparation and issuance of audit reports.
  - Performing other duties as required.

  The board must adopt an audit standard to implement the internal control review required by Section 404.
- **Section 105: PCAOB Investigations.** Information received or prepared by the PCAOB shall be "confidential and privileged as an evidentiary matter (and shall not be subject to civil discovery or other legal process) in any proceeding in any Federal or State court or administrative agency, unless and until presented in connection with a public proceeding or [otherwise] released." No sanctions report will be made available to the public unless and until stays pending appeal have been lifted.
- **Section 107(d): PCAOB Sanctions.** The SEC has the right to require the board to carry out additional responsibilities, such as keeping certain records, and it can inspect the board as necessary.
- **Section 107(c): Review of Disciplinary Action Taken by the PCAOB.** The SEC can change, cancel, reduce, or increase sanctions applied by the board.
- **Section 108: Accounting Standards.** The SEC recognizes GAAP and all the principles therein, and any new procedures must adhere to the GAAP principles.

- **Section 201: Prohibited Activities of Professional Service Providers.** The firm that supplies auditing services to a client cannot provide bookkeeping or other accounting record service to the audit client; financial information systems design and implementation; appraisal or valuation services; actuarial services; internal audit outsourcing services; management functions or human resources; brokerage, investment adviser, or investment banking services; legal services; or any other service that the board determines, by regulation, is impermissible.
- **Section 206: Conflict of Interest.** The CEO, controller, CFO, and so on cannot have worked for the company's external audit firm in the year preceding the audit.
- **Section 301: Public Company Audit Committees.** The audit committee is to be made up of board members who are guaranteed to be independent and free of interests that conflict with those of the corporation.
- **Section 302: Certification.** CEOs and CFOs must certify in each reporting period that the information presented is accurate and fairly represents the financial position of the company and operational results. Certifying officers will face penalties for false certification of $1 million and/or up to 10 years' imprisonment for a "knowing" violation and $5 million and/or up to 20 years' imprisonment for a "willing" violation.
- **Section 304: Forfeiture of Certain Bonuses and Profits.** If an issuer is required to prepare an accounting restatement due to a material noncompliance of the issuer, as a result of misconduct, with any financial reporting requirement under the securities laws, the CEO and CFO of the issuer shall reimburse the issuer for any bonus or other incentive-based or equity-based compensation received by that person from the issuer during the 12-month period following the first public issuance or filing with the SEC (whichever first occurs) of the financial document embodying such financial reporting requirement; and any profits realized from the sale of securities of the issuer during that 12-month period.
- **Section 306: Blackout Periods.** Officers, directors, and other insiders may not purchase or sell stock during blackout periods.
- **Section 401(a): Disclosures in Periodic Reports.** All financial reports are to be prepared according to GAAP and shall "reflect

all material correcting adjustments . . . that have been identified by a registered accounting firm . . . ."

- **Section 401 (c): Off-Balance Sheet Disclosures.** The SEC shall study off-balance sheet disclosures to determine the extent of the transaction and whether GAAP rules were applied such that the transactions are transparent to investors.
- **Section 402: Prohibition of Personal Loans to Executives.** No public company, except consumer credit institutions, may loan or renew a loan of a personal nature to its executive officers or directors. A credit company may issue consumer loans and credit cards to its directors and executive officers if it does so in the ordinary course of business on the same terms and conditions offered to the general public.
- **Section 403: Disclosures of Insider Trades.** Directors, officers, and 10 percent owners must report insider trades within two business days of the transaction.
- **Section 404: Internal Controls.** Management must state their responsibility in establishing, maintaining, and analyzing the internal control structure, and must assess the effectiveness of such processes.
- **Section 406: Codes of Ethics.** A corporation is required to have a code of ethics that addresses financial data and record integrity. If a corporation does not have a code of ethics it must justify its position.
- **Section 407: Financial Expert.** At least one member of the audit committee must be a "financial expert," a person who has education and experience as a public accountant, auditor, principal financial officer, controller, or principal accounting officer.
- **Section 409: Real-Time Disclosure.** Issuers must disclose information on material changes in the financial condition or operations of the issuer on a rapid and current basis.
- **Title VIII: Corporate and Criminal Fraud:**
  - It is a felony to "knowingly" obstruct a federal investigation by tampering with documents or other such actions.
  - Auditors are required to maintain records for five years.
  - Section 806—Employees are given "whistleblower protection" that prohibits the employer from taking retaliatory action against employees who disclose information relevant to a fraud claim.

- **Title IX: White-Collar Crime:**
  - Maximum imprisonment for mail and wire fraud is increased from five to ten years.
  - Tampering with a record or otherwise obstructing a proceeding is a crime.
  - A CEO or CFO who knowingly or willfully certifies financial reports that are misleading faces a fine of up to $5 million and/or imprisonment of up to 20 years.
- **Section 1102: Tampering with a Record.** It a crime to alter, destroy, or conceal any document with the intent to obstruct an official proceeding; the penalty is up to 20 years in prison and a fine.
- **Section 1105: Prohibited Board Members.** A person who has committed securities fraud may be prohibited by the SEC from serving as a board member.

IMPACT OF THE ACT

The Sarbanes-Oxley Act of 2002 requires public companies to validate the accuracy and integrity of their financial accounting and reporting processes, and the management thereof. The processes and documentation required for compliance are rigorous and require a commitment from all members of the organization. From the CEO to the accounting clerk to the information specialist, all employees must operate using ethical and accurate standards, and those standards must be communicated through, and reinforced by, the corporate culture.

SARBANES-OXLEY AND CORPORATE CULTURE

It is one thing to create new laws and regulations and expect companies to follow them, but it is an entirely different matter to efficiently implement those changes. That is where corporate culture comes into play. The "tone from the top" is a crucial element in achieving change of this magnitude and importance.

The message prior to Sarbanes-Oxley was primarily profit driven; now corporate communication needs to emphasize realistic expectations and goals for the company and staff. This means that, from setting sales targets to planning budgets, all goals must be fundamentally achievable without cutting corners or concealing information. Crucial to this process are managers who walk the talk and encourage open lines of communication between management and staff.

To ensure open communication, ethics programs should be implemented and followed. No longer a gratuitous (and often ignored) function of the human resources (HR) department, ethics programs will serve as the vehicle through which employees can report suspected misconduct without fear of penalty or reprisal. Section 301 of the Sarbanes-Oxley Act requires each audit committee of a public company to establish procedures for the receipt of confidential and anonymous submissions by employees regarding questionable accounting or auditing matters. Section 806 requires corporations to set up a formal whistleblowing program that protects the anonymity of informants and protects them from reprisals. Employees must understand corporate rules and regulations and have a clear idea of how their role fits within their departments and with the overall mission of the company. It is imperative that all employees feel connected to, and part of, the business.

This connection also means understanding that strict penalties can be imposed on individuals, throughout the ranks, for not properly reporting financial matters. Because management must certify that the financial information they are presenting to the public is accurate, they will expect their accounting, finance, and information professionals to adhere to the highest professional and ethical standards. Managers need to set this example and incorporate a best-practices routine for their staff to model. That means taking the time to review documentation, asking questions about the numbers and information sources, and addressing issues as they arise. Rubber-stamping is no longer acceptable. Due diligence does not indicate distrust in a colleague's work; rather; it reinforces the importance of accurate reporting and attending to issues at the source so that they can be rectified and abated.

SARBANES-OXLEY AND THE FINANCE DEPARTMENT

The finance department will undergo enormous change as Sarbanes-Oxley–related reforms roll out. The Act is viewed by many as, primarily, a finance act; though that is not entirely true, finance carries the burden of proving to the rest of the company, the board, the auditors, and the investors that the corporation is in compliance. Regardless of who sits on the committees or who else makes certifications, when it comes to financial reporting the go-to person will be the CFO.

The most obvious and potent change for the CFO is the responsibility status of the position. The CFO and the CEO have joint responsibility for certifying that all reports of financial information are accurate and truthful, and that the systems that generated the reports are effective and reliable. The CFO no longer has one more chain of command to report to in terms of information integrity; his or her neck is on the line with liability equal to that of the CEO. Even if CFOs had formerly considered themselves to be the second-in-command, now there is no doubt that the stakes of the position have been raised. The added pressure of this level of responsibility and accountability is daunting at best and terrifying at worst. The whole transacting, data-recording, data-manipulating, report-generating machine is in need of a tune-up or major overhaul—and the consequences of failure include personal, criminal liability. The role of the CFO will be integral and highly influential in the change process.

Change management is discussed often enough, but the fact is, for many companies, changes to get in line with Sarbanes-Oxley will be the most significant they have ever experienced. Change of this magnitude requires paramount leadership ability and, as a leader in this process, the CFO will need a big bag of tricks. The sheer number and diversity of people that must be involved in the process will make for very lively discussion in the conference rooms, halls, offices, and cubicles throughout the corporation. Many executives think of change as an organizational dynamic that the HR department deals with; to keep from being steamrolled in this process, the CFO requires some change management skills of his or her own.

To mange change, the people in charge have to be leaders in all senses of the word. Visionary, inspiring, motivating, dedicated—all those qualities will be necessary for the CFO and the compliance team to accomplish their task. They will also have to have a great deal of confidence in fellow team members to carry out their duties, and pay attention to whom they will delegate duties. Likely, the CFO will be working closely with people with whom he or she previously had little contact. The information technology (IT) department is the most obvious inclusion in this group, but HR, marketing and sales, and heads of the other strategic business units (SBUs) may also be unfamiliar teammates. The divergent nature of the cross-functional team will present many challenges and opportunities for all members of the organization to gain an understanding and appreciation of the value each department brings to the table. Because Sarbanes-Oxley reform goes way beyond finance and essentially dictates a new way of doing business, the corporation has a prime opportunity and responsibility to make the most of the changes.

Instituting broad-sweeping, corporate-wide reform will take a concerted effort from all departments, and will thrust the CFO into a main leadership role. Aside from personal liability, the CFO will have high visibility in the process, so this is the perfect venue in which to prove (or disprove) his or her leadership ability. The CFO will have to transform the entire finance department into a transparent, team-oriented unit; unfortunately, this will be quite a leap for many. The finance department will be looked at as a model for the new and open atmosphere that is necessary for the data integrity and accuracy demanded by Sarbanes-Oxley.

To ensure dependable data and transparent operations, it will be necessary to shift the focus of finance from being the department that controls the money to being the department that ensures forthrightness. Rather than being seen as the gatekeeper of the money and the approver of expenses, the CFO will need to establish an environment that is forgiving of over-budgets and understanding of unforeseen expenses. These are the situations that drive many of the less-than-accurate transactions that are recorded and are what motivate otherwise honest managers to fudge the numbers a little. Of additional concern are HR policies that rely on aggressive financial and sales targets for pay incentive programs. All of the executives, the board, and corporate programs will need to embrace the new idea of operational integrity by supporting the CFO and communicating the message to the employees.

Because all data recording processes eventually entail human intervention, the best way to mitigate dishonesty is to remove the motivators. The CEO and the CFO have added motivation to ensure that this occurs because Sarbanes-Oxley sets out very foreboding, personal consequences for them if the system fails. Sarbanes-Oxley provisions that affect the CFO directly include:

- CEOs and CFOs are required to certify all reports that contain financial statements.
- CEOs and CFOs are required to certify both annual and quarterly reports. Furthermore, they must certify that all facts in the annual report are true and that no significant information or facts have been left out.
- If a corporation must restate its financial information, those CEOs or CFOs found to be in violation of the rule will lose any bonuses and all other incentives for the one-year period prior to the first filing of the misleading financial information.
- It is the responsibility of CEOs and CFOs to identify, establish, and maintain internal controls, and to make sure that they are apprised of all material information.
- Any CEO, CFO, or other individual found to have destroyed, falsified, or changed records after a company declares bankruptcy, or during a federal investigation, may be fined, imprisoned for up to 20 years, or both.

These responsibilities and sanctions directly discourage the top two sources of fraudulent human intervention. It is the responsibility of the CEO and the CFO to demonstrate and drive down the tenets of honestly, integrity, and ethics to the rest of the company.

The CFO can approach Sarbanes-Oxley with negativity, viewing it as a migraine headache on steroids; or he or she can embrace the revolutionary reforms as a perfect opportunity to grow the profession and improve U.S. corporations. The fallout bonuses include a richer understanding of the corporation and all its departments, an opportunity to drive up the value of finance, and a chance to reap the many benefits that come with increased responsibility and respect.

SARBANES-OXLEY AND THE IT DEPARTMENT

Sarbanes-Oxley, the new financial reporting law, likely means huge changes to information systems technology. One of the principal ways in which corporations and corporate executives can reduce their corporate, and now personal, liabilities is to implement changes to the IT infrastructures that support the compliance and disclosure demands of Sarbanes-Oxley. Some industry analysts are saying that bringing systems into compliance with the Act may overshadow the time and expense invested in Y2K fixes. Addressing Y2K was a single task, but the changes necessary to achieve Sarbanes-Oxley compliance are expected to take place on an evolutionary basis as systems are updated and integrated. Even companies whose systems appear to comply with the Act are uncertain as to exactly what some provisions mean; ultimately, costly overhauls to budgeting, reporting, and decision-support systems across the company may be necessary. The result is that many companies are expecting to implement major systems changes related to governance and compliance issues.

Corporate responsibility is foremost in the changes mandated by Sarbanes-Oxley. Section 302 requires the CEO and CFO to sign statements verifying the completeness and accuracy of financial reports. This means that executives who are liable at report-signing time will demand systems that are accurate, timely, and tamper-proof. The accuracy demanded will place enormous pressure on the multitude of information systems running in a company. Because this section requires executives to sign off not only on their companies' financial statements, but also on the control processes that surround the collection of the data behind them—down to the transaction level—the IT department will be charged with auditing and verifying each step in a transaction, from order, to payment, to storage of data, to aggregation into financial reports. This will also require a process for monitoring each step, and includes a procedure to alert key people to breaches in or failures of the system. This may necessitate the enhancement of current systems or the incorporation of systems that can enforce business rules and transform data without human intervention, or software that can report exceptions and alert internal or external auditors when something goes awry.

Although complete tamper-proofing is probably impossible, given the fact that any minor error in any of the thousands of processes involved in the system will have to be fixed to ensure accuracy; financial data must be made as secure as humanly possible. This will require absolute diligence in creating secure systems that manage financial information separate from the places where data is stored. Because systems are only as secure as the people who have access to them, users should be limited to those systems that are essential to their job function; only system administrators should maintain the underlying database of information.

Accuracy is one element of the changes required and speed is another. Section 409 requires that companies report changes in financial condition "on a rapid and current basis" and that they have systems for "real-time disclosure." Sarbanes-Oxley significantly reduces the time allowed for filing of reports:

- Quarterly reports must be filed within 35 days of quarter-end (down from 45 days) by 2005.
- Annual reports must be filed within 60 days of year-end (down from 75 days) by 2005.
- Disclosure of "material events" and insider trades must be filed within two days.

The speed of a system and its integration processes must be able to keep up with these rigorous information demands. Older systems, such as legacy Cobol-based transaction processing systems or terminal-based order entry systems, will not allow for such fast processing, and flat-file batches or other periodic data transfer methods may hamper efficient integration.

Companies that have been proactive with financial-consolidation software systems have likely focused on integrating budget, reports, planning, and analysis tools. Thus, many of the systems needed to provide a complete view of the operation's functions will have been left out. Financial data and nonfinancial indicators will have to be interfaced to provide the detail that the SEC requires under Sarbanes-Oxley. To accomplish this task, many internal processes will have to be put in place to facilitate it. Essentially, an entire organization will require change, and the organization will expect IT to lead, not stand in the way.

This is a huge undertaking that will involve many person-hours and, sometimes, prohibitive budgets. The accuracy of the reports coming out is an absolute requirement, and a great deal of money will be spent accomplishing that objective; the need to tighten the time frame for reporting will put even greater pressure on IT resources stretched thin by these other commitments. Large companies will just have to find the money and other resources somewhere; smaller companies that are still relying on spreadsheet-based solutions face huge obstacles and costs that have the potential to affect business operations and efficiencies.

Sarbanes-Oxley will require radical changes to the manner and speed of information flow within the corporation: IT and its value position will change forever.

Financial system overhauls will have to address all the control, monitoring, and reporting processes of a company, meaning that a top-to-bottom examination of any and all systems, from inventory control to payroll, will be required. IT departments and the company will likely face higher labor costs as they prepare to meet the compliance regulations and then maintain the systems afterward. Requests for system changes will likely come fast and often, and projects that might have seemed unjustifiable from a cost-benefit standpoint in the past will likely take on new significance under Sarbanes-Oxley rules.

As daunting as the task of overhauling a company's IT system is, the CIO faces an even stronger legal hazard from the rollout of the Sarbanes-Oxley Act. As it becomes more and more apparent that IT is an integral link in the financial reporting system, CIOs will likely be held to the same liability standards as CEOs and CFOs when it comes to assuring the accuracy of reports. In April 2003, Health-South's CIO, Kenneth Livesay, was fired and pleaded guilty to federal charges of falsifying financial information and conspiracy to commit wire and securities fraud. He and seven other financial employees, including the CFO and Chief Controller, admitted their guilt in the scheme to artificially inflate HealthSouth's earnings and assets during the past several years. The information coming out is only as good as the information going in, and the onus will be on the IT department to ensure data integrity, reliability, and accuracy.

SARBANES-OXLEY AND CORPORATE MANAGEMENT

Despite the grumbling about the cost to deploy systems that will enable corporations to comply with Sarbanes-Oxley–initiated reforms, the consensus among senior executives is that the outcome will benefit corporations as much as investors. By leveraging the controls put in place under Sarbanes-Oxley, corporations will have much more accurate and timely data with which to make all business decisions. Benefits of this process include:

- Improved flow of information, allowing better business decisions.
- Better management of resources.

- Streamlined operations.
- Improved investor relations.
- Enhanced reputation for integrity and reliable financial reporting.

The notion that accurate and timely data will improve operating efficiency is certainly not new, and the ideal of transparent and ethical treatment of business data has always been lauded. Sarbanes-Oxley is the catalyst that has brought all these elements to the forefront, out of theoretical posturing and into actual solutions. All three factors will work together to ultimately create stronger corporations that have greater sustainability in economic downturns.

Accurate data is an obvious necessity when making any business decision, from the mundane to the momentous. Senior management will need to instill this into every employee and every process so that accuracy becomes paramount, even over staying on budget. This certainly does not mean that assets should be used recklessly to maintain accurate records; rather, it simply means that the generally accepted business practice (GABP) is to choose the most accurate method rather than the cheapest method. This will mean a shift in focus for many corporations across all industries and of all sizes; however, the long-term benefits will outweigh the initial costs.

Second only to accurate information is the need for timely information. Accurate figures are most useful when they can be used to determine future practices rather than analyze historic events. With periodic reports coming out weeks and months after the closing date, many business decisions are made using insufficient forecasts and outdated information. Linking day-to-day operations with anticipated results will enable the management team to identify and react to divergences much quicker and much more effectively. Many hours are put into strategic planning, and timely information is key to keeping the corporation on course.

There will be little argument that timely and accurate data improves business efficiency. Transparency is the third factor that will ensure operational sustenance. Transparent accounting and reporting are key to investor satisfaction, and investors will ultimately keep the corporation healthy and prosperous. Investors want to have confidence that the information presented to them is historically correct, currently relevant, and future oriented. The difficulty will be in aligning these factors and bringing them together at the same time—both to meet Sarbanes-Oxley requirements and to meet future regulatory and economic challenges.

Compliance Committee

Integral to bringing this compliance effort to fruition will be an empowered, capable, and diverse compliance committee. The CEO in a small to mid-size organization and the CFO or other designate in a larger corporation will likely chair this committee. It will be extremely important to include the CIO and other key information and technology staff, because IT solutions will drive most of the changes required to achieve compliance reporting. Because this committee will identify and spearhead the reform movement, it will be extremely important that the whole organization know and understand the purpose and function of the committee and its authority to lead change.

To be effective, the compliance committee should team with other risk-management functions in the organization. This will broaden the perspective and give the various departments or business units the opportunity to contribute their expertise. The internal auditors will certainly be able to suggest many effective ways to identify and monitor areas that require attention.

Manufacturing and sales will be able to alert the committee to potential sources of error emanating from their departments. Human resources will be invaluable in the communication and rollout phases, and will provide necessary resource support for actual implementation of the plan. Sarbanes-Oxley compliance is a corporate-wide issue, and corporate-wide involvement will be required to develop new and improved systems for integrating and controlling the flow of information within and outside the company.

Centralized versus Decentralized Strategies

When attempting change that requires corporate-wide involvement, it will be necessary to employ a more centralized approach to the management of the process. This is not to imply that Sarbanes-Oxley requires a centralized structure; it does mean that the tenets of centralization (such as uniform policies and procedures and hierarchical access controls) must be observed to assure the CEO and CFO that the reports they are certifying are correct. Improved controls usually mean more or tighter controls, and this will be necessary in the new reporting environment. It will be a fine line between control and autonomy.

While the pendulum keeps swinging on the centralized-versus-decentralized debate, the key factor in successful implementation of these new corporate governance standards will be acceptance by line and staff employees. The control systems put in place are only as trustworthy as the people who operate within them. Taking away too much autonomy alienates staff; giving them too much discretion and access creates too many risks. This is, again, where the "tone from the top" figures in. The board, the executives, and the compliance committee will need to communicate changes effectively and openly, and must create systems that employees will embrace and that will not create operational inefficiency or unnecessary burdens.

PROCESSES OR SYSTEMS?

The short answer is "Both." To further complicate the situation, the question of which will drive the other is analogous to the chicken-and-egg argument. Sarbanes-Oxley requires a shift in governance focus. The bottom line takes second place to honesty. Stakeholders will no longer tolerate incorrect, misleading, or fraudulent information or activity, so reform is needed that will cover business processes and control systems. As the two areas that drive how corporations operate and how employees make decisions, they are inextricably intertwined; changes in one will spur changes in the other, and vice versa. The important thing to keep in mind throughout the reform process is that the intention of Sarbanes-Oxley is to improve.

Analyzing business processes at the micro-level was not seen as a cost-effective activity prior to this legislation. As a result, there are likely a plethora of inefficiencies and unnecessary activities that go on daily because that is just how it has always been. The processes and procedures can now be looked at from an effectiveness standpoint and the systems can be analyzed for integrity; the opportunity to gain operational efficiency is enormous. Process deficiencies will lead to system failures and system failures will require the elimination of unnecessary or redundant processes. Sarbanes-Oxley unwittingly (or perhaps purposefully) gives corporations permission to examine their operations, and forgives the potential income losses related to the initial expenses of compliance.

For Sarbanes-Oxley to achieve the largest impact, even the smallest components of the organization require attention. Though much of the Act focuses on and discusses control systems, it is important to remember that systems and processes function together. The best controls can be put in place, but if operational processes do not support the new system, employees will act based on method rather than control. In the medium to long term, improved processes and systems will lead to improved corporate function, and ultimately will lead to more satisfied investors—a large feat based on the compound effect of many small process and system changes.

CONSEQUENCES OF NONCOMPLIANCE

Human nature being what it is, the Act seeks to ensure compliance through harsh sanctions. Sarbanes-Oxley creates new federal crimes, or broadens the scope of existing definitions, for obstruction of justice and securities fraud, with maximum prison time of 20 or 25 years, respectively. Sentences for many existing federal crimes were enhanced. Mail and wire fraud maximum penalties were quadrupled, from 5 to 20 years. The maximum sentence for some securities law violations was doubled from 10 to 20 years, and the maximum fine against a company for the same offense was increased from $2.5 million to $25 million.

The strength of the criminal penalties portion of Sarbanes-Oxley will depend on the government's success in prosecuting specific individuals. The statute's harsher penalties cannot be applied to crimes committed prior to passage of the law, so only time will tell their true effectiveness. For Sarbanes-Oxley to have the bite intended, corporate officers (considered the prime perpetrators of corporate misdeeds) are expected to have to serve prison time in addition paying to the hefty fines imposed.

CIVIL AND CRIMINAL PENALTIES

Sarbanes-Oxley has made a number of actions sanctionable under the Act. A list of the activities deemed criminal under the Sarbanes-Oxley Act, as well as by the New York City Office of the Comptroller, is found in Exhibit I.2.

EXHIBIT I.2   Actions and Penalties

Action	Penalty
Altering, destroying, or concealing any records with the intent of obstructing a federal investigation.	Fine and/or up to 10 years' imprisonment.
Failure to maintain audit or review "workpapers" for at least five years.	Fine and/or up to 5 years' imprisonment.
Anyone who "knowingly executes, or attempts to execute, a scheme" to defraud a purchaser of securities.	Fine and/or up to 10 years' imprisonment.
CEO or CFO who "recklessly" violates his or her certification of the company's financial statements.	Fine of up to $1 million and/or up to 10 years' imprisonment.
If the violation is "willful," the penalty increases.	Fine of up to $5 million and/or up to 20 years' imprisonment.
Conspiracy by two or more persons to commit any offense against, or to defraud, the United States or its agencies.	Fine and/or up to 10 years' imprisonment.
Any person who "corruptly" alters, destroys, conceals, etc., any records or documents with the intent of impairing the integrity of the record or document for use in an official proceeding.	Fine and/or up to 20 years' imprisonment.
Mail and wire fraud.	Penalty increase from 5 to 20 years' imprisonment.
Violating applicable Employee Retirement Income Security Act (ERISA) provisions.	Various lengths depending on violation.

ENDNOTE

1. Division of Corporation Finance, Office of the Chief Accountant, U.S. Securities and Exchange Commission, *Staff Statement on Management's Report on Internal Control over Financial Reporting* (May 16, 2005), *http://www.sec.gov/info/accountants/stafficreporting.htm* (accessed October 1, 2005).

PART I

Sarbanes-Oxley for the Finance Professional

CHAPTER 1

Scope and Assessment of the Act

Some pervasive themes emerge from the Sarbanes-Oxley Act, which is built on the following basic and key principles:

- Integrity
- Independence
- Proper oversight
- Accountability
- Strong internal controls
- Transparency
- Deterrence
- Corporate process management

INTEGRITY

The process of reporting and disclosing material information to stakeholders must be honest and truthful. The stability of the U.S. market depends on investor trust in the corporations and the systems in which they operate; Sarbanes-Oxley is the means to guarantee trust and integrity.

INDEPENDENCE

For a system to function reliably, it must have a certain degree of autonomy. For corporations, this means that the people entrusted to ensure fair and accurate representation must be impartial and independent. The auditors and board members must be free to operate objectively and in the best interests of investors to maintain stability in, and accuracy of, corporate reporting.

PROPER OVERSIGHT

Guidance and supervision are key elements at any level of management. This means that the executives (CEO, CFO, CIO, COO), the board, and the auditors need to have explicit means to evaluate the effectiveness of their governance and compliance systems. This also means ensuring that all systems are linked and that all departments and functions have effective methods of sharing compliance information.

ACCOUNTABILITY

All stakeholders, from investors to employees to customers, deserve accountability from the executives who manage the corporation in which they have a vested interest. Accountability breeds responsibility, and the tough, new standards of the Sarbanes-Oxley Act ensure that someone is accountable for the daily operations of the company and disclosure of the company's performance.

STRONG INTERNAL CONTROLS

To be effective, any system requires assiduous control systems. Internal controls are the measures against which corporate effectiveness is judged. Essentially, controls are the framework that an auditor will use to determine compliance, and Sarbanes-Oxley makes it absolutely necessary for corporations to design and implement explicit, effective internal controls that will guarantee that compliance.

TRANSPARENCY

The corporation's movements must be open to scrutiny from all angles. When all transactions are subject to public disclosure, transparency of the system acts as its own control system. Sarbanes-Oxley mandates transparent operations, which enhance corporate responsibility and governance.

DETERRENCE

Unfortunately, corporate executives, officials, and employees are human; thus, suitable and significant deterrents are required to discourage unacceptable behavior. Sarbanes-Oxley has introduced strong, new measures that introduce harsh penalties for white-collar crime and criminalize activity intended to obstruct justice or commit securities fraud.

CORPORATE PROCESS MANAGEMENT

Who is best suited to ramp a company up for Sarbanes-Oxley compliance? Is it the CFO, the CIO, both, or neither? See Exhibit 1.1.

The notion of IT irrelevance is at the core of who is best suited to lead the Sarbanes-Oxley challenge. The CIO is the keeper of the corporate data and it is the IT systems that will determine how financial information is recorded, tracked, and disclosed—yet many executives (CIOs included) view compliance with Sarbanes-Oxley as a finance issue, not a systems issue. Some recognize that IT has a role to play, but the focus is still on the finance department to lead the way.

EXHIBIT 1.1 Who Leads?

Joe, the CFO at XYZ Corporation, has been charged with implementing the changes necessary to comply with Sarbanes-Oxley and the new regulations imposed by the SEC. The current financial systems rely on spreadsheet solutions and, after much research, Joe has decided that the financial information must be consolidated and the whole process sped up. He knows he will need IT support to create the changes necessary and provide the software and hardware, but he is confident that he can design a control-system framework that IT can work with. He does not want to bother the CIO with his finance problems related to Sarbanes-Oxley, so he goes about the process of creating a wonderful, theoretical system that will allow information to flow through the company accurately and quickly. He presents his findings to the CEO, who is delighted, but when it comes times for application, the CIO comes up with many reasons why the plan is not practical or doable. "Trust IT to always be the stick in the wheel," Joe says.

Role of IT

Sarbanes-Oxley is financial legislation, but its implementation and compliance rest with the IT department. Sarbanes-Oxley requires a sophisticated set of internal controls that guide the creation of financial documents and disclosure of financial information in a timely and accurate manner. Because IT systems are used to generate, change, house, and transport that data, CIOs have to build controls that ensure that the information stands up to audit scrutiny.

If CIOs are considered ancillary to the process, how will the necessary systems be developed and controls put in place? It is imperative that IT be an integral component of Sarbanes-Oxley compliance; hence, the CIO will need to demonstrate a thorough understanding of the issues related to Sarbanes-Oxley. CFOs may resist letting the technology department play a central role in implementing the changes necessary to ensure data integrity. From finance's perspective, IT is a cost center, and therefore the CFO needs to manage this process in terms of value to the corporation rather than simply spending money on some requisite system upgrades. The CIO is in the unique position of understanding the importance of stringent controls and the functional difficulties of attaining them. Finance and IT are tightly bound in this process, so it is important that the corporation enable the two departments to work together to address the challenges of Sarbanes-Oxley.

Note: The idea that a *404* is a clueless person (as in a 404 message, meaning "file not found") is rapidly being replaced by the notion that being a 404 means you need to find the information fast, to comply with Section 404 of Sarbanes-Oxley.

Companies spend an enormous amount of time developing business plans and forecasts on which to base important decisions. It is critical that the information that drives their strategic decision making be accurate and timely. A 2003 survey by the Hackett Group found that 47 percent of companies used stand-alone spreadsheets for planning and budgeting.[1] Considering the importance of the information that comes out of these spreadsheets, it is alarming that a study by Rajalingham, Chadwick and Knight[2] found that 90 percent of the spreadsheets analyzed had significant errors. Actual or potential spreadsheet error will be unacceptable to CEOs and CFOs who must personally certify that the information in financial reports is true.

A critical challenge for Sarbanes-Oxley compliance will be to reduce the reliance on human processes in the flow of information and record management. This responsibility falls firmly on IT's shoulders, and the CIO will have to document usage rules and an audit trail for each system that contributes financial information. CIOs need to work closely with the Sarbanes-Oxley auditors to make sure that they know what their companies' weaknesses are and then take immediate action to remedy any problematic situations.

Analyst's Opinions and Recommendations

According to analysts, to meet compliance requirements, companies will want to:

- Determine whether the members of the audit committee and the majority of the board of directors meet the definition of *independent*.
- Review the existing code of ethics, making changes to meet Sarbanes-Oxley standards, if necessary.
- Put a code of ethics in place if one does not already exist.
- Determine the financial expertise of the members of the audit committee.
- Ensure that the company's benefit plans comply with restrictions during blackout periods.
- Ensure that any nonaudit services being performed do not violate Sarbanes-Oxley.
- Ensure that the CFO outlines what information must be reported and how quickly it must be reported.
- Ensure that computer technology has the ability to get information to the CFO in a timely fashion.
- Establish a process whereby the CFO will be able to inform the IT department of compliance issues in a timely manner.
- Identify internal processes that could possibly pose risks for the company.
- Consider having all directors, officers, and their families go through preclearance procedures before conducting transactions.
- Appoint an executive(s) to receive a power of attorney, which will allow him or her to sign off on reports.

- Appoint a disclosure committee, if one is not already in place, to help ensure that disclosures are accurate and complete. Appoint an individual from each part of the company, so all departments are covered. Then ensure that:
  - Everyone understands what the committee is accountable for.
  - A committee charter has been written and communicated to the appropriate personnel.
  - The committee has an agenda.
  - All committee members know their specific responsibilities.
  - The company is aware of the specific roles of members of the committee.
  - A process for resolving disputes is instituted among the disclosure committee, the CEO, and the CFO.
- Create a disclosure policy that is tailored specifically to meet the needs of the company.
- Ensure that if a policy is adopted, it will be adhered to.
- Ensure that the company practices and written policies are compatible. If you are doing something as a company practice that is not in the written form, change the written form so that you are in compliance.
- Test the effectiveness of controls and assess how they are doing overall.
- Have an internal audit function in place.
- Create and put into place a process, in compliance with the whistleblower mandate, that will allow employees to voice their concerns about possible company violations; this process should also allow them to express concerns about financial or business practices.
- Have the executive officers and audit committee ensure that the internal controls are effective and make efforts to correct any weaknesses.
- Implement dates by which completion of strengthening of weaknesses should be achieved; also, identify the plan of action that will lead to completion.
- Inspect liability insurance and coverage to ensure proper coverage and protection.
- Have the CFO outline, as clearly as possible, the internal processes of financial reports. This will allow the CFO to make determinations on where the company needs to improve its per-

formance to comply with Sarbanes-Oxley. According to one analyst, "The level of detail you have to get down to is pretty significant. You have to get down to the level of Excel spreadsheets and determine whether the people using them know what they are doing and whether or not they are being appropriately monitored and reviewed."

■ Create a protected hotline that will allow whistleblowers to call in with information.

ENDNOTES

1. The Hackett Group, Press Release, "Hackett Group Survey Reveals That Nearly Half of All Companies Ignore IT in Critical Elements of Sarbanes Oxley Compliance Efforts," December 16, 2003, Atlanta, GA.
2. K. Rajalingham, D. Chadwick, B. Knight, and D. Edwards, *Quality Control in Spreadsheets: A Software Engineering-Based Approach to Spreadsheet Development,* Thirty-Third Hawaii International Conference on System Sciences (Maui, Hawaii, January 4–7, 2000).

CHAPTER 2

Internal Controls

Good internal controls are no longer just best practice.
Internal control means different things to different people. Fortunately, the proposed SEC rule on Section 404 specifically discusses the definition of internal controls offered by the Committee of Sponsoring Organization (COSO), an independent group sponsored by five major accounting organizations, including the American Institute of Certified Public Accountants and the Institute of Internal Auditors.

COSO's definition of *internal control* is:

> *a process, effected by an entity's board of directors, management, and other personnel, designed to provide reasonable assurance regarding the achievement of objectives in the following categories:*
>
> - *Effectiveness and efficiency of operations;*
> - *Reliability of financial reporting;*
> - *Compliance with applicable laws and regulations.*

In 1992, COSO issued a report examining corporate fraud and what procedures could be put together to combat it. It recommended that companies adopt a framework within which all transactions are properly authorized, there are safeguards against improper use, and all transactions are recorded and reported. What that means is that every division in a company needs a documented set of internal rules that control how data is generated, manipulated, recorded, and reported.

In August 2003, the SEC introduced the term *internal control over financial reporting*, which is a version of the COSO definition specific to Sarbanes-Oxley requirements. *Internal control over financial reporting* is:

> *A process designed by, or under the supervision of, the issuer's principal executive and principal financial officers, or persons perform-*

ing similar functions, and effected by the issuer's board of directors, management and other personnel, to provide reasonable assurance regarding the reliability of financial reporting and the preparation of financial statements for external purposes in accordance with generally accepted accounting principles and includes those policies and procedures that:

- *Pertain to the maintenance of records that in reasonable detail accurately and fairly reflect the transactions and dispositions of the assets of the issuer;*
- *Provide reasonable assurance that transactions are recorded as necessary to permit preparation of financial statements in accordance with generally accepted accounting principles, and that receipts and expenditures of the issuer are being made only in accordance with authorizations of management and directors of the issuer; and*
- *Provide reasonable assurance regarding prevention or timely detection of unauthorized acquisition, use or disposition of the issuer's assets that could have a material effect on the financial statements.*

The last relevant requirements are the SEC's Disclosure Controls and Procedures, which are "designed to ensure that information required to be disclosed by a company in the reports filed by it under the Exchange Act is recorded, processed, summarized, and reported within the time periods specified by the SEC." The disclosures that must be made to stay in compliance with Sarbanes-Oxley must be certified just as the internal control systems are.

It is apparent that much of a company's success in compliance with Sarbanes-Oxley hinges on the establishment and management of effective and efficient internal controls and controls that regulate how information is disclosed. Although there is overlap, these controls are distinct and distinguishable. Internal control includes such things as signature requirements or periodic data checks, whereas a disclosure control relates to ensuring that information is tracked, recorded, summarized, and reported as required by the SEC.

COMPONENTS OF INTERNAL CONTROL

Internal control consists of five interrelated components that are derived from the way management runs a business, and are integrated with the management process.

Control Environment

The control environment is the foundation for all other components of internal control. It emanates from the corporate culture and it sets the tone for how employees view control and the way an organization deals with discipline and structure. Control environment factors include:

- Integrity, ethical values, and competence of the employees
- Management philosophy and operating style
- Assignment of authority and responsibility within the organization
- Organizational structure
- Training and development opportunities
- Degree of board involvement

Because the control environment sets the stage for all other elements of control within an organization, it is the crucial element in determining how effective the internal controls are. The best laid-out system will not survive if the environment it operates in does not support and encourage the various processes and rules.

Risk Assessment

All organizations are subject to internal and external risks that must be continuously assessed. *Risk assessment* involves identifying and analyzing risks that are relevant to the objectives of the firm, and it forms a basis for determining how the identified risks should be managed. Because risks will change with the economic, industrial, regulatory, and operating environments, mechanisms must be put in place to identify and deal with the risk of change.

Control Activities

Control activities are the policies and procedures that management develops to ensure that its objectives are met and its directives are carried out. They are the rules and regulations that guide employees to complete their tasks, and are established to maintain consistency and reliability within the organization. Control activities occur throughout the organization and include such things as approvals, authorizations, verifications, reconciliations, and reviews of operating performance, as well as security of assets and segregation of duties.

Information and Communication

Relevant information must be gathered and communicated to employees in a timely fashion to enable them to perform their duties. Information systems are charged with producing reports for operational, financial, and compliance-related programs, thus making it possible to run and control the business. Information systems gather both internal and external data, and assimilate that information into reports that are used to determine an appropriate course of action.

All communications must flow freely through the organization so that all employees have a clear understanding of what management expects from the control system and the type of control environment management wants to foster. Bottom-up flow is just as crucial to prevent blockages at lower levels, which have the potential to shut executives out of significant information loops. Regulation and control are also needed for the area of communication with external suppliers, customers, shareholders, and regulators.

Monitoring

Internal control systems have to be monitored diligently. Ongoing monitoring occurs in the course of operations, and includes regular management and supervisory activities, and other actions personnel take in performing their duties. The scope and frequency of evaluations will depend primarily on an assessment of risks and the effectiveness of ongoing monitoring procedures. Internal control deficiencies should be reported upstream, with serious matters reported to top management and the board. Control system development is not a static process; effectiveness should be evaluated over time and adjusted as necessary.

A continuous process of risk assessment, communication, risk management, and evaluation forms an effective internal control system. This continuous process ensures that the five components of an internal control system are in place and functioning, and it reinforces the importance of controls to the corporation's infrastructure. Built-in controls support quality and empowerment initiatives, avoid unnecessary costs, and enable quick responses to changing conditions. All components of internal control are relevant to each other, and they must all be present and functioning effectively for anyone to conclude that internal control over operations is effective.

PURPOSE OF INTERNAL CONTROL

The purpose of internal control is to aid the organization's efforts to achieve its operating goals and objectives and to assist in reliable financial reporting and compliance with regulations set out by law or other external sources. Essentially, a good control system is what leads the organization through its day-to-day operations, providing rules or guidelines for activities and identifying risks. Internal control is there for guidance, but it will not ensure absolute success or definite achievement of business goals. Even the most effective systems are subject to human management and changing regulatory, economic, and competitive environments.

Unfortunately, internal control systems cannot guarantee that financial reports are accurate or that the reports comply with all regulations. Achievement of these objectives is affected by things outside the sphere of internal control, including judgment errors, simple miscalculations, and plain old human mistakes. The need for an ability to override the system in case of such a mistake also opens the system up to error and corruption.

Roles and Responsibilities

Everyone in an organization has responsibility for internal control.

- **Management.** The CEO is ultimately responsible for the internal control system. He or she must provide leadership and direction to senior managers and review the way they are controlling the business. Senior managers then assign responsibility for establishment of more specific internal control policies and procedures to their employees, and the process repeats itself down to the control activities of the line and staff workers.

- **Board of Directors.** Management is accountable to the board, the members of which are objective and knowledgeable about the organization's activities. A strong and effective board needs to ensure that management cannot override the controls that have been put in place or suppress information that is significant to operations in an attempt to cover its tracks or claim ignorance later. This type of diligence requires good communication throughout the corporation, especially upward lines.
- **Internal Auditors.** Internal auditors, by their job description and expertise, play a crucial role in monitoring and evaluating the effectiveness of control systems. It is critical that they have enough autonomy and objectivity to report honestly; therefore, they should not be under any undue influence from executives.
- **Other Employees.** If internal control is to be effective, everyone in the organization must take some responsibility for it. Almost every employee will create or manipulate information that is input into a control system, so they must be aware of and understand the ramifications of mistakes or poor judgments. It is important that all employees have an avenue of communication to report problems or noncompliance; Sarbanes-Oxley's protection for whistleblowers is an explicit recognition of this.

DEVELOPING AN INTERNAL CONTROL SYSTEM

Fundamental steps in developing an internal control system that addresses the requirements of Sarbanes-Oxley are:

1. Establish a compliance committee.
2. Assess risk.
3. Set reporting objectives.
4. Prepare a formal implementation plan.
5. Communicate the procedures.
6. Provide training.
7. Document processes and risk management.
8. Perform continuous evaluation.

Establish a Compliance Committee

To manage the process of compliance with Sarbanes-Oxley, the corporation will need to develop collaborative committees that include, at a minimum, the CEO, the CFO, and the heads of any distinct business units. The compliance committee should also consist of executives and/or key staff in the finance, IT, legal, and internal audit departments.

Depending on the size of the organization, this may not be feasible; the bottom line is to have personnel on the committee who are committed to Sarbanes-Oxley compliance and can take a company-wide perspective when identifying risks and coming up with solutions. The corporation itself should commit to providing a workplace forum that is conducive to a coordinated effort. Effective communication and resource deployment will be critical; relying on e-mail communication will not be sufficient. The compliance committee should focus on:

- Communicating program objectives and initiatives.
- Managing the overall process and activities.
- Providing training, assessment resources, and tools as necessary.
- Engaging the various departments or business units to identify risks and solutions.
- Keeping the goals of the committee visible and compelling.

Assess Risk

As noted earlier, *risk assessment* is the process of identifying and analyzing both internal and external risks and threats to achievement of identified goals and objectives. It can be performed on any specific process within the organization, at all levels of the organization, and for the organization as a whole. Common sources of risk include:

- Changes in operating environment
- New technology
- New or changed information systems
- New employees (executives)

- Rapid growth
- New lines, products, or services
- Corporate restructuring, mergers, and acquisitions
- Foreign operations
- Regulatory changes

The process of risk assessment involves the following five key components, which are all interrelated and work together to form a continuous evaluation cycle:

1. Determine control objectives
2. Prioritize requirements
3. Identify risks
4. Determine likelihood of the risk
5. Manage risk

To meet the standards of Sarbanes-Oxley, risk must be assessed at the corporate-wide level, as well as at the individual-application level. The SEC has stated that financial report certification will involve more than just financial data; it includes documentation and assessment of the internal control systems as well. Corporate-wide risk assessment will address strategic risks, whereas application-level risk assessment focuses more on transaction and business process services. These risk-assessment levels should be linked so that the company can develop a systematic and complete measurement tool that addresses all of the control points and objectives.

Control objectives are the specific goals that the corporation wants to achieve at all levels, from the organization as a whole to the specific applications. Examples of control objectives that will meet Sarbanes-Oxley compliance include:

- Satisfactory business planning and needs analysis
- Confidentiality and integrity of transaction systems
- Satisfactory information accuracy and speed of access
- Reliable, valid, authorized, and timely transaction processing
- Proper system implementation and integration
- Satisfactory end-user support and training
- Satisfactory system and data protection

Set Reporting Objectives

After thoroughly analyzing the risks and developing control objectives, it is necessary to determine the likelihood of error and then set decision rules and reporting objectives to address the potential risk. If a control activity is deemed necessary, the activity chosen for use should be the most cost-effective and least likely to disrupt operational efficiency. The specific elements of internal control should be recorded in an official policies and procedures manual; this manual should articulate not only the specific practices the entity employs to achieve its control objectives, but the enforcement policies as well. The following types of controls are the most common and most effective:

- Preventive (stop), detective (catch), and corrective (fix) controls.
- Personnel controls.
  - Separation of duties.
  - Careful hiring, assignment of duties, training, and supervision.
  - Performance reviews.
- Physical controls—access to hardware components of system.
- Logistic controls—access to and authorization of system.
- System controls—document order, internal validity, checks and balances.

Corporate-wide control focuses on the directives and support that upper management provides to achieve established goals. These controls make it possible for the corporation to be successful and its employees to be productive. The following strategic planning controls are examples for Sarbanes-Oxley compliance:

- Establishing steering committees.
- Identifying opportunities provided by enterprise resource planning (ERP) systems.
- Evaluating and balancing the level of skills and outside resources required to complete IT projects satisfactorily.
- Evaluating automated systems for internal control.

Specific business/transactions services controls include:

■ Policies and procedures.

■ Document validation and matching.

■ Transaction detail calculation.

■ Account summary comparison.

■ Periodic ledger reconciliations.

■ Help and incident reporting and support.

■ Management reports.

Prepare a Formal Implementation Plan

A formal implementation plan includes the identification, capture, and exchange of information in a form and time frame that enable personnel to carry out their responsibilities. It can incorporate methods for recording, processing, summarizing, and reporting the entity's transactions, events, and conditions in order to maintain accountability for each respective control activity. A direct and systematic reporting process through the various chains and lines of command must be established, as well as a means of providing an understanding of individual roles and responsibilities in the organization.

Communicate the Procedures

Communication is the key to any successful change or management endeavor, and compliance with Sarbanes-Oxley may be one of the biggest changes a corporation will ever face. The compliance committee is responsible for managing the communication process. Because Sarbanes-Oxley will likely require increased control measures, it will be important to address the reasons for the changes (the "whys"). The success of internal control ultimately relies on each and every employee's performance, so the new procedures must be presented clearly and effectively, with as much input into the process at lower levels as possible. If only one corporate communiqué gets buy-in from the masses, Sarbanes-Oxley compliance should be it— all the more reason to focus on collaboration and setting a cultural tone that will facilitate employee understanding, acceptance, and observance.

Provide Training

Once a system is developed and tested, employees will require varying degrees of training to implement, operate, and maintain it. Again, the compliance committee will lead this process and provide the resources that all employees will need to function successfully in the new environment. The training efforts may consist of both internal and external components, depending on what type of system is put in place. Sophisticated, prepackaged IT solutions may necessitate intensive training at various levels, and it will be the committee's responsibility to secure the needed training. The training program created should address internal policies, procedures, and practices to ensure that each is being performed correctly, including:

- Classifying and recording authorized transactions in the proper period.
- Making operational and financial disclosures.
- Protecting company assets from improper, unauthorized use.

Through this process, some employees' jobs will change very little, whereas others will require whole new job descriptions. The committee will need to apprise management of these changes so that management can make personnel decisions accordingly. Furthermore, increased responsibility may lead to promotions, pay increases, and the like, and the HR function will have to be managed effectively to eliminate any staff dissatisfaction or inequity (both prime sources of risk).

Document Processes and Risk Management

To comply with Section 404, the CEO and CFO will have to certify that the internal controls systems of the corporation are sufficient and that they have been monitored within 90 days of the report being filed. To do this with any degree of confidence, the controls must be documented diligently. The executives will require detailed descriptions and analyses of all systems, clear enough that any audit of the system can be conducted easily and efficiently. Additionally, risks will have to be documented, both as a reason why the controls were put in place and to assist in identification of new or changing sources of risk.

The SEC mandates that, as part of the reporting process, a company maintain "evidential matter," including documentation, to provide reasonable support for management's claim that the internal control system is effective. It is important to remember that the CEO and CFO are responsible for (that is, directly supervise) the design of the internal control system relating to financial reporting. Tracking, documenting, and analyzing every stage of the process will make the internal control report easier to process and easier for top executives to sign off on.

Perform Continuous Evaluation

The quality of the internal control process must be continuously evaluated and modified to fit the corporation's changing environment and needs. Detection and timeliness of response are two key factors in maintaining and monitoring a system of internal controls. It is management's responsibility to establish and maintain controls that operate as intended or are modified as appropriate.

Early analysis, including detection and resolution of problems, can begin as a reactive process and ultimately develop into a formal procedure. Integration and coordination between different levels of management and functional areas should support firm violation enforcement provisions. These can include disciplinary and corrective actions to help reinforce established codes of practice throughout the organization. Exhibit 2.1 illustrates these steps graphically.

Business Process Controls

Sarbanes-Oxley requires top executives to confirm that their internal control structure is functioning effectively. This means they will need to be very attuned to the various business process controls and stay well informed. To accomplish this, they must establish a link between the control activities of the organization and the governance activities of the board and executives. Sarbanes-Oxley requires a bottom-up approach to controls, with line managers along the way certifying (formally or informally) that the information received and passed on is complete and accurate.

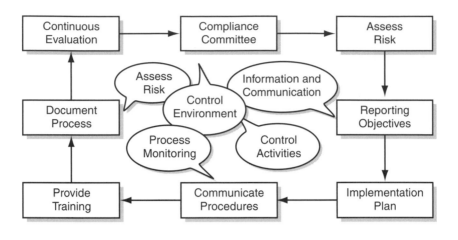

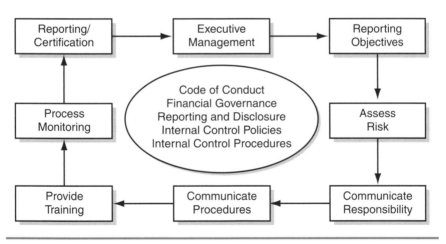

EXHIBIT 2.1   Developing an Internal Control System

This link will be facilitated by effective communication, and this emphasis on communication will have broad-reaching effects on all aspects of business. Strong internal controls have long been touted as necessary best practice, but unfortunately, implementation was often nixed based on cost-benefit analysis. Now, Sarbanes-Oxley provides a strong impetus to revive those internal control plans, and the bonus will be a greater chance of business success. Company management is responsible for creating and maintaining thorough internal control structures and identifying how effective the internal control structure and financial reporting procedures are (at the end of the most recent fiscal year). The company's auditor is required to confirm the validity of the internal control report.

Information Technology Controls

Management must first set the criteria for scope decisions (i.e., financial reporting elements, process documentation, and the depth of management's assessment of controls design and effectiveness):

- Define documentation and assessment methodology to support assertions about internal control, and provide a basis for the independent public accountant's review and testing.
- Break down the organization to evaluate entity-level and process-level controls.
- Identify the technology and tools needed to support the controls evaluation process. The method should be robust, to ensure enterprise-wide consistency.
- Agree to and validate an approach with external, independent public accountants to ensure that all involved concur with the choice of approach.
- Define and distribute a communications plan during the project.

Control Processes

Control processes address multiple objectives:

- Financial reporting.
- Regulatory compliance.
- Internal operations.

Management is not required to evaluate internal controls over operations, except to the extent that operational control overlaps with financial and regulatory compliance. When operational procedures are defined, documented, and implemented, these controls more often relate to financial reporting activities. Also, some compliance controls may be affected by SEC rules and regulations (assessing impact of changes, articulating reporting policies, and communicating such policies throughout the organization).

Process owners must document and communicate policies and procedures regarding IT, which is managed by control owners and other assigned personnel. Relevant and reliable information is necessary to understand and control external and internal business processes. Performance measures regarding communication processes are essential to proper internal control. IT and the process owner must be responsible for:

- Access control over sensitive and critical applications and data files supporting the process (including security for preventing viruses and hacker intrusion).
- Authorization, documentation, testing, and organization of the implementation of new applications that affect the process.
- Backup and recovery procedures for all critical applications and data files supporting the process.
- Commitment to assurance that all pertinent information is captured close to sources, accurately recorded and processed, and promptly reported for analysis, evaluation, and use in financial reports.
- Capture of adequate information—with full executive management support—from external sources to assess the effects on the process of external environmental changes, any effects on performance, and the information about that performance (e.g., customer needs and desires; competitive, technological, and regulatory issues, and general economic and industry trends and conditions).
- Access to information about changing conditions and trends affecting the performance of the process.
- Provision of relevant information on a timely basis, in detail, to control owners and other process personnel, to enable them to carry out their responsibilities.
- Communication of process objective to control owners and other process personnel; facilitation of communications within the process and the realm of stakeholders; and support of a process for control owners and other personnel to convey upward issues regarding process performance and control.

Assessing Internal Control

Management and the CEO and CFO must perform an internal control evaluation and prepare a report attesting to the effectiveness of the controls as of the end of the fiscal year. Material changes in the internal control system must be reported during the fiscal quarter in which they occurred if they are likely to affect financial reports. The report must address the design and effectiveness of the system, and management must demonstrate that it performed actual tests on the controls. It is important to note that the effectiveness of the system must be confirmed; a "negative assurance" or statement that "nothing has come to management's attention" is not sufficient.

Although the SEC has not prescribed any one method of evaluating internal control, it does require that a suitable, recognized framework be used. For a framework to be suitable, it must be free from bias, be qualitatively and quantitatively consistent, be sufficiently complete, and be relevant. The most common and most recommended system is COSO (some advocate for it to become the mandated system). The five criteria used and recommended by COSO to assess reliability are:

1. Extent of documentation
2. Awareness of system (communication)
3. Monitoring
4. Design effectiveness
5. Operating effectiveness

With the five components of internal control listed along the top and the elements of reliability on the side, the grid shown in Exhibit 2.2 can be used to assess the reliability of the entire control system.

Design effectiveness refers to whether a control is able to prevent or detect material inaccuracies in specific financial statement items. It involves consideration of the financial reporting objectives that the control is meant to achieve. *Operating effectiveness* refers to whether the control is functioning properly and as intended. During the evaluation of operating effectiveness, management gathers evidence regarding how the control was applied, the consistency with which it was applied, and who applied it.

EXHIBIT 2.2 Control Systems Evaluation

	Control Environment	Risk Assessment	Control Activities	Information, Communication	Monitoring
Extent of documentation					
Awareness of system/communication					
Monitoring					
Design effectiveness					
Operating effectiveness					

CHAPTER 3

Control Environment

The control environment is the control consciousness of an organization; it is the atmosphere in which people conduct their activities and carry out their control responsibilities. An effective control environment is an environment in which competent people understand their responsibilities, know the limits to their authority, and are knowledgeable, mindful, and committed to doing what is right and doing it the right way; in short, they are committed to following an organization's policies and procedures and its ethical and behavioral standards. The control environment encompasses both technical competence and ethical commitment; it is an intangible factor that is essential to effective internal control.

It is necessary to evaluate the entire organizational environment to determine if broad-based controls are working and are being followed. For example, management may evaluate the design of a code of conduct by considering whether the code is comprehensive and detailed enough to guide ethical decisions. It may verify that the code of conduct is sent to all personnel and that all personnel sign off on the policy. This is one way to ascertain that the code is actually contributing to compliance, and this investigation allows management to evaluate the operating effectiveness of this control. Another example is to consider if job descriptions are adequately designed, so that they include all relevant tasks of a position in sufficient detail. Determining whether employees are aware of the job descriptions, participate in updating them, and adhere to them may provide evidence of the operating effectiveness of job descriptions.

RISK ASSESSMENT

Risk assessment is the identification and analysis of risks associated with the achievement of operations, financial reporting, and compliance goals and objectives. This, in turn, forms a basis for determining how risks should be managed. Risk assessment is one of management's responsibilities and enables management to act proactively in reducing unwanted surprises. Failure to consciously manage risk can result in a lack of confidence that operational, financial, and compliance goals will be achieved.

A *risk* is anything that could jeopardize the achievement of an objective. Asking the following questions helps to identify risks:

- What could go wrong?
- How could we fail?
- What must go right for us to succeed?
- Where are we vulnerable?
- What assets do we need to protect?
- Do we have liquid assets or assets with alternative uses?
- How could someone steal from the department?
- How could someone disrupt our operations?
- How do we know whether we are achieving our objectives?
- On what information do we most rely?
- On what do we spend the most money?
- How do we bill and collect our revenue?
- What decisions require the most judgment?
- What activities are most complex?
- What activities are regulated?
- What is our greatest legal exposure?

It is important that risk identification be comprehensive, both at the department level and at the activity or process level, for operations, financial reporting, and compliance objectives. An assessment should consider both external and internal risk factors.

Usually, several risks can be identified for each objective. Management may consider if its risk assessment includes the effects of intense competitive pressures on revenue recognition practices. In evaluating the design of the risk assessment process, management may consider: the thoroughness of procedures to identify business units experiencing competitive pressures, and the likelihood of inappropriate revenue recognition practices occurring as a result; whether accounting personnel are involved in the risk assessment; and whether there are procedures for implementing follow-up control activities or monitoring.

Inspecting risk assessments to determine whether relevant risks were identified, and inquiring of personnel to determine the appropriateness of follow-up actions, may provide the basis for an evaluation of operating effectiveness. Management may review the policies and procedures that articulate when and how often IT risk assessments are required, as well as the planned program of risk assessments. Operating effectiveness may be evaluated by examining the results of risk assessments performed, conclusions reached, and documentation of activities to mitigate risks.

Control Activities

Control activities are actions supported by policies and procedures that, when carried out properly and in a timely manner, manage or reduce risks. Controls can be preventive, detective, or corrective. The intent of each type of control is different. *Preventive controls* attempt to deter or prevent undesirable events from occurring. They are proactive controls that help to prevent loss. Examples of preventive controls are separation of duties, proper authorization, adequate documentation, and physical control over assets.

Detective controls, in contrast, attempt to detect undesirable acts. They provide evidence that a loss has occurred, but do not prevent a loss from occurring. Examples of detective controls are reviews, analyses, variance analyses, reconciliations, physical inventories, and audits.

Corrective controls are used to ensure that, once an error has been detected, the mistake is corrected and the accounting records are made accurate. Examples of corrective controls include clearing reconciling items, reversing incorrect accounting entries, and reclassifying items that were improperly classified.

All three types of controls are essential to an effective internal control system. From a quality standpoint, preventive controls are essential because they are proactive and emphasize quality. However, detective controls play a critical role in providing evidence that the preventive controls are functioning and actually preventing losses. Finally, corrective controls restore the accounting records to a state of accuracy.

Control activities include approvals, authorizations, verifications, reconciliations, reviews of performance, security of assets, segregation of duties, correcting entries, and controls over information systems, as further explained herein.

Approvals, Authorizations, and Verifications (Preventive)

Management authorizes employees to perform certain activities and to execute certain transactions within limited parameters. In addition, management specifies which activities or transactions require supervisory approval before they are performed or executed by employees. A supervisor's approval (either manual or electronic) implies that he or she has verified and validated that the activity or transaction conforms to established policies and procedures.

Reconciliations (Detective)

Employees relate different sets of data to one another, identify and investigate differences, and take corrective action when necessary.

Reviews of Performance (Detective)

Management compares information about current performance to budgets, forecasts, prior periods, competitors, or other benchmarks to measure the extent to which goals and objectives are being achieved and to identify unexpected results or unusual conditions that require follow-up.

Security of Assets (Preventive and Detective)

Access to equipment, inventories, securities, cash, and other assets is restricted; assets are periodically counted and compared to amounts shown on control records.

Segregation of Duties (Preventive)

Duties are segregated among different people to reduce the risk of error or inappropriate action. Normally, responsibilities for authorizing transactions, recording transactions (accounting), and handling the related asset (custody) are divided.

Correcting and Reversing Entries (Corrective)

Once the detective controls have identified incorrect entries or errors in transactions, the originating department should either correct or reverse the entry to make certain the financial records are accurate. In automated systems, the corrections may be performed in real time.

Controls over Information Systems (Preventive and Detective)

Controls over information systems are grouped into two broad categories: general controls and application controls. *General controls* commonly include controls over data center operations, system software acquisition and maintenance, access security, and application system development and maintenance. *Application controls*, such as computer matching and edit checks, are programmed steps within application software; they are designed to help ensure the completeness and accuracy of transaction processing, authorization, and validity. General controls are needed to support the functioning of application controls. Both are needed to ensure complete and accurate information processing.

Control activities must be implemented thoughtfully, conscientiously, and consistently. A procedure will not be useful if performed mechanically, without a sharp, continuing focus on the conditions to which the policy is directed. Further, it is essential that unusual conditions identified as a result of performing control activities be investigated and that appropriate corrective action be taken. For instance, management may consider the design of online authorizations for purchases and investigate whether all types and values of purchases are included in the authorization. Operating effectiveness may be evaluated by queries to authorization tables in the system.

The evaluation may include consideration of general controls, such as system access, and program change controls. Management may consider the segregation of duties between personnel who deposit cash receipts and those who prepare bank reconciliations. Operating effectiveness may be evaluated by inspecting signatures indicating which personnel deposit cash receipts and which prepare bank reconciliations.

INFORMATION AND COMMUNICATION

Information and communication are essential to effecting control; information about an organization's plans, control environment, risks, control activities, and performance must be communicated up, down, and across an organization. Reliable and relevant information from both internal and external sources must be identified, captured, processed, and communicated to the people who need it, in a useful form and within a useful time frame. Information systems produce reports containing the operational, financial, and compliance-related information that makes it possible to run and control an organization.

Information and communication systems can be formal or informal. Formal information and communication systems, which range from sophisticated computer technology to simple staff meetings, should provide input and feedback relative to operations, financial reporting, and compliance objectives; such systems are vital to an organization's success. Nevertheless, informal conversations with customers, suppliers, regulators, and employees often provide some of the most critical information needed to identify risks and opportunities. When assessing internal control over a significant activity (or process), the key questions to ask about information and communication are:

- Do departments get the information they need from internal and external sources in a form and time frame that are useful?
- Do departments get information that alerts them to internal or external risks (e.g., legislative, regulatory, and developmental matters)?

- Do departments get information that measures their performance? That is, do they get information that tells a department whether it is achieving its operational, financial reporting, and compliance objectives?
- Do departments identify, capture, process, and communicate the information that others need (e.g., information used by customers or other departments) in a form and time frame that are useful?
- Do departments provide information to others that alerts them to internal or external risks?
- Do departments communicate effectively, both internally and externally?

Information and communication are simple concepts. Nevertheless, communicating with and getting information to people in a useful form and time frame is a constant challenge. Management may, for example, consider the design of procedures for involvement of the accounting department in changes to a company's enterprise resource planning system, including signoffs on changes.

Operating effectiveness may include inquiry as to whether the accounting department was actually involved and what level of involvement was reported, and inspection of evidence (such as signoffs or project plans) indicating the personnel involved. A typical class of transactions a company may process is payroll, which involves the capture of payroll changes and the recording of payroll liabilities in the general ledger. Management may consider whether the design of the process ensures that the right information is provided, in sufficient detail and on a timely basis, to ensure that payroll liabilities are complete and accurate (including, for example, vacation accruals).

Evaluation of operating effectiveness may be performed by asking personnel about the timeliness and accuracy of the information received, and by inspecting payroll and accounting records. Management may consider the design of decision processes related to business expansions, acquisitions, and contractions and the extent to which timely and relevant information is passed to the tax department for consideration of tax effects and applicability. Operating effectiveness may be evaluated by reviewing meeting minutes or other documentation as evidence of the required participation, information flow, and analysis.

MONITORING

Monitoring is the assessment of internal control performance over time. It is accomplished by ongoing monitoring activities and by separate evaluations of internal controls such as self-assessments, peer reviews, and internal audits. The purpose of monitoring is to determine whether internal controls are adequately designed, properly executed, and effective. Internal controls are adequately designed and properly executed if all five internal control components (i.e., control environment, risk assessment, control activities, information and communication, and monitoring) are present and functioning as designed. Internal controls are effective if the board of directors or trustees and management have reasonable assurance that:

- They understand the extent to which operational objectives are being achieved.
- Published financial statements are being prepared reliably.
- Applicable laws and regulations are being complied with.
- The internal controls are operating effectively. The effectiveness of an internal control system can be determined by its ability to prevent material errors in the financial accounting records and to ensure that the financial accounting records present an accurate picture of the organization's business operations and its financial status.

Although internal control is a process, judging its effectiveness involves an assessment of the condition of the process at one or more points in time.

Just as control activities help to ensure that actions to manage risks are carried out, monitoring helps to ensure that control activities and other planned actions to effect internal control are carried out properly and in a timely manner and that the end result is effective internal control. Ongoing monitoring activities include various management and supervisory activities that evaluate and improve the design, execution, and effectiveness of internal control.

In contrast, separate evaluations, such as self-assessments and internal audits, are periodic evaluations of internal control components, resulting in a formal report on internal control. Department employees perform self-assessments; internal auditors who independently appraise internal control perform internal audits.

Management's role in the internal control system is critical to the effectiveness of that system. Managers, like auditors, do not have to look at every single piece of information to determine that the controls are functioning; rather, they should focus their monitoring activities on high-risk areas. The use of spot checks of transactions or basic sampling techniques can provide a reasonable level of confidence that the controls are functioning. Operating effectiveness may be evaluated by considering instances of follow-up action when tolerances were exceeded, the level of tolerances used, and the frequency of analysis. In evaluating design, management may consider whether deficiencies have been identified and the nature of those deficiencies. To evaluate operating effectiveness, management may review supporting documentation indicating evidence of follow-up and corrective action, such as changes in policy, to correct control deficiencies.

CHAPTER 4

Material Weaknesses

The SEC, relying on Auditing Standard No. 60, states that a control system, or part thereof, is judged ineffective if there is any "material weakness"; it defines *material weakness* as "a reportable condition in which the design or operation of one or more of the internal control components does not reduce[,] to a relatively low level, the risk that misstatements caused by errors or fraud in amounts that would be material in relation to the financial statements being audited may occur and not be detected within a timely period by employees in the normal course of performing their assigned functions." Any material weakness must be reported in the management report on internal control. The SEC has further stated that an aggregation of reportable conditions could constitute a material weakness.

SPECIFIC INTERNAL CONTROLS TO EVALUATE

The SEC has suggested certain types of controls that should be included in the evaluation process. Its list includes, but is not limited to:

- Initiation, recording, processing, and reconciliation of account balances.
- Classes of transactions and disclosure-related assertions contained in the financial statements.
- Initiation and processing of nonroutine and nonsystematic transactions.
- Selection and application of accounting policies.
- Prevention, identification, and detection of fraud.

DISCLOSURE COMMITTEE

The SEC has recommended that companies create a disclosure committee to consider the significance of information, review the disclosure requirements, identify relevant disclosure issues, and coordinate the development of infrastructure. The disclosure committee would report to and include senior management, specifically the certifying officers. When certifying officers sign certifications, they are representing that they possess or have access to the collective knowledge of the company regarding all information that is significant to investors. They are also certifying management's internal processes; therefore, control over financial reporting is integral to the certification process. Important activities for the disclosure committee include:

- Ensuring that disclosure guidelines are in place.
- Making sure that the organization identifies and discloses its compliance with legal and regulatory requirements.
- Setting an appointment to meet alone with the audit committee at least twice each year.
- Setting up verification of work plans with auditors, and then seeking approval of plans from the CEO and audit committee.
- Ensuring that a documentation system is in place that will allow the corporation to meet the requirement of disclosing any changes in finances or operations within the required two-business-day time frame.
- Establishing how frequently controls should undergo self-assessment to ensure continued compliance with the Sarbanes-Oxley Act.
- Finding out what the external auditor requires and expects from internal control documentation.
- Determining how the external auditor plans to measure the level of effectiveness of internal controls.
- Creating a positive and nonthreatening disclosure atmosphere by frequently communicating what the disclosure expectations are.

Auditing Standard

On October 7, 2003, the PCAOB put forth a proposed standard on the "Audit of Internal Control over Financial Reporting Performed in Conjunction with an Audit of Financial Statements." After receiving feedback on the proposed Audit Standards, the PCAOB presented three Standards recommendations. On May 14, 2004 *Audit Standard No. 1—Preferences in Auditors' Reports to the Standards of the Public Company Accounting Oversight Board* was released for use and was quickly adopted as the accepted report process.

On March 9, 2004 *Audit Standard No. 2—An Audit of Internal Control Over Financial Reporting Performed in Conjunction with an Audit of Financial Statements* was released. This document provided a recommended standard and included a framework for audit and controls. Based on user feedback, conformance amendments were released for the adopted standard on September 15, 2004 (PCAOB Rel. No. 2004-008) and again on May 15, 2005 (PCAOB Rel. No. 2005-009).

On June 9, 2004 *Auditing Standard No. 3—Audit Documentation* provided a standard for documenting the audit process.

- The standard refers to an "internal control audit" rather than an attestation, and it specifies that such an audit is to be performed in conjunction with a financial statement audit.
- The standards are based on the evaluation of "management's assessment of internal controls." This means that the auditors must satisfy themselves that management has an evaluation process in place and that the process yields accurate results. Even though the auditor is using management's assessment as its guide, it is understood that the auditor may perform actual tests of the system.
- The standard provides a specific framework for determining the significance of a deficiency. It provides examples on how to apply the framework.
- The standard addresses, the issue of cost versus benefit of the internal control assessment. It also recognizes that a one-size-fits-all standard is not necessarily appropriate, given the resource and economic disparities between large corporations and small to

mid-sized ones. This is even more evident when the conformance amendments are related to the original standards proposed.

- The standard indicates the rotation process that auditors should apply when auditing the corporation from year to year.
- The standard requires auditors to follow a specified process from original recording through to the financial statement.

When used, this standard is extremely useful for corporations and will level the playing field on which all companies assess themselves.

Limits of Internal Control

Because control systems are designed and built by humans, human fallibility is a continuing issue. Internal control can always be circumvented by fraudulent abuse, decreased through carelessness, and eliminated by resource constraints. The benefits of internal control must be continuously monitored and the processes changed to maintain effectiveness and diligence.

Remember: Internal control can help to mitigate risks, but it does not eliminate them.

CHAPTER 5

Implementing Sarbanes-Oxley: What Does Compliance Look Like?

Complying with Sarbanes-Oxley is complex; compliance requires a multifaceted approach involving many departments and many people. The process of designing and implementing the compliance effort has to be managed diligently. This is not the type of project that can be worked on in discrete units, because the activities required to meet the demands of one Act section most likely affect the compliance demands of at least one other section. To keep the process flowing, and to maintain control of the project, an organization must draw up and execute a detailed time line that includes critical dates for compliance and checklists for specific activities required to comply with each section. Sarbanes-Oxley compliance is a very large project consisting of many interrelated components that all exert influence on one another in a dynamic way; thus, the ability to effectively manage projects is absolutely critical.

TIME LINE

The changes required for compliance with Sarbanes-Oxley are being phased in. This provides corporations with sufficient time to implement the new systems necessary to ensure compliance, as well as time to absorb the full scope and intent of the Sarbanes-Oxley Act. The deadlines for compliance with the various sections of the Act are set out in Exhibit 5.1. *Note that the deadlines are subject to change.* (Please review current documentation at *www.sarbanesoxleyguide. com.*)

EXHIBIT 5.1 Provisions

Section	Provision	Status as of August 2005
101	PCAOB Recognition	Effective for annual filings for the first fiscal year ending after December 15, 2003
201	Nonaudit Services	Adopted January 28, 2003; services that were contracted before May 6, 2003, are allowed so long as they are completed by May 6, 2004.
301	Audit Committee— Independent Director and Responsibilities	Compliance is required by the earlier of the first annual meeting after January 15, 2004, or October 31, 2004.
302	CEO/CFO Certification	Effective for all reports due on or after August 14, 2003.
906	CEO/CFO Certification	Effective for all reports due on or after August 14, 2003.
304	Forfeiture of Bonuses and Profits	Effective July 30, 2002.
306	Blackout Periods	Effective January 26, 2003.
401	Off-Balance Sheet Disclosures	Off-balance sheet disclosures required on statements for fiscal years ending on or after July 15, 2003.
		Contractual obligation disclosure is required on statements for fiscal years ending on or after December 15, 2003.
402	Prohibition of Loans to Executive	Effective July 30, 2002.
403	Disclosure of Insider Trades	Effective January 26, 2003.
404	Internal Control Report	Accelerated filers are required to include the annual report for the first fiscal period ending on or after November 15, 2004. All others are required to include the annual report for the first fiscal period ending on or after July 15, 2007.

(continues)

EXHIBIT 5.1 *(Continued)*

Section	Provision	Status as of August 2005
406	Code of Ethics	Required disclosure (or waiver of requirement) in annual reports for fiscal years ending on or after July 15, 2003.
407	Financial Expert on Audit	Required compliance for annual Committee reports with fiscal periods ending on or after July 15, 2003 (December 15, 2003 for small business).
409	Real-Time Disclosure	The SEC is not required to adopt specific rules.
806	Whistleblower Program	New civil and felony provisions in place as of July 30, 2002.

CHECKLISTS

To avoid being overwhelmed by the complexity of Sarbanes-Oxley compliance, an organization should develop a checklist of specific activities that must be accomplished for each section of the Act. These detailed checklists can then be used to guide the action and direction of the compliance effort. Without a prescribed system to follow, the potential for missing crucial steps is too large. Good project management breaks large objectives down into manageable pieces and details the tasks required to complete the overall goal. The following sections present key tasks ensuring compliance with each of the sections of the Act.

Audit Committee Compliance (Addresses Section 301)

- Confirm that the external auditor has registered with the PCAOB.
- Set up a periodic confirmation that external auditor complies with the mandates of, and is in good standing with, the PCAOB.
- Establish a charter for the audit committee (may be a committee separate from the board of directors), and ensure that the committee is responsible for reviewing:
  - Critical accounting practices.
  - Alternative treatments of financial information under GAAP.

- Material communication between the auditor and management.
- Ensure that the audit committee is composed of independent board members as defined by the SEC.
- Arrange for a financial expert (as defined by the SEC) to be on the audit committee.
- Ensure that the audit committee is responsible for approving all nonaudit services provided by the audit firm, and has set procedures in place to do so.
- Rotate the lead audit partner every five years.
- Prohibit the hiring of employees from the audit firm for 12 months after they leave their positions; have the audit firm prohibit the hiring of employees from the corporation for 12 months after those employees leave the corporation.
- Establish procedures for the audit committee to evaluate all practices of management and the board, to ensure integrity and ethical behavior.
- Establish procedures to deal with forfeiture of bonuses and profits or other sanctions imposed for noncompliance.
- Develop a procedure to respond to employee concerns.
- Meet with the CFO and the auditors separately at least twice a year.
- Ensure that management evaluates business risks and internal control systems at least once a year, and conduct a separate review of management's assessment process.
- Evaluate trades occurring during blackout periods, to ensure compliance with the Act.
- Keep current on all regulatory and governmental matters and actions that affect the corporation and the board.

Compliance Committee Compliance (Addresses Section 302)

- Ensure that the CFO is on the compliance committee, and that the committee also includes the CEO, CIO, and other key executives (HR, legal, operations, sales, etc.) whenever possible.
- Assess and document identified risks.
- Establish objectives.

- Confirm that all policies and procedures comply with the Sarbanes-Oxley Act and are reasonable given industry norms. Communicate and enforce these policies and procedures.
- Provide training as necessary to ensure understanding.
- Draft and communicate policies related to:
  - Financial statement preparation.
  - Involvement of internal auditors with the external auditor.
  - Off-balance sheet transactions.
  - Evaluation of internal control systems.
  - Code of ethics.
  - Real-time disclosure.
- Establish procedures to disclose material changes in financial positions or operations within two business days.
- Ensure that the company web site addresses material changes within the disclosure time frame.
- Reevaluate key performance indicators to ensure that they are reasonable and attainable within an ethical and transparent work environment.
- Address and implement all audit recommendations.
- Establish a whistleblower program and communicate details of the program and employee protection provided thereunder.
- Document all processes and internal control systems.
- Manage the change process through open communication and fair practice.
- Consider hiring an external party to assess these compliance activities.

Internal Control Report Compliance (Addresses Section 404)

- Ensure that the compliance committee understands its roles and responsibilities.
- Ensure that the compliance committee consistently applies a zero-tolerance policy to any activity that is not in compliance with the Sarbanes-Oxley Act.
- Review compliance efforts for appropriateness and completeness.
- Ensure that the definitions of *independent* and *financial expert* have been met.

- Ensure that the compliance plan and all processes have been documented.
- Ensure that the documentation is standardized across the corporation.
- Ensure that the documentation is easily accessible and current.
- Establish a process to monitor operations and the environment, and to ensure continuous improvement.
- Test the firm's ability to meet disclosure deadlines (e.g., simulate a material event and ensure disclosure within two business days).
- Monitor the effectiveness of the compliance committee:
  - Are there a charter and agenda?
  - Are the committee members satisfied with their roles and progress?
  - Has the committee's purpose been effectively communicated?
- Ensure that all elements of the certifications for internal and disclosure controls can be attested to. Exhibits 5.2 and 5.3 are samples of certification documents prescribed by the SEC.

You will find the following certifications and other useful information at the SEC's web site: *http://www.sec.gov/rules/proposed/33-8212.htm*

Build an Effective Whistleblower Program. "Approximately one third of American employees have witnessed unethical or illegal conduct in their workplace. Of these, over half did not disclose what they observed."[1]

"71 percent of respondents expected that people who reported corruption would suffer for reporting it."[2]

Section 301 of the Sarbanes-Oxley Act requires audit committees to establish procedures for receiving and handling complaints related to "accounting, internal accounting controls, or auditing matters; and the confidential, anonymous submission by employees of the issuer of concerns regarding questionable accounting or auditing matters." Effective whistleblower programs will help organizations meet these requirements.

EXHIBIT 5.2   Certification: Internal Controls

CERTIFICATION (internal controls)

I, [identify the certifying individual], certify that:

1. I have reviewed this annual report on Form 20-F of [identify registrant].
2. Based on my knowledge, this report does not contain any untrue statement of a material fact or omit to state a material fact necessary to make the statements made, in light of the circumstances under which such statements were made, not misleading with respect to the period covered by this report.
3. Based on my knowledge, the financial statements, and other financial information included in this report, fairly present in all material respects the financial condition, results of operations and cash flows of the registrant as of, and for, the periods presented in this report.
4. The registrant's other certifying officers and I are responsible for establishing and maintaining disclosure controls and procedures (as defined in Exchange Act Rules 13a-15 and 15d-15) for the registrant and have:
   (a) Designed such disclosure controls and procedures to ensure that material information relating to the registrant, including its consolidated subsidiaries, is made known to us by others within those entities, particularly during the period in which this report is being prepared;
   (b) Evaluated the effectiveness of the registrant's disclosure controls and procedures as of a date within 90 days prior to the filing date of this report (the "Evaluation Date"); and
   (c) Presented in this report our conclusions about the effectiveness of the disclosure controls and procedures based on our evaluation as of the Evaluation Date.
5. The registrant's other certifying officers and I have disclosed, based on our most recent evaluation, to the registrant's auditors and the audit committee of registrant's board of directors (or persons performing the equivalent functions):
   (a) All significant deficiencies in the design or operation of internal controls which could adversely affect the registrant's ability to record, process, summarize and report financial data and have identified for the registrant's auditors any material weaknesses in internal controls; and
   (b) Any fraud, whether or not material, that involves management or other employees who have a significant role in the registrant's internal controls.
6. The registrant's other certifying officers and I have indicated in this report whether there were significant changes in internal controls or in other factors that could significantly affect internal controls subsequent to the date of our most recent evaluation, including any corrective actions with regard to significant deficiencies and material weaknesses.

* Provide a separate certification for each principal executive officer and principal financial officer of the registrant.

Date: _____ Place: _____   [Signature] _____
                                               [Title]

EXHIBIT 5.3 Certifications: Disclosure Controls

CERTIFICATIONS (disclosure controls)

I, [identify the certifying individual], certify that:
1. I have reviewed this annual report on Form 40-F of [identify registrant].
2. Based on my knowledge, this report does not contain any untrue statement of a material fact or omit to state a material fact necessary to make the statements made, in light of the circumstances under which such statements were made, not misleading with respect to the period covered by this report.
3. Based on my knowledge, the financial statements, and other financial information included in this report, fairly present in all material respects the financial condition, results of operations and cash flows of the registrant as of, and for, the periods presented in this report.
4. The registrant's other certifying officers and I are responsible for establishing and maintaining disclosure controls and procedures (as defined in Exchange Act Rules 13a-15 and 15d-15) for the registrant and have:
   (a) Designed such disclosure controls and procedures to ensure that material information relating to the registrant, including its consolidated subsidiaries, is made known to us by others within those entities, particularly during the period in which this report is being prepared;
   (b) Evaluated the effectiveness of the registrant's disclosure controls and procedures as of a date within 90 days prior to the filing date of this report (the "Evaluation Date"); and
   (c) Presented in this report our conclusions about the effectiveness of the disclosure controls and procedures based on our evaluation as of the Evaluation Date.
5. The registrant's other certifying officers and I have disclosed, based on our most recent evaluation, to the registrant's auditors and the audit committee of registrant's board of directors (or persons performing the equivalent functions):
   (a) All significant deficiencies in the design or operation of internal controls which could adversely affect the registrant's ability to record, process, summarize and report financial data and have identified for the registrant's auditors any material weaknesses in internal controls; and
   (b) Any fraud, whether or not material, that involves management or other employees who have a significant role in the registrant's internal controls.
6. The registrant's other certifying officers and I have indicated in this report whether there were significant changes in internal controls or in other factors that could significantly affect internal controls subsequent to the date of our most recent evaluation, including any corrective actions with regard to significant deficiencies and material weaknesses.

* Provide a separate certification for each principal executive officer and principal financial officer of the registrant.

Date: _____ Place: _____ [Signature] _____
                                           [Title]

Factors that Contribute to Employee Disclosures

Protection.   Employees are usually reluctant to blow the whistle for fear of retaliation, which may take the form of discrimination, harassment, intimidation, alienation, targeted supervision, and in some cases even termination. Reassurances that management will protect whistleblowers from retaliation, and that legal safeguards are in place, will help create an environment in which employees feel that disclosing their concerns is acceptable and encouraged.

Accessibility.   Making the disclosure must be easy and convenient. Ideally, there will be a few different options for the employee to choose from.

Tone at the Top.   A management team that sends a clear and consistent message about behaving ethically, with integrity, fairness, and openness, and in compliance with the law will foster a workforce that will police itself. The corporate culture will promote intolerance of fraudulent or inappropriate behavior, and employees will expect honesty from their coworkers and supervisors.

Awareness.   Awareness and acceptance of the whistleblower program, the rationale for its existence, and management's support will create an environment in which employees know immediately what to do if they ever encounter a questionable situation.

Steps for Building Effective Whistleblower Programs: Development Stages

Assessment

- Assess employee characteristics and the needs of the organization.
- Ensure that all locations across the country or worldwide have access to the program.
- Ensure that the program operators can deliver support in any language needed.
- Make access to the program free (or very inexpensive), uncomplicated, and anonymous whenever possible. A toll-free

number, fax access, e-mail, or program ombudsmen are all options.

■ Provide availability 24 hours a day, 7 days a week.

■ Evaluate whether to insource or outsource the program.

■ Establish a protocol for the program staff to follow.

■ Establish a committee to oversee the appropriate handling of disclosures.

■ Provide a reasonable budget.

Design

■ Build a program that addresses the corporation's needs as established during assessment.

■ Provide training for staff (if insourcing) and the committee that will oversee the program.

■ Develop policies and procedures making the whistleblower program an official component of the organization's system of internal controls.

Implement

■ Communicate the program effectively. The preferred method is a face-to-face meeting with employees describing the program and its development. Other options include e-mail, memo, video conferencing, or a computer-based training (CBT) program.

■ Initiate or release the program throughout the organization at the same time.

Evaluate

■ Conduct surveys to obtain feedback and make sure that employees remain aware that the program is in place and working effectively.

■ Use the committee to gather statistics on program use, effectiveness, and outcomes.

■ Keep the audit committee apprised of the program.

■ Keep the program visible. Mention it at staff meetings, in newsletters, on bulletin boards, and the like.

REPORTING, DOCUMENTATION, AND ARCHIVING

Sarbanes-Oxley requires an unprecedented amount of documentation, which must be accessible and easy to follow if and when an audit of the corporation's processes, systems, reports, or statements occurs. This mandate presents a dilemma in that it will be important to maintain records, but only to the point where those records do not become a liability. The idea that all records should be kept forever is an extreme reaction, and the possession and retention of all these records is a source of business risk.

Records management is a driver of a successful compliance effort. E-mails, forms, reports, images, web content, and office documents are all records that must be managed, and all are considered information assets. Policies and procedures that outline how these records are to be stored, and for how long, will be very important to ensure Sarbanes-Oxley compliance and also to ensure that incorrect information is *not* stored. Policies and procedures will have to be written to ensure standardized reporting; best practice dictates a continuous documentation process with rules regarding how long information is to be kept and what type of information is to be archived or destroyed.

DISCLOSURE

As an effort to mandate transparent operations, Sarbanes-Oxley requires that many business activities be presented and explained to the public and stakeholders. Aside from reporting internal control systems and disclosure controls and procedures, compliance with the Act requires the following disclosures:

- Companies are required to disclose whether a financial expert serves on its auditing committee, to disclose that person's name, and to disclose if that person is independent.
- Public accounting firms must disclose whether they have a code of ethics for executive officers.
- All brokers, analysts, and securities analysts are required to disclose:
  - If they have any investments or debt with the company their firm is working with or reporting on.

- If the compensation they are receiving is both beneficial to the public's interest and allows protection of the investors.
- If the issuer has been a client of the broker or dealer.
- If the analyst was compensated for any research reports based on investment banking revenues.
- Issuers must disclose, in understandable plain English, pertinent information, including quantitative and trend, regarding material changes in the issuer's financial situation or operations.
- Disclosures must be made in real time.
- All annual and quarterly reports must "disclose material off-balance sheet transactions, arrangements and obligations (this includes contingent obligations) in addition to other relationships the issuer has with unconsolidated entities and other individuals that may have an impact on material current or future effect on the issuer's financial condition, results of operations, liquidity, capital expenditures, capital resources or significant components of revenue or expenses."

ENDNOTES

1. S. Dawson, *Whistleblowing: A Broad Definition and Some Issues for Australia* (Working paper) (Victoria University of Technology, 2000), *http://www.uow.edu.au/arts/sts/bmartin/dissent/documents/Dawson.html* (accessed September 30, 2005).
2. L. Zipparo, "Encouraging Public Sector Employees to Report Workplace Corruption," *Australian Journal of Public Administration* 58, no. 2 (1999): 83–93, quoted in S. Dawson, *Whistleblowing.*

CHAPTER 6

Technology Implications

Sarbanes-Oxley Sections 302 and 404 require companies to evaluate the *effectiveness* of their internal controls over information reported to the financial markets. The SEC has issued rules to implement these statutory requirements, which apply for financial year-ends on or after November 15, 2004 (for most companies), and on or after July 15, 2007, for others. This has a direct effect on the IT sector, CIOs, CTOs, and other IT professionals. Charged with analysis and design, systems development, and maintenance responsibilities, IT professionals must be cognizant of the following:

- Compliance efforts must cease being just tactical exercises and become true, value-creating strategic IT initiatives.
- Enterprise resource planning (ERP) provides a foundation for compliance, performance, and quality.
- Systems based on spreadsheets are insufficient for the demands of Sarbanes-Oxley; procedures must be foolproof, automated, integrated, and auditable.
- Compliance systems should have adequate virus and hacker security protection, backup schedules, backup restore testing, and documented disaster recovery plans.
- Business-critical processes should reside on one platform.
- Real-time information must be accessible in case of problems, from anywhere, at anytime.
- Defined policies, procedures, and processes must be actively integrated into all entities, enterprise-wide.
- Application standards in target processes, day-to-day work, problem resolution, system controls, and risk management must be implemented at all levels throughout the organization.

Section 404 compliance has a definite effect on IT management, in that processes are carried out by information systems—and those systems are owned by IT. The first year of compliance will be the costliest, as companies use consultants and new technology to document and evaluate processes. However, companies are positioning themselves to go forward on a self-sustaining basis. Most are not likely to hire new employees dedicated solely to Section 404 compliance.

Ideally, the professional used for compliance system development is a project manager (PM) with a background in finance. Seasoned PMs are skilled and capable of matrix managing across multiple departments and time lines. Whether from internal audit, accounting, treasury, or another finance area, the PM's expertise will be extremely valuable. Internal audit, corporate, and international finance experience are advantages for the PM. The normal cycle for compliance systems development is depicted in Exhibit 6.1.

STORAGE SYSTEMS

Sarbanes-Oxley will have significant long-term effects on the storage industry. Analysis indicates a significant impact on enterprise storage environments and those who manage them (see Exhibit 6.2).

- Scalability of storage subsystems will be required for compliance, especially for large enterprises with high volumes of financial transactions.
- Automatic capture and storage of financial data will be required.
- Compliance certification of storage infrastructure will be a critical factor.
- It will be difficult for organizations to extract data stored in unaltered form, because of changes in applications software, operating systems, and storage devices.
- Communications between IT management and senior management will become more vital, be more policy based, and require more system resources.
- Compliance requirements and reporting requirements will force a tighter integration of mainframe and open systems and data stores.

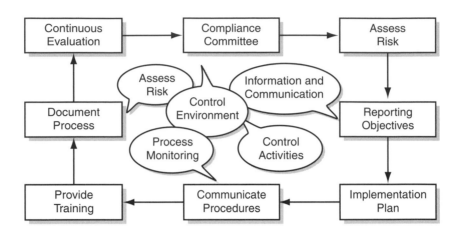

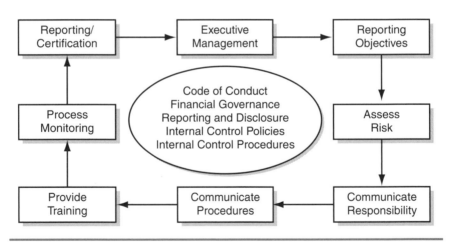

EXHIBIT 6.1   Developing an Internal Control System

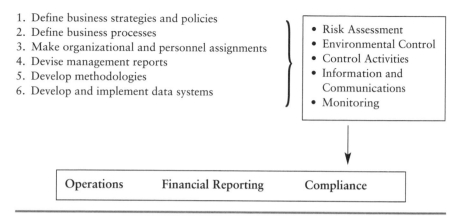

1. Define business strategies and policies
2. Define business processes
3. Make organizational and personnel assignments
4. Devise management reports
5. Develop methodologies
6. Develop and implement data systems

- Risk Assessment
- Environmental Control
- Control Activities
- Information and
  Communications
- Monitoring

| Operations | Financial Reporting | Compliance |

EXHIBIT 6.2 Compliance

IT SOLUTIONS

For most, the Section 404 solution will serve as a central repository for internal control documentation. It will also facilitate the testing of internal and external audit controls and serve as a portal for executive review. Like most rollouts, Section 404 software requires education in processes and internal controls.

Most products offered by vendors are Web-enabled, allowing clients with multiple locations to use the software with a minimum of IT staff. The use of Extensible Markup Language (XML), Extensible Business Reporting Language (XBRL), Java, and middleware languages is a success factor. These languages, particularly XBRL, bring the publication, exchange, and analysis of the complex financial information in corporate business reports into the interactive realm of the Internet.

XBRL provides a common platform for critical business reporting processes and improves the reliability and ease of communicating financial data among users, whether internal or external to the reporting enterprise. XBRL is an XML-based, royalty-free, open standard that is being developed by a consortium of more than 170 companies and agencies; the intent is to deliver benefits to investors, accountants, regulators, executives, business and financial analysts, and information providers.

Commercial packages typically include word-processing, spreadsheet, diagramming, and flowcharting tools to document processes and internal controls; these features allow users to custom-design their software. Some solutions facilitate certification testing of controls by the business owner and the auditor. Others allow a view of best practices for internal controls or the Committee of Sponsoring Organizations (COSO) Integrated Framework.

Various packages offer users the ability to resolve significant accounts from financial statements. Processes associated with selected accounts are identified and then assigned to process owners. Internal controls are documented and tested, and process owners can sign certifications for each process on a quarterly basis.

CHANGES IN IT MANAGEMENT

Compliance with requirements of Sarbanes-Oxley represents a unique opportunity to pursue and implement best practices for planning, executing, reporting, and analyzing business performance. It involves both processes and systems; solid business rules and requirements; system specifications, development, and documentation; proper implementation; and enterprise-wide training. At a minimum, the software development life cycle (SDLC) methodology must:

- Model the processes.
- Automate the processes.
- Manage and monitor the processes.
- Analyze the processes.
- Integrate the processes with relevant systems.

The optimal methodology is to adopt capability maturity model (CMM) practices. During the Year 2000 scare, the fact that companies had to search for software date bugs using a definite methodology forced them to clean up packages in the process. The same is true of the Sarbanes-Oxley initiative: reporting systems will have to become more robust, have more integrity, be more flexible, and be under tighter management controls on corporate destiny.

CHAPTER 7

Sarbanes-Oxley–Related Bodies

Many regulatory bodies are involved with the Sarbanes-Oxley Act, and it is important to understand the role that each plays in the compliance process. The Sarbanes-Oxley Act itself created the main governing body, called the Public Company Accounting Oversight Board (PCAOB). The PCAOB in turn influences the Securities and Exchange Commission (SEC), and deals with issues related to the Committee of Sponsoring Organizations (COSO) and the Financial Accounting Standards Board (FASB). The relationships among these bodies can be complex; hence, we next explore the depth, breadth, and influence of each entity as it relates to Sarbanes-Oxley.

PUBLIC COMPANY ACCOUNTING OVERSIGHT BOARD

The Public Company Accounting Oversight Board was established to ensure that covered individuals and entities fully comply with the Sarbanes-Oxley Act of 2002. The PCAOB is charged with setting audit firm standards and overseeing quality control, ethics, and independence issues. The PCAOB also has the power to discipline accountants.

Implementing and enforcing the new standards will take time, perseverance, and money. Though it is currently funded by the federal government, the PCAOB is a not-for-profit board that levies fees on publicly traded companies (based on the corporation's size) to sustain itself. (Companies with a market capitalization of less than $25 million are exempt from the fees.) The fees are not optional; some observers estimate that the largest companies could pay up to $1 million annually to support the PCAOB.

This board consists of five members, appointed by the Securities and Exchange Commission, and must include a maximum of two CPAs. Members of the PCAOB cannot be involved professionally in any other business activity and must be independent and full-time. The PCAOB will cooperate with advisory groups and professional accounting groups to help increase effectiveness of standards and setting standards. One of its main roles is to ensure auditor independence, and it has not shied away from hotly contested issues such as whether accounting firms should be allowed to participate in the lucrative business of performing tax services for an audit client. The PCAOB's activities and responsibilities include:

- Registering public accounting firms.
- Inspecting public accounting firms.
- Investigating all claims and bringing disciplinary actions.

All domestic and foreign public accounting firms that prepare or issue audit reports for any public company *must* register with the PCAOB. If information pertaining to the registration application changes, the company must report that information. The PCAOB can and may implement sanctions against registered accounting firms, including revoking a firm's registration, suspending or limiting its auditing activities, or imposing censure or monetary penalties.

Although it was created with a very narrow scope of jurisdiction—namely, the oversight of Sarbanes-Oxley—the PCAOB's mission is to create standards, register and inspect audit firms, and discipline officers of organizations and their external auditors for SEC registrants' audit problems. This means that the PCAOB's influence could extend to others, who will undoubtedly look at what the board does and argue that its standards and processes should also be applied to private companies and other non-SEC registrants. Because the provisions of Sarbanes-Oxley are not necessarily relevant or applicable to non-SEC registrants, this has the potential to create a two-tiered system of auditing standards and peer review.

COMMITTEE OF SPONSORING ORGANIZATIONS

COSO is a voluntary organization that was formed in 1985 to sponsor the National Commission on Fraudulent Financial Reporting. Its mandate is to improve the quality of financial reporting through business ethics, effective internal controls, and corporate governance; it does so by studying the factors that lead to fraudulent reporting and developing recommendations to combat it.

COSO is backed by the American Accounting Association, the American Institute of Certified Public Accountants, the Financial Executives Institute, the Institute of Internal Auditors, and the National Association of Accountants (now the Institute of Management Accountants). The original chair of the National Commission was James C. Treadway; hence its popular name, the "Treadway Commission." The current chairman is John Flaherty, the retired vice president of and general auditor for PepsiCo Inc.

COSO authored *Internal Control—Integrated Framework*, which set out a model for establishing and then evaluating internal control systems. Control activities are centered on financial applications to protect integrity, confidentiality, and availability, but they go beyond finance to address systems in all departments of an organization. This model is well respected and widely used, and has been loosely adopted by the SEC as an appropriate model for developing and evaluating internal control for Sarbanes-Oxley purposes. COSO developed its model and evaluation system based on four key concepts:

1. Internal control is a process, and as such is not static; it requires continuous assessment, evaluation, and modification.
2. Internal control is more than written policies and procedures; it requires buy-in and acceptance from employees at all levels of the organization.
3. Internal control does not guarantee results; rather, it provides reasonable assurance that the information is accurate. Because systems ultimately rely on human interaction or intervention, there is always room for error.
4. Internal control is objective based; the objectives are achieved by controls in overlapping areas.

COSO has been very influential in both the initial development and the continuing evolution of Sarbanes-Oxley. Its model has been proposed by the SEC as a standard for evaluating internal controls, and COSO is looked upon as a leader in corporate governance issues.

SECURITIES AND EXCHANGE COMMISSION

The U.S. Securities and Exchange Commission was established to protect investors and maintain the integrity of the securities markets. Investing is risky; members of the public must have access to reliable information in order to make good decisions and protect their money to the best of their ability. To ensure that investors have access to such information, the SEC requires public companies to disclose meaningful financial and other information to the public. The SEC also oversees other investment organizations, including stock exchanges, broker-dealers, investment advisors, mutual funds, and public utility holding companies. For the SEC to be effective, it was given the authority to pass (per federal legislation) and enforce securities laws.

The SEC has adopted many of the provisions set out in the Sarbanes-Oxley Act, and it oversees the PCAOB. Sarbanes-Oxley "requires the SEC to promulgate rules and regulations on the retention of any and all materials related to an audit, including communications, correspondence, and other documents created, sent or received in connection with an audit or review." The following is a list of additional SEC authorities:

- The SEC oversees the PCAOB.
- The SEC appoints the members of the PCAOB.
- The SEC can request a court order to bar a person from becoming or remaining as a director or an officer of an issuer if the person's behavior makes him or her unfit to serve in such a position.
- The SEC reviews company filings at least once every three years.
- The SEC has provided a set of standards that attorneys must follow, including:
  - Any lawyer who works for a public company must report to the CEO or the chief counsel of the company if the lawyer has evidence of a securities violation or any violation by the company.
  - The lawyer then must ensure that the chief counsel or CEO takes action regarding the evidence. If neither of these persons does so, the lawyer must advise the board of directors or audit committee of the evidence.

The SEC has been given a great deal of authority for implementing the specifics of Sarbanes-Oxley, so it is important to note that the SEC is susceptible to political pressures. Lawmakers have praised the SEC for its commitment to forwarding some of the most groundbreaking corporate reform since the 1930s. Advocates for investor groups, however, feel that the SEC has softened almost all of the provisions in the Act in response to pressure from the accounting and legal professions.

A particularly glaring example is the fact that the SEC allows audit committees to preapprove nonaudit services. Congress clearly wanted strict auditor independence, yet the SEC put in the preapproval caveat to quiet the protests of accounting firms. It did, however, ban audit firms from also providing financial-system implementation and internal audits. Although the SEC has adopted many of the provisions of Sarbanes-Oxley, it is clear that the SEC works under its own agenda and biases.

FINANCIAL ACCOUNTING STANDARDS BOARD

The Financial Accounting Standards Board was formed in 1973 to establish standards of financial accounting and reporting for private industry. Although the SEC has statutory authority to establish these standards for publicly held companies, its policy is to rely on the private sector so long as it demonstrates the ability to function in the public interest. To guarantee this public-interest focus, the FASB is independent of all other business and professional organizations. The FASB also participates in international activities in an effort to improve comparability and quality standards between statements issued internationally and those issued in the United States. The budget for the FASB comes from annual fees paid by public accounting firms, and it also receives independent funding under Sarbanes-Oxley.

CHAPTER 8

Opportunities and Challenges Created by Sarbanes-Oxley

Certainly, the Sarbanes-Oxley Act presents many challenges as companies scramble to comply with the implementing regulations in a timely manner. From those areas designated as needing reform, though, come many opportunities. Sarbanes-Oxley will have its supporters and detractors, and the people within those camps may change over time as the legislation matures and evolves, but the issues will always be there. Here is a look at the current climate surrounding Sarbanes-Oxley.

OPPORTUNITIES

The most obvious opportunities stem from the new human resource capabilities that are required to ensure compliance. Sarbanes-Oxley demands new skills in terms of internal control, and it will push people in managerial roles to expect excellence in every aspect of the workplace. The skill set for Sarbanes-Oxley compliance will likely become highly specialized, thus paving the way for outsourcing opportunities: rather than have in-house compliance experts, companies will hire specialists to manage the compliance process.

Job Opportunities

Most of the employment opportunities created by Sarbanes-Oxley compliance efforts center on finance, accounting, IT, and auditing roles. Whether firms choose to supplement their internal staff or decide to outsource some of the compliance activity, there will be a surge in the need for experienced, qualified professionals to lead or implement the required change. The stringent requirements of the Act mean that high-level executives want more experts on their staffs, to ensure that the company's compliance efforts are effective and that they are designed properly.

Many companies are creating a new position of Chief Compliance Officer (CCO). The person in this position takes charge of leading the compliance committee, thus alleviating some of the pressure on the CFO and CIO and enabling them to focus more on their staff's needs during the process. Where companies choose not to add to the executive team, the CIO and CFO will have new or more complex job descriptions and greater pressures. This may lead to a reevaluation of their job descriptions and compensation. See Exhibit 8.1.

The need for public and corporate accountants is also expected to rise dramatically because of the vigorous demands of Sarbanes-Oxley. The level of detail required of both internal and external auditors means that adding extra staff is inevitable. The standards for these professionals will also be strictly enforced, and there will likely be an increased focus on training and professional development. Sarbanes-Oxley forces companies to uncover fraud on a more aggressive basis, so forensic accounting is an area of growth and demand. Already 40 percent of the top 100 accounting firms in the United States have expanded their forensic/fraud services.

An interesting twist to the employment opportunities created by Sarbanes-Oxley is the reluctance of many finance professionals to serve as directors or members of audit committees since inception of the Act. Many retired accountants, financial consultants, and CFOs are hesitant to accept the "honor" of being asked to sit on a board for

EXHIBIT 8.1   Wanted: Sarbanes-Oxley Compliance Manager

Wanted: Sarbanes-Oxley Compliance Manager
Public Company seeks Sarbanes-Oxley Compliance Manager. In this internal controls function, the qualified candidate will be responsible for ensuring ongoing compliance with Sarbanes-Oxley as related to different business units. Focus on adequacy of internal controls and developing recommendations for improvement. Degree in Accounting and Public Audit preferred. CPA, MBA or CSOX a plus.

fear of the legal liabilities they face from the strict new standards. Sarbanes-Oxley has placed a much greater level of responsibility and accountability on the audit committee members, so it is imperative that all members assess the risk associated with their duties in that capacity.

Lawyers are cautioning all potential board members to make sure that the board carries sufficient directors and officers (D&O) liability insurance and that it has a completely independent counsel. It should be very apparent from this guide that Sarbanes-Oxley means business and has significant bite; it is, therefore, prudent to thoroughly evaluate one's own liability in relation to potential corporate misconduct.

Outsourcing

Outsourcing is expected to increase in the IT field as companies look to service providers who concentrate on Sarbanes-Oxley reform. Rather than develop sophisticated internal systems, it may make economic sense to hand a large portion of record management over to an outside company. Rather than reinvent the wheel, companies are likely to explore ways to use other people's technology to accomplish their objectives. The problem with increased outsourcing is the fact that the firm loses some of its control.

With the focus on control systems, this risk factor must be thoroughly assessed before any decision to outsource is made. The rules and regulations surrounding outsourced contracts will likely become very strict and will involve a coordination of internal control and external controls to ensure data integrity. As it is, the CEO and CFO have to certify that statements are accurate and that internal controls are effective; because of this, the level of accountability and scrutiny between partner companies will increase tremendously.

CHALLENGES

Aside from the overall challenge of achieving compliance, the main issues that people see stemming from Sarbanes-Oxley are the impact the Act will have on the global community and what this Act will mean to the viability of U.S. public companies in the future. Once the mechanics of compliance have been sorted out, the challenge for legislators will be to ensure that Sarbanes-Oxley accomplishes what it was intended to do (improve financial reporting and investor confidence) while balancing the need for businesses to remain viable in a global economy.

Global Impact

Some provisions of Sarbanes-Oxley conflict with the laws of other countries, and that could pose big problems for non-U.S. companies listed on the New York Stock Exchange (NYSE) and other U.S. exchanges. Noncompliance could result in delisting, and some companies considering entry into a U.S. exchange may put off that entry. Thirty percent of the NYSE consists of non-U.S. companies, and the loss of even just a few would have a negative effect on both U.S. and foreign economies; also, U.S. investors would have less access to foreign companies and foreign companies would have less access to U.S. capital.

Though the chance of a major worldwide departure from U.S. markets is low, German companies will have a very difficult time complying with Sarbanes-Oxley. By law, their supervisory boards must include employee representatives who will not be able to pass any Sarbanes-Oxley test for independence. This was a major factor in Porsche's decision not to list in the United States. The other main problem for foreign companies is the restriction on loans to corporate directors; this prohibition conflicts with many countries' customs and practices. The SEC has relaxed a few restrictions for foreign issuers, but the sentiment of the majority is against allowing too many concessions. Japan and Germany want to see foreign exemptions, and they do not think that their companies' management structures and in-house controls should have to conform to U.S. standards.

In fact, Sarbanes-Oxley does apply U.S. norms and culture to foreign subsidiaries or business units of U.S. multinationals. This creates conflict among the countries and within international corporations:

■ Sarbanes-Oxley creates a conflict between Japan's goals in the market, which are to expand power, market share, and size; and the goals of the United States and the United Kingdom, which are to maximize shareholder profits.

- Europeans, for the most part, met Sarbanes-Oxley with objections and proceeded to lobby for exemptions.
- The finance ministers of the European Union oppose the requirement that foreign public accounting firms must register with the PCAOB, and called for the negotiation of a transatlantic mutual recognition agreement based on home-country control.
- In a survey by LexisNexis, the majority of lawyers surveyed (700 worldwide) admitted that they are concerned about the impact of Sarbanes-Oxley on the legal profession.[1] They believe that clients will be fearful of being open and candid with their lawyers.
- Only one in ten lawyers—a considerably low number—believes the Act will bring more honesty from corporate executives.
- Lawyers in the United States fear they will not get the opportunity to work with lawyers abroad until those lawyers understand the Sarbanes-Oxley Act intimately.
- According to LexisNexis, of 600 foreign attorneys surveyed, most were "confused and uncertain of the effects of Sarbanes-Oxley and the SEC rules."
- According to the LexisNexis report, lawyers from foreign countries are concerned that the Act will attempt to prevail over national regulatory authorities in their respective countries.
- Ultimately, foreign issuers will likely have to adapt to the new regulations if they want to maintain access to the rich U.S. capital market; a sacrifice most will be willing to make.

Future

Two of the big questions relating to Sarbanes-Oxley are:

1. Will it restore public's faith in public accounting firms?
2. Will it restore investors' faith in public corporations?

Obviously, the hope is for an affirmative answer on both counts. It is undeniable that the public lost faith in both institutions as a result of the enormous fraud perpetuated by some highly respected and well-regarded companies. Though faith that the reforms will work is generally high, half of the executives surveyed said they believed it would take time to regain the public's trust. This is as expected; the onus is on every employee of every public company and every accountant to govern themselves in accordance with the principles of honesty and integrity. No one thinks that Sarbanes-Oxley will be an instant fix. "The last ten years dug a very, very deep hole," says Lynn E. Turner, an accounting professor at Colorado State University and former chief accountant for the SEC. "Usually you aren't able to crawl out of a hole overnight. It's a three- to five-year process."[2]

Sarbanes-Oxley has already had some positive effects. Analysts' reports usually recommended investors sell in 1 percent of the situations discussed; now that figure has increased to 20 percent. This is a strong indication of more independence and less collusion between interested parties. The percentage of shareholders winning proxy fights has also increased, and more shareholders brought motions against excessive compensation increases at companies' annual general meetings. Although the costs of compliance are high, in comparison to the astronomical losses suffered in the fall of Enron they are quite insignificant. Many of the reforms were not legally required until well into 2005, or as far into the future as 2007, so the results of this revolutionary Act will take a few years to be thoroughly assessed. Regardless, 81 percent of the CEOs of United States' fastest growing companies believe the costs of compliance will only grow in the coming years.

ENDNOTES

1. *http://www.lexisnexis.com/about/whitepaper/LexisNexis_Exec Summary.pdf*
2. *http://www.forbes.com/technology/corpgov/2003/07/22/cz_af_ 0722sarbanes.html*

CHAPTER 9

Summary for the CFO

In various polls and surveys of executives that have been conducted over the past few years, it has been observed that:

- An estimated 45% feel that Sarbanes-Oxley is a step in the right direction, but that compliance costs place an excess burden on companies.
- An estimated 30% feel that Sarbanes-Oxley is a good start but is not sufficient in and of itself.
- An estimated 15% feel that the Act was pushed through too quickly without enough consideration.
- An estimated 10% feel that the Act is adequate to address the current accounting and reporting issues.

It is not surprising that legislation as revolutionary as Sarbanes-Oxley produces divergent opinions, and it will take time to assess the actual outcomes and effects of the Act. In general, based on various polls and surveys, about one-third of executives believe that Sarbanes-Oxley will restore public confidence in the capital markets, while half think it will have no effect.

CHANGES TO CORPORATE GOVERNANCE

Regardless of the final outcome of Sarbanes-Oxley, what is certain is that it will change the face of corporate governance in the United States forever. Some of what is already taking place includes the following:

- Management certifications are being integrated into routine business and financial reporting processes.

- CEO involvement in financial reporting processes has increased.
- Companies are increasingly using technology in current systems or new systems that leverages their ability to analyze and identify potential and actual inaccuracies.
- There has been reinforcement of cultures that support accountability, responsibility, and financial and business integrity across all levels of the organization.
- There is increased engagement with external auditors, including more extensive discussions about accounting, reporting, internal controls, and audit-related matters.
- Policies, procedures, and standards are being created or formalized to identify and address all actual or potential violations of organizations' ethical, professional, or financial reporting values.
- There is an increased commitment from management to provide business information that has potential financial consequences in a timely manner.
- Internal audit responsibilities are shifting more toward oversight of financial integrity, including greater emphasis on the evaluation of finance-related internal controls and the reliability of financial systems.
- Executive management is linking the effectiveness of its internal controls over financial reporting to its certification under Section 302 of the Act; many companies are working on complying with Section 404 as a way to further support the certification process.
- Parent-company management certification processes and corporate governance principles are being replicated and leveraged at the subsidiary level, including in overseas subsidiaries.
- Disclosure committees that include representation from all departments and relevant strategic business units have been formed; they are meeting quarterly to discuss business events, transactions, and conditions requiring disclosure in the quarterly and annual reports.

CATALYST FOR IMPROVEMENT

The compliance effort will not come without pain and stress and fumbling. Yes, the costs of compliance may be hefty at first, but the inevitable outcomes are more accurate financial reporting and quicker access to pertinent information—two things that should certainly improve investor confidence at least a little bit. Still, executives are currently under great pressure to understand and apply Sarbanes-Oxley, and to maintain a corporate environment that continuously supports the basis of that Act: accurate, timely, and transparent information.

Although Sarbanes-Oxley itself focuses on financial data and information, the eventual consequence of the efforts to comply is that each corporation will become stronger, healthier, and more cohesive. The operational overhaul that is required will bring together all the disparate departments, business units, and functions, forcing them to discover the value that each brings to the organization as a whole. This understanding and awareness of how all the pieces fit together is a rich source of growth potential that can spur the organization to accomplish objectives and develop strategies never before explored. Reform as broad and revolutionary as Sarbanes-Oxley is expected to cause some hardship; after all, as the saying goes, "no pain, no gain." Fortunately, what corporations stand to gain at the end is definitely worth the initial pain.

PART II

Sarbanes-Oxley for the IT Professional

The goal of this part is to help a CIO or other senior-level IT professional understand the process to follow, from a technology perspective, to assist the CEO and the CFO in making the organization Sarbanes-Oxley compliant. It is designed to help the IT professional:

- Understand the key issues in Sarbanes-Oxley compliance.
- Visualize the IT infrastructure from the holistic perspective of an enterprise technology ecosystem, specifically:
  - The key business processes of the enterprise.
  - The interaction of the key business processes with each other.
  - The flow of value across the enterprise.
  - The flow of information across the enterprise.
  - The ecosystem of business applications inhabiting the enterprise.
  - The ecosystem of key technologies inhabiting the enterprise.
  - A vision for the future of the enterprise technology ecosystem aligned with the strategic goals of the enterprise.
- Understand the contributions of the key enterprise technologies in facilitating Sarbanes-Oxley compliance.
- Follow a well-defined process to enable the IT professional to create a Sarbanes-Oxley Compliant Key Enterprise Technology (SOCKET™) team. This SOCKET team will interact with the Sarbanes-Oxley compliance committee under the Chief Compliance Officer (CCO) or Chief Risk Officer (CRO) and will cover all aspects of the enterprise technologies relevant to Sarbanes-Oxley.

The basic premises of this part are as follows:

- In many ways, Sarbanes-Oxley matters are no different from "IT as usual"; all the things that IT will do to become Sarbanes-Oxley–compliant are really things the department should have been doing anyway.
- The Sarbanes-Oxley compliance effort is an opportunity to get systems in place to streamline organizational processes, as well as to simplify and streamline reporting mechanisms.
- Of U.S. companies, 80 percent already have 80 percent of the technology they need to achieve Sarbanes-Oxley compliance.

CHAPTER 10

Impact of Sarbanes-Oxley

The impact of the Sarbanes-Oxley Act on IT can be arrived at logically through the process of ripple-effect reasoning:

- Sarbanes-Oxley affects the CEO and CFO directly, as they must certify the authenticity and accuracy of certain documents, both financial and other.
- This certification responsibility, in turn, affects the corporate finance, governance, and knowledge management systems that support the CEO and the CFO in generating those documents.
- This, in turn, affects the technology infrastructure that, to a large extent, encapsulates and automates the finance, governance, and knowledge management systems.
- The design and operation of a technology infrastructure are the responsibility of the IT department, which is headed up by a CIO and/or CTO.

The ripple effect of Sarbanes-Oxley on the CIO and his or her IT department has to be examined through various intermediate stages if we are to obtain any insight into the exact nature of its impact. The following sections explore this.

IMPACT ON THE ENTERPRISE, THE CEO, AND THE CFO

The primary impact on the CEO, the CFO, and the enterprise as a whole arises out of Sections 302 and 404. Section 302 requires the CEO and CFO to personally certify the authenticity, accuracy, and reliability of the organization's financial reports. Section 404 requires them to certify the status of the company's internal controls.

Further, Section 409 mandates real-time disclosure of material events. The SEC has now listed nearly 20 material events. Also, if we adhere to the spirit of the Act rather than its letter, it is clear that the Sarbanes-Oxley Act is intended to maximize the factual representation of all financial information about a public company of which management is aware (or should be aware). This includes projections, forecasts, and all events or trends that will affect the company in the short or long term.

In summary, then, the major impact of Sarbanes-Oxley on the CEO, the CFO and, in general, on the enterprise is in the following six areas:

1. Accelerated reporting requirements:
   a. Reporting deadlines for filing periodic reports will arrive earlier.
   b. Faster reporting of significant internal or external "events" affecting the business's condition is required (Section 409).
   c. Insider trading is to be reported much faster.
2. Certification requirement:
   a. Review, accuracy, and authenticity certifications must be made by the CEO and CFO of all company filings (Sections 302 and 404).
3. Internal controls (Section 404):
   a. Internal controls must be effective and strong and they must be verified in the company's annual filings with the SEC.
   b. CEOs and CFOs must inform their boards if significant internal control deficiencies exist.
4. Recordkeeping:
   a. Auditors must maintain all documents and records pertaining to an audit for seven years (Section 103).
   b. Strong criminal penalties for altering, destroying, or falsifying records are imposed.
5. Conflict of interest:
   a. Audit firms cannot provide services for financial information systems design or implementation (Section 201).
   b. Each company must create an independent audit committee.
6. Communication: Whistleblowers must be allowed to communicate independently with the audit committee (Section 301).

IMPACT OF SARBANES-OXLEY ON CORPORATE MANAGEMENT SYSTEMS

The CEO and the CFO rely on the corporate financial, governance, and knowledge management systems when obtaining the financial and related information and documents they need to fulfill the certification and other requirements of Sarbanes-Oxley (described in the preceding section). In this section, the implications of Sarbanes-Oxley for the corporate management system are analyzed from an essence, spirit, or holistic perspective, as well as from a more reductionist perspective.

The Spirit of the Act: A Holistic View

In spirit, the Sarbanes-Oxley Act is aimed at providing accurate, "real-time"[1] corporate performance information to the investor. The ideal is that all relevant information that the CEO and the CFO observe during the normal course of business, and that could affect the company's financials by changing the direction of its strategic or operational course, should be disclosed to investors. Further, the Act is also aimed at ensuring that all important and significant information reaches the CEO, the CFO, and the investors in real time; that is, that no important information be tampered with, hidden, or delayed.

True implementation of real-time reporting to the investor would create a situation in which investors would effectively be able to participate in corporate decision making by "voting" on important events through means of the stock market. Positive information would immediately result in a rise in the stock price; negative information, such as the possibility of losing a large client, would result in an immediate drop in the company's stock price. This is the corporate democracy through which investors would be able to influence a company's decision making in real time. It would also ensure that the CEO has the confidence of the board, as well as of the majority of the investors.

Thus, the Sarbanes-Oxley Act has implications far beyond sending CEOs to jail. In actuality, it makes the theoretical or philosophical foundations of public companies and stock markets practical.

A Reductionist Perspective

The precise impact of Sarbanes-Oxley on corporate management systems is analyzed from a reductionist perspective in the following subsections.

Accelerated Reporting Requirements. The accelerated reporting requirements mean that reporting has to be done faster; hence, all relevant data must be consolidated in the reporting system more quickly and reports must be generated faster. This requires that mechanisms exist in the enterprise to quickly[2] assemble all relevant data and information in a centralized data repository.[3]

This centralized data repository should then be connected to an information and analysis system, through which the corporate analysts will quickly be able to analyze, judge, and report on the effect of any new event or information affecting the strategy and operations of the enterprise. A report distribution system or document management and workflow system will disburse the analysts' reports to the CEO and the CFO within the prescribed time frame and allow them enough time to make their own final judgments about the situation.

Finally, a public information distribution system should exist to quickly issue this information, if deemed important by the CEO and the CFO, to the investors and other stakeholders or relevant authorities prescribed by Sarbanes-Oxley.

Certification Requirements. The various certification requirements of Sarbanes-Oxley place the following requirements on corporate management systems:

- An accurate data capture system and a document capture system, to capture data and relevant information at the point of generation of the information.
- Secure data and document travel from the point of generation to the point of storage.
- A centralized data repository and document repository to securely store the relevant and prescribed data and documents.

- A secure data and document retrieval system with hierarchical access control.
- Data and document retention, destruction, and management systems based on the corporate data and document policies.

Internal Controls. The internal control requirements entail:

- Seamless integration of all systems through which financially relevant data, information, and documents travel.
- Security systems to implement hierarchical access control policies.
- Workflow management systems to implement the proper control for financially relevant business decisions, so that such decisions are made through the appropriate chain of command.
- Business process monitoring and management systems to implement and monitor the key business processes of the enterprise and provide control over them to top management.

Recordkeeping. Recordkeeping requirements are prescribed for auditors. Auditors will be required to maintain the relevant records for seven years. It makes good business sense to internally replicate the auditor's records for the same period of time. This forces the corporate management system to include or develop a records management system that allows secure, long-term storage of important documents; establishes document destruction and retention policies; and provides for implementation of those policies.

Communications. IT can fulfill the Sarbanes-Oxley communications requirements by implementing a secure and anonymous communication system between potential whistleblowers (meaning all employees) and the audit committee. The system should be conveniently and anonymously accessible to all employees, and information put into that system should reach the audit committee within a reasonable time frame. Further, the audit committee should be able to archive all the complaints securely and be able to investigate and provide status reports on the investigations through that system. Once an investigation is closed and the final report is deposited, it should be stored securely and for the long term.

IMPACT OF SARBANES-OXLEY ON THE TECHNOLOGY INFRASTRUCTURE

Most of the corporate management systems listed in the preceding section are encapsulated and implemented in enterprise applications and technologies.[4] Crucial requirements of the Sarbanes-Oxley Act are thus translated into requirements for a company's technology infrastructure, and therefore directly affect IT's core responsibility areas.

A company can be fairly straightforward in assigning the various available (and most likely already deployed) enterprise applications and technologies according to the requirements of the corporate management systems, as described in the following sections.

Accelerated Reporting Requirement

Quickly Assembling Data. The requirement regarding data assembly speed is fulfilled mostly through transaction processing systems, such as enterprise resource planning (ERP), supply chain management (SCM), and customer relationship management (CRM). In these systems, each transaction in which the enterprise is involved is captured at the point of the transaction itself. The systems are structured such that a transaction cannot go through unless all the relevant data is incorporated into them.[5]

In many corporations, this kind of data might be captured through legacy or functionally dedicated (single-module) transaction processing systems, such as sales order management systems, procurement systems, billing systems, and so on. In these cases, the data is usually routed in some form to the "mother-ship" ERP system. However, if the integration is not done properly, there is the possibility of a weakness at this point.

If the enterprise uses several such disparate legacy or functionally dedicated systems,[6] it is important to closely audit their integration with the core financial and accounting or ERP system.

Centralized Data (or Centrally Accessible Data) Repository. This kind of data repository is inherently available in corporations that have an integrated ERP system in place. For other organizations, with heterogeneous technologies and business applications, the repository would exist if data warehouse systems (especially extraction, transformation, and loading [ETL] tools) have been deployed and the appropriate metadata architecture has been implemented (i.e., centralized for small- and medium-sized enterprises, decentralized for large enterprises, or distributed for enterprises that have gone through several mergers and acquisitions).

For very large organizations with multiple transaction systems and data overlap problems,[7] this centralized repository can be supplemented with enterprise repositories.

Reporting and Analytical Systems.   The reporting systems deployed in the corporation are likely to be much more sophisticated than a typical management information system (MIS). However, an MIS would fulfill a lot of the Sarbanes-Oxley reporting requirements. This does mean that the analysts have to take the MIS reports, feed them into spreadsheets, and then do their own analyses. Although this process is prone to error and is person-dependent, it is a reasonably good solution for small and medium-sized enterprises.

An alternative approach would be to import a lot of the analyses into preprogrammed business intelligence (BI) tools (such as OLAP, data mining, and related decision support tools) and let the analysts work out various analyses.

A new category of enterprise applications can be highly useful for providing reporting of "material events" in "real time": namely, business activity monitoring systems. Various enterprise applications have a module that falls into this category, and several dedicated applications in this category also exist.

Related classes of applications that will put real-time information at the fingertips of the CEO and the CFO are "Executive Dashboards" and the various business performance monitoring and operational intelligence systems.

Report Distribution System or Document Management and Workflow Systems.
Although reporting requirements would be satisfied with a report distribution system, it is best to go for an integrated (and versatile) document management and workflow system (DMS). A DMS combined with a workflow system would enable the same solutions to be uti-

lized for multiple requirements of Sarbanes-Oxley. Hence, this would be an ideal choice for Sarbanes-Oxley compliance; together with ERP and enterprise application integration (EAI), it may even be a "must-have" system.

Public Information Distribution System.   The Sarbanes-Oxley requirements regarding public distribution of information can be taken care of by deploying enterprise information portal systems. These portals can disburse information to the appropriate stakeholders and investors, as well as to regulatory authorities. The portals do the job of publishing the appropriate documents and real-time alerts through proper access control systems, after going through the predefined approval hierarchy, by posting them automatically on to the enterprise web sites on the Internet and any intranets. Most portal systems also allow automatic notification e-mails and short message service (SMS) alerts to be sent to subscribed users.

A simplified alternative is to have a basic web site where important information is published, and through which e-mail notifications to various agencies and regulatory authorities are sent, in addition to electronic and hard-copy filings. Further, notification of investors and stakeholders via e-mail newsletters can also fulfill several important requirements of Sarbanes-Oxley.

Certification Requirement

Data Capture System.   Automated solutions for data capture are usually implemented using transaction processing systems, either integrated applications such as ERP, CRM, and SCM, or functionally dedicated ones, such as sales order management system, billing systems, lead management systems, and so on.

Document Capture System.   Several document imaging and capture solutions are available with optical character recognition (OCR), intelligent character recognition (ICR), and intelligent mark recognition (IMR) capabilities. Further, solutions exist for form identification and recognition, as well as for structured and unstructured document information capture.

Secure Data and Document Transfer.   There are several solutions for secure data and document transfer, such as various kinds of encryption technology and digital rights management.

Internal Controls

Integration of Enterprise Applications.   Having an integrated ERP is the conceptually cleanest way of satisfying the requirement of seamless integration. Depending on where these systems are in terms of technology, this may or may not be a feasible option at present.

Fortunately, there are several other means of satisfying this requirement. Sharing data and documents in a centralized repository is one way to partially achieve this. A number of technologies for enterprise integration are currently available, including enterprise application integration, web services and web integration, data integration, middleware, XML (or its various versions such as ebXML and XBRL), and business process integration.

Security Systems.   Systems such as the role-based access control system, security audit system, encryption system, policy management software, and vulnerability management software provide the basic security infrastructure required for Sarbanes-Oxley compliance.

Communications

The communications system required for whistleblower protection and communication should be based on e-mail, telephone, and secure document management. Any system deployed must ensure the anonymity, accessibility, and objectivity of the communication and complaint tracking process established for whistleblower communications between employees and the audit committee.

Business Processes Affected by Sarbanes-Oxley

Six key business processes of the enterprise are:

1. Marketing and sales:
   a. Invoicing
   b. Collections
   c. Sales forecasting
2. Research, design, and development
3. Purchasing and subcontracting (supply chain):
   a. Ordering
   b. Payments
   c. Material logistics
4. Production planning and control:
   a. Raw material and work in progress (WIP) inventory management
   b. Quality system
   c. Labor management
5. Distribution and warehousing:
   a. Finished goods inventory management
   b. Warehouse management
   c. Dealer logistics
6. After-sales service

These are the core processes of a live enterprise. With the exception of processes 5 and 9 (that is, research, design, and development and after-sales service), all these business processes are directly affected by Sarbanes-Oxley. The systems that are used to manage these processes, whether manual or automated, will thus also be affected. Further, comprehensive, confident, and convenient compliance with Sections 302 and 404 will dictate that these systems be seamlessly integrated with each other; ideally, they would be incorporated into one single system (for example, an integrated ERP).

However, many large public companies are the product of several mergers or acquisitions, and their operations are spread out globally and involve many diverse product lines. This typically results in a jigsaw of incompatible, legacy IT systems from the merged companies. Further, each geographic location can typically be expected to have a different IT system, and each product-line function may be treated as a different business unit and thus have its own IT system. This complexity poses its own set of challenges.

ENDNOTES

1. "Real time" implies a predefined time interval. Thus, the information should reach the investor within a prescribed time after the information is generated. The time frame prescribed by Sarbanes-Oxley differs for different kinds of information.
2. See the definition of *real time* in note 1. Here, it is recommended that *quickly* be understood to mean much less than the minimum "real-time" time interval specified in the Sarbanes-Oxley Act, which is two days.
3. Or centrally accessible data repository. This allows a distributed data architecture with centralized access, possibly through a centralized metadata repository.
4. Of course, it is possible to continue implementing several of the corporate management systems without much technology. However, this will make them highly inefficient, ineffective, slow, and prone to errors and deficiencies.
5. This provides a form of control on the transaction, as well as on the data, at the point of generation.
6. This is quite possible for a large organization with a long history that has gone through numerous mergers and acquisitions.
7. For example, the same customer information is available in slightly different formats in the ERP, CRM, and SCM systems, but there is no simple automated way to determine whether this is so.

CHAPTER 11

Technologies Affected by Sarbanes-Oxley: From Sarbanes-Oxley to SOCKET

Even in a simplified IT environment, it is expected that the CRM system (managing sales and distribution), the SCM system (typically managing the procurement supply chain and sometimes the distribution or demand chain), the ERP system (managing the financials and accounting), internal controls, inventory, and production will all be using different IT systems. Add to these the numerous supporting IT systems for the several subsidiary business processes, and the real picture of the various data islands in the enterprise begins to emerge. It is to be expected that the data from these disparate systems will not reflect the same view of reality. What data represents the true picture of reality is anybody's guess.

However, the CEO and the CFO, subject to personal liability and risk, must sign and certify that the financial reports are accurate and reflect the true picture to the best of their knowledge; furthermore, they must certify that they have checked the internal controls supporting the financial processes. This puts the pressure on the CIO in turn to ensure that the key business processes are properly implemented and that the data is accurate and secure. How to accomplish this is the focus of the remaining chapters in this book.

SEPARATE VENDOR HYPE FROM REALITY

For obvious reasons, Sarbanes-Oxley carries with it some fear, uncertainty, and doubt (the FUD factor).

Fear exists because Sarbanes-Oxley legislates personal liability and prescribes fines for and imprisonment of the CEO and CFO who deviate from the Sarbanes-Oxley–prescribed rules and regulations.

Uncertainty exists because the exact steps to be taken to comply with Sarbanes-Oxley are still unclear. According to AMR Research, about 80 percent of CIOs are not sure of the exact significance of Sarbanes-Oxley for their company.

Doubt exists about the precise impact of Sarbanes-Oxley on the enterprise, the CEO, the CFO, and the CIO. There is also considerable doubt about the extent to which Sarbanes-Oxley will be enforced, and the sections that the SEC will choose to enforce.

Many vendors are appearing, hoping to cash in on this Sarbanes-Oxley–created FUD factor. The way to separate vendor hype from reality is to *do your own analysis*. There is no simple way to separate hype from reality. In general, even with established vendors, there is a fine line between hype and reality. Nevertheless, vendors are an important source of relevant information and a lot of that information cannot be dismissed as mere hype. However, especially when the issue is of compliance with laws such as Sarbanes-Oxley, it is important for the CIO, CEO, and CFO to keep an extremely skeptical mindset to prevent the implications of noncompliance from clouding their thinking.

The way to cut through the vendor hype, or any other hype, is to ask specific questions and get into the details of the service and product offerings. The devil of hype hides within the details. The questions in Exhibit 11.1 are provided as a guideline for querying a vendor about its products and/or services.

SARBANES-OXLEY COMPLIANCE AS AN IT PROJECT

It is imperative that Sarbanes-Oxley compliance be viewed by the CIO as an IT project. A *project* can be defined as a list of activities undertaken to achieve a desired outcome or goal using predefined, fixed resources, and completed within a given time frame. This will help in the implementation of Sarbanes-Oxley, as IT will be used according to the desired time line, with well-understood goals and within budget. The risk of project failure is reduced. Sarbanes-Oxley compliance is one project where failure is not an option.

EXHIBIT 11.1   Vendor/Product Due-Diligence Checklist

Which section(s) of Sarbanes-Oxley does the product/service relate to?

How does the product/service support compliance with those sections of Sarbanes-Oxley?

Are there other classes of products from other vendors that also claim to provide compliance?

Will the vendor provide a written statement that the product/service provides compliance with Sarbanes-Oxley?

How does the product/service improve upon the existing system? What deficiency in the existing system does it address?

Is there a simpler and more inexpensive way to rectify this deficiency?

Has the vendor worked with Sarbanes-Oxley experts to develop the system?

What other changes will have to be made if the product is purchased and implemented? Will it affect other systems that are already in place? Will any or all of these have to be changed?

Have any Sarbanes-Oxley experts certified or endorsed the product/service as "Sarbanes-Oxley compliant"?

However, although the initial project to achieve Sarbanes-Oxley compliance must have a fixed time frame, organizations must also set up ongoing programs that monitor and take corrective actions to maintain compliance with Sarbanes-Oxley. This will have a profound effect on the way an organization coordinates its financial accounting system development with its IT organization.

PERSPECTIVE ON SARBANES-OXLEY GOALS

How the CIO chooses the goal of the Sarbanes-Oxley compliance project for IT is itself an important decision. There are several goals the CIO may choose from:

- **The obvious.** The goal for Sarbanes-Oxley compliance using IT as set by the CEO or the CFO.

- **The easy.** Vendor-recommended Sarbanes-Oxley–compliant product implementation.
- **The mandatory.** Foolproof implementation of Sarbanes-Oxley Compliant Key Enterprise Technologies (SOCKET) across the organization. Any change in the SOCKET ecosystem should be arrived at via a structured approach, without affecting the Sarbanes-Oxley compliance of the system.
- **The proactive.** Achieve strategic enterprise goals through proper encapsulation of key business processes (KBPs) in a SOCKET ecosystem.

A CIO will have to choose the goal that is appropriate for the company's current situation and constraints. However, given sufficient resources and operational freedom, it is best to choose the proactive goal. The easy goal might be the one to go for if the vendor's claims have been verified by the corporate Sarbanes-Oxley compliance team and have been found to result in Sarbanes-Oxley compliance, *and* the vendor has successfully implemented its product/service in a company in a similar industry sector. The obvious goal will have to be achieved in any case. The mandatory goal is the best way to ensure that all important processes for Sarbanes-Oxley compliance using technology have been followed.

STEPS FOR SARBANES-OXLEY COMPLIANCE

The detailed process for Sarbanes-Oxley compliance for IT is provided later. Here, we give a brief overview of the main steps involved.

The process toward compliance begins with a broad-level conversation with the compliance team, led by the Chief Compliance Officer (CCO)[1] or equivalent. The compliance team should include the CEO, the CFO, the CIO, the CCO, and other relevant personnel. This team should prepare a *vision for compliance* document, a *timeline for compliance* document (the internal time frame for compliance with various sections of Sarbanes-Oxley), and a *resources for compliance* document (the resources and costs the company is able and willing to commit to the compliance effort). They must then follow a *strategy for compliance.*

This compliance strategy will prescribe the mix of people, processes, and technology that will be required to achieve compliance. The processes will have to be audited and analyzed. The extent of automation, the number of IT systems, and the number of people required to implement each of these processes will have to be studied.

The processes themselves might have to be modified to make them fundamentally more secure and controlled. The control features in each of the IT systems will have to be configured to attain the desired controls. The remaining control deficiencies can either be addressed through implementing new IT systems, or can be done manually by creating new control procedures, documenting them, and assigning responsibilities to the appropriate personnel. The basic principle underlying proper design of these controls is that a sufficiently large number of people be involved in the controls to prevent the possibility of collusion that is able to circumvent the control. However, this requirement has to be balanced against the requirement that the process be efficient.

There is another possibility for fundamentally changing the architecture of the IT system and acquiring completely new software (possibly a single-instance ERP) into which all the processes and the data are migrated. The chances are high that this kind of system will be Sarbanes-Oxley compliant. However, the chances of a single-instance ERP being able to take care of all the diverse needs of a global, multiproduct, highly diversified enterprise are very low.[2] Even if such an ERP exists, migrating to it will be an extremely high-risk, time-consuming, and costly venture—exactly the kind of thing Sarbanes-Oxley, in spirit, was designed to save investors from!

Ten Steps to Sarbanes-Oxley Compliance

Exhibit 11.2 provides a step-by-step process for achieving Sarbanes-Oxley compliance in an enterprise. (To download a copy of this worksheet, visit *www.SarbanesOxleyGuide.com*.) In general, an initial business process analysis (BPA) usually identifies:

- Inefficiency in information flow.
- Inaccuracy and security vulnerabilities in the transaction, analysis, and reporting systems.

EXHIBIT 11.2 Process Steps

	Process Step	Time Frame	Budget
1.	Understand key sections of Sarbanes-Oxley, especially Sections 302 and 404.		
2.	Decide to create a Sarbanes-Oxley Compliant Key Enterprise Technology (SOCKET) ecosystem.		
3.	Develop a project plan for the SOCKET ecosystem.		
4.	Get the approval of the CEO and the CFO for creating the SOCKET ecosystem.		
5.	Identify and select the top level of the SOCKET compliance committee.		
6.	Conduct a Sarbanes-Oxley requirements analysis.		
7.	Implement a "Sarbanes-Oxley Compliance for IT" or SOCKET process at the pilot site.		
8.	Replicate this success story at all locations.		
9.	Audit and confirm that Sarbanes-Oxley compliance has been achieved.		
10.	Put an ongoing SOCKET audit and implementation process and team in place to ensure continued Sarbanes-Oxley compliance.		

■ Ineffective internal controls.

■ Deficiencies in real-time reporting and control monitoring capability for CEOs and CFOs.

■ Inappropriate data, document, and record storage; appropriate data storage for the long term (at least seven years); and disaster recovery infrastructure requirements.

■ Communication systems inefficiency or security vulnerability.

The BPA exercise should be followed by business process reengineering (BPR) to correct the identified deficiencies and then a business process management (BPM) system to help implement the new business processes and monitor them.

Total Cost of Compliance

The total cost of compliance (TCC) should be calculated in a manner similar to calculating the total cost of any project or product. For this, we need to look at the complete process for compliance. Of course, we will restrict discussion here to the costs of the IT department.

The IT department will want to form a SOCKET team, which will spend time, effort, and resources on the compliance project. Further, the SOCKET team may need to acquire IT products and/or services that will require additional investment. Total cost is calculated taking into account the required people, processes, and technologies. Cash flow, internal rate of return (IRR), and other related calculations are done for financial justification.

This is one of the most crucial steps in a SOCKET implementation. All the inputs related to people, processes, and technology must be fully understood. Each gap, risk-control area, and internal control systems area is analyzed in detail, and a detailed project plan is made for each identified initiative. For each project, the requirements of resources, time frame, deliverables, budget, and control measures are worked out. (For more details, refer to the SOCKET TCC Calculator spreadsheet at *www.sarbanesoxleyguide.com*. It is one of the most valuable tools you can get for use in your Sarbanes-Oxley compliance journey.)

SARBANES-OXLEY AND THE SEC

A number of recent articles suggest that the SEC has watered down the Sarbanes-Oxley requirements and that not much need be done to comply with the SEC rulings. Is this the best approach, or is the best approach yet to come? The SEC might have weakened the Sarbanes-Oxley Act in implementation, but whose organization would you like to risk being the first to test these waters?

To play it safe, the best recourse is to take the strong interpretation of Sarbanes-Oxley and to comply with that. This is recommended, as what Sarbanes-Oxley mandates is good business practice in any case. However, given financial or other resource constraints, it might be a reasonable decision to adhere to the bare minimum required by SEC recommendations. When choosing the latter strategy, it is important to understand the risks involved and commit to a strong interpretation of Sarbanes-Oxley compliance in the long term.

ENDNOTES

1. The CCO is usually a senior professional, with a legal background, who has an understanding of enterprise operations at the broad or big-picture level as well as at the ground level. The CCO should have the appropriate authority within the company, and the CEO, the CFO, and the CIO should be accessible to him or her. The key personnel in the enterprise should also believe in this person's capability and expertise. The CCO can be either a consultant or a homegrown officer with a long history in the organization.
2. This might, however, be a longer-term goal for medium-sized companies while achieving compliance.

CHAPTER 12

Enterprise Technology Ecosystem

The SOCKET methodology can be viewed from an "ecosystem" perspective. This means that all the components of the ecosystem are treated as important and critical. A change in any one of the components will result in a change in the way the ecosystem works. At any particular point in time, the ecosystem may be optimized or tuned for accomplishing a certain set of business or technology objectives, or for delivering a particular set of functionalities exceptionally well. As the business environment changes, the ecosystem should be optimized in accordance with those changes.

ORGANIC IT ARCHITECTURE

The ecosystem perspective gives an organic and evolving view of the enterprise architecture. In contrast, the conventional enterprise architecture view is static and mechanistic. In the conventional view, the business objectives are assumed as a given and the technology architecture is developed to optimize achievement of business objectives.

In the technology ecosystem, it is recognized that the business ecosystem[1] itself is dynamic and that the business objectives are therefore always changing. Further, the technology components themselves are continuously evolving. Hence, the enterprise architecture should be designed to evolve and adapt; thus, it has to be viewed as an ecosystem.

In a static, inorganic view of the enterprise technology infrastructure, change requires a company to completely redesign the new architecture from scratch, while hoping to keep as much of the existing technology unchanged as possible. This static viewpoint yields an infrastructure that is then optimized for the new conditions—but by the time the changes are in place, the conditions have changed again. The technology infrastructure always lags behind the business objectives.

The solution to this dilemma is to view the enterprise as a dynamic, organic ecosystem. The ecosystem perspective emphasizes the idea that the technology infrastructure is dynamic, and though it may be stable or tuned or optimized at any given point in time, it will eventually change again. The key is to change it in a controlled manner, at a rate of change suitable to the enterprise, and in a direction dictated by the enterprise business objectives.

This requires viewing the technology ecosystem as a whole. The technology ecosystem has to be seen as an infrastructure layer supporting the business processes of the enterprise in the entire business ecosystem, both within and outside the enterprise. The purpose of the technology ecosystem is to make the business processes faster, more efficient, and more effective.

ECOSYSTEM AND SARBANES-OXLEY

When the business requirements change, such as in the case of new laws like Sarbanes-Oxley, the technology ecosystem must be reviewed in the context of the new business ecosystem. The new business process ecosystem also has to be analyzed. The SOCKET ecosystem, for example, dictates these four rules:

1. **Section 103.** Documents and records should be preserved for seven years to mirror the storage requirements for auditors.
2. **Section 302.** All the financial data should be accurate.
3. **Section 404.** The internal controls must be in place and auditable.
4. **Section 409.** There should be real-time reporting of "material" events that affect current and projected financials. This makes it important to apply these newly important business requirements to the ecosystem and change it accordingly.

Should this be taken to mean that a completely new technology infrastructure is required? The short answer is no. One of the fundamental premises of this guidebook is that *80 percent of companies already have at least 80 percent of the technology required to achieve Sarbanes-Oxley compliance.*

However, adapting an ecosystem to new business and regulatory stimuli (or requirements) will necessitate a detailed audit of the infrastructure. The output or work product of that audit will be a report with a gap analysis of what the ideal system for the current business requirement of Sarbanes-Oxley compliance looks like and how well the current system provides for compliance.

The next step is to compile a reengineering report. This report outlines how many of the requirements identified by the gap analysis can be satisfied by reorganizing the existing technology infrastructure, and which of them may require new technology. With this report in hand, the reorganized technology infrastructure is created and then the remaining gaps are filled using new technologies. Even here, a lot can be accomplished by procuring or developing simple patches or fixes; usually, only a few requirements will demand completely new technology.

The enterprise technology ecosystem is designed to adaptively and continuously align the enterprise business and technology goals and operations in the continuously changing business ecosystem. The technology ecosystem allows the CIO to visualize the enterprise IT infrastructure from a holistic perspective and to see its interaction or relationship to changes in the business ecosystem (for example, Sarbanes-Oxley and the financial business processes that it affects).

ENDNOTE

1. See J. Moore, *The Death of Competition: Leadership and Strategy in the Age of Business Ecosystems* (Chichester, UK: John Wiley & Sons, 1996); M. Zeleny, R. J. Cornet, and J. A. F. Stoner, "Moving from the Age of Specialization to the Era of Integration," *Human Systems Management* 9 (1999): 153–170.

CHAPTER 13

Implementing the SOCKET Methodology

Sarbanes-Oxley has changed the existing business ecosystem by affecting some key business processes, which have, in turn, had an effect on the accuracy of financial reports and internal controls on financials. These business processes create or capture relevant financial information through software applications running on specific technology platforms. The SOCKET methodology enables us to visualize how all these aspects work together. Specifically, the SOCKET methodology assists and enables the CIO to visualize the enterprise IT infrastructure holistically and to gain insight into its interaction with and relationship to both Sarbanes-Oxley and financially relevant business processes.

SPECIES OR COMPONENTS OF THE ENTERPRISE TECHNOLOGY ECOSYSTEM

The business ecosystem, including the regulatory environment, defines the fundamental requirements of the enterprise technology ecosystem. The enterprise technology ecosystem is an interdependent system of various technology components, including hardware, software, networks, standards, and protocols, among others.

The enterprise technology ecosystem has to be designed so as to allow for frequent and continuous changes in the business ecosystem. Newly important business processes should be automated easily and made available through the existing technology ecosystem; at most, the company should have to buy only a limited number of new technology components to accommodate a particular set of business processes. In the most challenging case, the company will want to acquire an IT system that seamlessly meshes with the rest of the existing technology ecosystem, without causing serious problems for the rest of the enterprise. This, in essence, is the goal toward which the enterprise technology ecosystem strives.

The species inhabiting the enterprise technology ecosystem are the hardware, the software, the network, the standards, and the protocols. The business processes that utilize these keep changing with time. Hence, these components should be flexible and adaptable enough to accommodate any new business processes that becomes important in the future.

Interaction of the Species

The components interact with each other through interfaces. These interfaces should be such that they can be made to interact easily with any of the other species or components, without restriction or significant effort. In general, this calls for following open standards or de facto industry standards. Further, if vendor lock-in is to be avoided, to avert potentially disastrous dependency on a single vendor, the company must choose appropriate standards that are supported by multiple vendors.

Organic and Evolving Nature

Every CIO is fully aware that the enterprise technology ecosystem components (species) are continuously evolving and changing. The vendors providing these components try to make them better and faster and try to provide more features with each new generation of the species. In itself, this is good progress. However, viewing the enterprise ecosystem as a whole, the introduction of new species causes instability in the ecosystem. Each new species requires changes in business processes and the other species with which it interacts, in terms of training for the personnel involved in implementation, use, and maintenance of the new components.

If the new species is a piece of software, it might require newer hardware, more disk space, and better and faster networks. Sometimes, it could require that different standards or protocols be adopted. Data might have to be migrated from older formats or systems to new formats and systems. The implementation teams will have to be trained on the configuration capabilities; users will have to be trained on the features and functionality; and the maintenance team will have to be trained on the new administration and maintenance requirements and functionality of the new species.

All of this results in decreased productivity during migration time, extra effort from IT personnel for deployment and system migration, and time and effort from other business personnel to adapt to the new way of conducting the business process.

Benefits of the Ecosystem Perspective

The ecosystem perspective keeps these issues firmly in the limelight, emphasizing foresight, synthesis, and analysis before any technology-buying initiative is undertaken. It brings a very high level of perspective to planning and buying decisions, keeping the technology decisions closely aligned to the business drivers. If the business ecosystem so dictates, the first attempt will be to reconfigure the existing technology ecosystem to achieve the desired effects. If this is not possible within existing constraints, then a buying decision can be made.

What is to be bought? How will it fit into the current technology ecosystem? Will it help or hinder the enterprise in changing business models or processes in response to the changing business ecosystem? What repercussions will the new species have on the existing ecosystem? The ecosystem concept forces reflection on such questions and issues before a new technology species is introduced into the existing enterprise technology ecosystem.

COSO FRAMEWORK

The SOCKET methodology has to be supplemented by the Committee of Sponsoring Organizations of the Treadway Commission (COSO) framework to achieve Sarbanes-Oxley compliance. The COSO framework for internal controls, which relates to Section 404 of the Sarbanes-Oxley Act, has been suggested by the SEC as a possible framework for evaluating internal controls.

There are three main objectives for determining which internal controls are to be applied:

1. Efficiency and effectiveness of operations.
2. Financial reporting reliability.
3. Regulatory compliance.

For each of these objectives, the five components of internal control are:

1. **Control Environment.** Corporate control culture and consciousness.
2. **Risk Assessment.** Assessment of risk factors for each objective.
3. **Control Activities.** Corporate policies, procedures, and processes that ensure the span of management control throughout the enterprise.
4. **Information and Communication.** Implementation of key business processes for efficient capture, storage, and distribution of relevant information required for efficient operations.
5. **Monitoring.** Ongoing or periodic internal control assessment processes.

These five components of internal control are evaluated for each objective at both the unit (functional) level and the activity (business process) level.

This framework is discussed to give you a feel for the overall internal audit that the corporate Sarbanes-Oxley audit team will have to carry out during its evaluation of internal controls. Because one of the core components of internal control, according to COSO, is information and communication; this will relate directly to the IT infrastructure of the enterprise. Further, the functional- and business-process-level assessments will also include assessment of the technology infrastructure in supporting those requirements. Hence, it is important that selected personnel (i.e., both the SOCKET audit team and the SOCKET implementation team) become conversant with COSO and how it applies to Sarbanes-Oxley and the technology infrastructure of the enterprise. IT controls such as security, physical access control over digital assets and corporate knowledge, business continuity and disaster recovery, control on the implementation of new applications and technology, modifications to existing applications and technology, retirement or maintenance of existing applications and technology, and authorization for personnel to access only relevant information technology assets are some of the pertinent enterprise-wide controls.

SOCKET TECHNOLOGIES

The following are some of the general principles to adhere to for achieving a SOCKET ecosystem:

- Centralized (or centrally accessible) data repository.
- Centralized (or centrally accessible) document repository.
- Pervasive logical and physical security infrastructure.
- Pervasive enterprise hierarchical access control to IT and information assets.
- Personnel access to information assets and IT restricted to the required domain of responsibilities.
- Secure and accurate mechanisms for the transfer of data, document, and other information assets from one layer or species of technology to another.
- Enterprise-wide business continuity plans and disaster recovery procedures for the enterprise technology ecosystem.

TRANSACTIONAL SYSTEMS: ERP, SCM, CRM

The key business processes of an enterprise, such as sales and procurement, can be automated using transactional systems. Earlier, and to some extent even today, businesses developed specialized software or systems that were dedicated to automating a particular aspect of a key business process, such as a sales order management system for processing sales orders. After the sales order was approved, it was passed on for further processing to the dispatch department, where the data was rekeyed into another transactional system for warehouse management.

Once the inventory levels in the warehouse reached a predefined level, the warehouse management system generated an alert and a predefined number of units were requested from the production department. The production department was then alerted and worked on replenishing the warehouse to the desired level. The production department then checked its own production planning system and ordered the required amount of raw material from the stores. Once the raw material inventory in the stores reached a certain level, the store's management system generated an alert, and a reorder of a predefined number of units of raw materials was passed on to the respective suppliers.

In this type of system, each stage added latencies in information transfer, and the business processes of the enterprise were implemented in a very inefficient manner. Further, many errors were made during the rekeying or reentry of data. The designs of the "source" systems' reports and the "target or sink" systems' input forms would inevitably be slightly different, resulting in a loss or distortion of data. Any enterprise-wide holistic analysis would be inherently difficult due to the sheer effort required to consolidate all the relevant data from all the separate legacy systems into a single system. Such an enterprise was not self-aware; only the subprocesses automated by single software were each self-aware and open to analysis and self-improvement.

To circumvent these problems, the concept of enterprise resource planning was born. *ERP* refers to an enterprise-wide transactional system that captures key business-process data at the point of generation. The core business processes of finance, production planning, and inventory management were automated and encapsulated in a single system. The dream of ERP was, of course, to embody all the key business processes and present a single transactional framework and database.

As it turns out, there were other key business processes as well, such as the sales process, customer interaction, supplier interaction, and so on. This gave rise to two other key categories of enterprise software: customer relationship management (CRM) and supply chain management (SCM).

Today, it is generally accepted that ERP is the core transactional system providing automation of the enterprise's internal business processes; SCM provides automation for the back end or supply side of the enterprise, and CRM provides automation for the front end or demand side of the enterprise. Thus, this trio of systems forms the core transactional system that completes the value chain and key business processes of the extended enterprise, forming a closed loop.

This closed loop of key business processes is what Sarbanes-Oxley affects the most. Any glitch, anywhere along this value chain, will immediately propagate through the rest of the value chain. This could result in a loss of revenue due to loss of sales, if some aspect of demand could not be fulfilled in time. In many cases, such a problem even threatens the very existence of the enterprise.

The case study in Exhibit 13.1 starkly demonstrates the crucial role that automation of the key business processes will play in Sarbanes-Oxley compliance. All of these processes have significant impacts on the financials of the company, because they affect sales, revenues, supply, inventory, and costs.

Even Alan Greenspan, in his testimony of the Federal Reserve Board's semiannual monetary policy report to the Congress, before the Committee on Banking, Housing, and Urban Affairs, U.S. Senate, February 13, 2001 emphasized the benefits of SCM and related software:

> *New technologies for supply-chain management and flexible manufacturing imply that businesses can perceive imbalances in inventories at a very early stage—virtually in real time—and can cut production promptly in response to the developing signs of unintended inventory building.*[1]

EXHIBIT 13.1   Before and After Sarbanes-Oxley

Before Sarbanes-Oxley

In 2000, Ericsson, the Swedish manufacturer of mobile phones, faced a sales shortfall of nearly $1 billion. This was partly the result of a fire in a factory of one of its crucial microchip suppliers. Ericsson found out about the fire more than a week later. Nokia came to know about it even before being formally informed by the supplier, by which time it had already taken action by contacting alternative suppliers.

After Sarbanes-Oxley

Suppose that a similar occurrence took place in a major corporation today. Would the CEO and CFO have to face a "challenging" situation? Possibly jail? Would the nonreporting of the significant event within two days be a violation of Section 409 of Sarbanes-Oxley?

The following is typically how the business cycle operates: CRM sales order creation triggers the value chain. The order goes to the fulfillment management module and a product is dispatched to the customer. Once the product leaves the warehouse, this information goes into the warehouse management module of the ERP system and triggers a requirement for one more piece of the just-dispatched product. This triggers a requirement in the production planning module of the ERP system and, in turn, in the stores module of the ERP system for the raw materials related to the product. Dispatch of the raw materials to the production line creates a requirement in the raw materials inventory management module of the SCM system, and this is propagated throughout the tiers of the supplier's enterprise systems.

The weak links in this information value chain are where the information leaves the CRM system and enters the ERP system, and where it leaves ERP and enters the SCM system. It is possible that data loss or distortion could take place at these points.[2]

There is also a risk of loss of internal controls, because it is possible for supplies to be ordered through the SCM system at costs for which there might be no customers in the marketplace; or for customer orders to be booked that cannot be fulfilled within the time period promised; or for products to be planned for which raw material cannot be obtained within the time period planned. These are inherent risks of having different systems for these processes. The case study in Exhibit 13.2 gives an example of these kinds of risks.[3]

These risks could result in violation of Section 404. Further, due to different information on, for example, the current finished goods, work in progress, and raw materials in the different systems, financial inaccuracies could result, thus violating Section 302. Also, if the glitches anywhere along the value chain of the three systems are not

EXHIBIT 13.2   Volvo

In the mid-1990s, the Swedish car manufacturer, Volvo, found itself with excessive stocks of green cars. To move them along, the sales and marketing departments began offering attractive special deals, so green cars started to sell. Unfortunately, nobody had told the manufacturing department about the promotions. It noted the increase in sales, read it as a sign that consumers had started to like green, and ramped up production.

brought to the immediate attention of the CEO and the CFO, there could be a loss of revenues, and this situation could end up in a violation of Section 409 because investors and regulatory agencies would not have been immediately informed by the CEO and CFO of "material events" occurring in the company.

The fact remains, however, that these three transactional systems have reduced the points of failure by orders of magnitude. Sarbanes-Oxley compliance will be much easier with these systems in place (or at least some of these in place, especially ERP) than without them.

CFP Research Services and Cap Gemini Ernst & Young surveyed 265 financial executives in 2002. The survey showed that 98 percent of the respondents had ERP systems that were not fully integrated with other applications; 71 percent felt that full integration could not be achieved even within the next three years.[4]

It is obvious that there is no way to obtain completely accurate financial reports without full integration between all ERP and financially relevant software applications. How companies will be able to address Sarbanes-Oxley Section 302 for accurate financial reporting without such integration is anybody's guess. Further, it seems difficult to comply with Section 404 in terms of proper internal controls when the financial systems themselves are not properly integrated. In fact, the lack of integration virtually assures that the internal controls will have weaknesses. The best course CEOs and CFOs have, then, is to conduct a proper assessment of the weaknesses and develop a plan with a projected time line for eliminating these weaknesses.

Any quick-fix attempts will only result in weak internal controls. However, there are solutions to these problems:

- Configure the controls already present in the existing software systems.
- Consolidate and reconcile, as far as possible, the data in the multiple ERP systems or other existing transaction systems.
- Use financial reporting and business intelligence systems that use data from centralized data repositories and that consolidate the data from the ERP, SCM, CRM, and other systems.
- Support ERP, SCM, CRM, and other system by using Executive Dashboards and business activity monitoring systems that are programmed to provide alerts upon the occurrence of material events.

ANALYTICAL AND REPORTING SYSTEMS

Even today, a majority of companies, including Fortune 500 companies, use spreadsheets to perform various analyses on their corporate data and create reports for management. Unfortunately, the likelihood of introducing errors in any reasonably large spreadsheet model is more than 90 percent.[5]

Section 302

According to The Hackett Group's 2003 survey, 91 percent of companies are not confident of their reporting and forecasting data, and 47 percent still rely on spreadsheets for their reporting. This means transferring data from a large number of sources into the spreadsheets. This in itself significantly increases the odds that there will be corrupt or incorrect data in the spreadsheets. Combine this with the research on spreadsheet errors, and you can see that the resulting reports are virtually guaranteed to be inaccurate. So, in fact, the CEO or CFO can confidently certify that the financial reports are *not* correct!

Further, Hackett Group data also reveals that 89 percent of the responding CFOs feel that spreadsheet-based systems cannot comply with the internal control and audit requirements. Hence, this exposes the CFOs and CEOs under Section 404 in addition to Section 302.

Under such circumstances, the CEO and the CFO cannot confidently certify the financial and internal control reports as mandated by Sections 302 and 404. The enterprise has to move toward a financial reporting model that does not involve data being transferred from application to application through manual rekeying or copy-and-pastes where errors can be introduced.

An ideal solution is to have good reporting that integrates data from all the major transactional systems or from the central data repository. Good reporting also provides data in a manner that allows consistency checks across the data from the various systems and audit traces of the source of the data.

The data entering a central repository has to be checked for accuracy and the repository must have access control and security. All the financial reports would then be generated out of this central repository.

Another strategy is to obtain a reporting tool that has good features for transformation and visualization and to use it in conjunction with a centralized data repository. Most online analytical processing (OLAP) tools have excellent reporting features, and it is often suggested that this may be the best approach to achieve compliance with Sections 302 and 404. OLAP tools also permit users to obtain business insights into the way the business is performing, thereby creating an infrastructure for sustained competitive advantage.

Real-Time Executive Reporting: Section 409

Disclosure of material changes to within two business days. The fundamental requirement for this is that the company and its management become aware of material changes in real time. For most enterprises, this in itself seems difficult to do, let alone filing the appropriate disclosures and making them public. The relevant information has to reach top management in real time, and proper analysis of the information or data must be carried out in real time as well. The analysis of sales and payment data in real time, for example, can help trigger appropriate alerts in real time and thereby enable management to file disclosures within the stipulated two business days.

Some think that the nature of a majority of the "material events" listed by the SEC is such that they would not be part of the IT systems, and that the CEO and CFO would come to know about them through some other means. Consider the following material events listed by the SEC:

- #1: Change in control.
- #6: Publication of financial statements and exhibits.
- #8: Any disclosure under Regulation FD.
- #11: Results of operations and financial condition.
- #12: "Other materially important events."
- #5 (new): Termination or reduction of a business relationship with a customer that constitutes a specified amount of the company's revenues.

- #9 (new): Events triggering a direct or contingent financial obligation that is material to the company, including any default on or acceleration of an obligation.

All of these can be interpreted broadly as events that could come to notice through IT systems in place in the enterprise. Number 1 could occur if access is granted to someone not authorized, either intentionally or unintentionally. Number 6 could occur through automated publications using enterprise portals, and numbers 11 and 12 could include almost any operational event if it has a large financial impact. For example, this could be interpreted to include anything that could materially affect the business of the company, including events like the fire at Ericsson's supplier factory that resulted in major supply problems.

Because 11 new material events have been added to the 9 material events already specified, reporting systems should be configured and tuned to track potential cases and alert management before such material events occur. This will help management be ready with disclosure reports almost immediately. The best course of action, when the event may not be favorable to the company's business, is to put management's focus on preventing such an event from taking place.

For example, if it appears that a major customer is reducing or is on the path to reducing its buying from the company, top management can be alerted so that they can focus on preventing this situation, or, if it cannot be prevented, being ready to find alternate customers and take appropriate actions (including filing disclosures) when the triggering event does occur. Similarly, if payment from a customer appears to be delayed, a real-time reporting system would track the delay before it reaches writeoff status. Another scenario involves a major supplier that was unable to supply a crucial component or part on time. This would, again, send a real-time alert and allow management to prevent a material event that could substantially reduce sales revenues.

Section 403

Reporting insider trading within two business days and posting it on the company web site within one business day. What is required here is a reporting system such as a business activity monitoring system, business performance monitoring system, or an Executive Dashboard. These systems can be configured to alert key executives to potential threats and assist them in understanding whether these are material events.

DATA WAREHOUSING

Throughout this book, one of the key points that keeps recurring is that a centralized data repository is a must-have tool for running a better business, as well as for achieving Sarbanes-Oxley compliance. A data warehouse provides such a centralized data repository, which can consolidate the data islands spread across the enterprise ecosystem in various transactional and other functional automation systems.

According to a 2001 survey by PricewaterhouseCoopers: "Three-quarters [of the 600 companies across United States, Australia, and United Kingdom surveyed] reported significant problems as a result of defective data, with a third failing to bill or collect receivables as a result (*www.pwc.com*)."[6] The problem of "data cleansing" will have to be addressed even after ETL tools for extraction, transformation, and loading of the data. This is not a trivial problem, and should be focused on very carefully before implementing a data warehouse. However, once this difficult exercise is completed and the enterprise is confident about its data quality, the Sarbanes-Oxley certifications of financial accuracy can be signed. Further, working with high-quality data will provide a competitive advantage to the company.

One data quality control problem occurs at the time of data entry: specifically, IT users who enter the data at the point of information or data creation. In most cases, this is done via input screens in ERP and other transactional systems. It is critical that these users be well trained and made aware of the importance of accurate keying; it is also critical that a monitoring and control system be put in place to enforce good data entry quality. This helps eliminate one major hindrance to confident certification of internal controls in accordance with Section 404.

These solutions require data warehouse systems that provide bidirectional interaction; that is, systems that put data into the warehouse as well as making the data from the data warehouse available to the transactional systems. This also ensures the reuse of preexisting information (e.g., customers who are already present in the CRM system), and thereby eliminates the risk of incorrect data entry in the ERP system (e.g., erroneous reentry of that customer information).

OLAP

In a Sarbanes-Oxley–compliant environment, the data warehouse would be connected to an OLAP engine and other business intelligence systems. The various financial and analysis reports would be generated from this OLAP engine. Depending on various criteria, trigger alerts would be generated and sent to the appropriate senior managers.

OLAP allows management to drill down to transaction-level data, which is the foundation of various aggregated information provided in disclosure reports to the regulatory authorities. This can provide tremendous confidence to the CEOs and CFOs as to the quality and accuracy of the financial reports.

Business intelligence and business performance management systems exist that make it possible for the board or C-level executives to get views on key performance indicators. These users can also drill down to the lower levels, to see where the data came from and then deconstruct it. This drill-down capability goes down to the actual transaction-level reports.

Data Mining

The tool or technique of data mining does not apply directly to any section of the Sarbanes-Oxley Act, but it helps improve the business performance of an enterprise that has a large amount of good-quality data in a centralized data warehouse. It thereby contributes to the intent of the Act.

Data mining can reveal new patterns and correlations between sets of data that might not seem to have any direct relationship to each other. This can potentially provide new hypotheses on cause-

and-effect relations throughout the enterprise value chain. This will help improve internal controls for compliance:

- **Section 404.** In the hands of a good forensic accountant, data mining can be a useful tool for internal auditing of the internal controls. It can reveal whether someone has tampered with the data, using the frequencies of real data.
- **Section 409.** Data mining can also potentially alert the enterprise by detecting unforeseen patterns, such as any material events that might already have taken place or be in the offing.

ENDNOTES

1. *http://www.federalreserve.gov/boarddocs/hh/2001/february/testi mony.htm* (accessed 11/28/05).
2. See J. Woods, A. White, K. Peterson, and M. Jimenez, "Demand Chain Management Synchronizes CRM and SCM" (Gartner Research Note, October 28, 2002); Simon Pollard, *Count the Money when Sales and Marketing Work with Logistics* (AMR Research, October 2001).
3. *http://www.economist.com/surveys/displayStory.cfm?Story_id= 949105* Hau Lee, *Ultimate Enterprise Value Creation Using Demand-Based Management* (Stanford Global Supply Chain Management Forum, September 2001).
4. Cap Gemini Ernst & Young, CFOs: Driving Finance Transformation for the 21st Century, *http://www.ca.cgey.com/knowledge_ centre/insights/findrivingfinancetransformation.pdf*
5. D. Freeman, "How to Make Spreadsheets Error-Proof," *Journal of Accountancy* 181, no. 5 (1996): 75–77; KPMG Management Consulting, "Supporting the Decision Maker: A Guide to the Value of Business Modeling," press release, July 30, 1998, *http://www.kpmg.co.uk/uk/services/manage/press/970605a.html*
6. PricewaterhouseCoopers, *Global Data Management Survey 2001.*

CHAPTER 14

SOCKET and Enterprise Information Management

According to some estimates, more than 70 percent of the documents owned by an enterprise are in digital format and might never be seen in hard copy. Enterprise information management, or document management, is perhaps one of the most important of the enterprise technologies that will provide a solution to the various requirements of Sarbanes-Oxley. Without proper systems for managing the information held within the company, compliance with Sarbanes-Oxley will be very difficult. This chapter presents the various Sarbanes-Oxley provisions and regulations that relate directly to effective document management.

DOCUMENT MANAGEMENT AND SARBANES-OXLEY

Several sections of Sarbanes-Oxley have a direct bearing on the manner in which the digital documents or records of the enterprise are created, reviewed, approved, stored, retrieved, transferred, and destroyed. According to Gartner, records management will become a "top 10" issue for many CIOs in the coming years.[1]

On the following pages, we discuss the particular sections of Sarbanes-Oxley for which a document management solution might help with compliance.

Section 302

According to Section 302, the CEO and CFO have to personally certify the financial statements and disclosures made by the company, vouching for their authenticity and accuracy. This requires a system to be in place that will make the CEO and the CFO confident that all the disclosures the company makes are in fact accurate and authentic. This can be done in two ways:

1. First is to trickle down the responsibility of the CEO and the CFO to the lower management levels, and in response bubble up the signoffs from lower management on all data and documents that become part of the company filings.
2. Second is to design comprehensive business processes that produce the company filings. The business processes must be designed in a very rigorous manner to comply with all the Sarbanes-Oxley provisions, and proper implementation and training of all personnel involving the business processes should initially be done thoroughly and tested thereafter on a periodic basis. Further, the business processes themselves should be open to the stringent internal audits that will be carried out from time to time.

A combination of both of these methods will go a long way toward ensuring compliance.

For both these options, it is clear that a strong, enterprise-wide document management system is needed as the foundation on which the compliance measures will actually be carried out. In the first case, the signoffs can be configured using a workflow module of the document management system (DMS). In the second case, the business process itself is configured in the DMS and all the relevant supporting or input documents are part of the DMS as well; this makes it easy to do the appropriate subordination and linking between the official company filings and the documents in the DMS.

As proof of the records supporting the final company financials, as filed or reported, it is important to archive all e-mails, spreadsheets, instant messages, and other communications and documents that were exchanged that led to a final certified filing by the CEO and CFO. This will safeguard the executives' claims that all the financial reports are true to their knowledge and that due diligence was carried out before they certified the reports.

Section 404

The CEO and CFO need to provide a report certifying that the company's "internal controls" have been assessed and are working fine, or that there are weaknesses and appropriate action is being taken. Complying with this requirement is one of the most difficult parts of Sarbanes-Oxley, and doing so requires a whole slew of people, processes, and technologies. However, DMS has an important role to play here.

All relevant e-mails and attached documents should be archived, preferably in chronological sequence, for the purpose of proving that the internal controls are appropriate. Ideally, a workflow module will provide added assurance that the internal controls are being implemented, and that they are being implemented properly.

Section 103

Section 103 requires an audit firm to store documents for a period of seven years. The company being audited should replicate this documentation to guard against any discrepancy, miscommunication, or mismanagement.

Section 409

Section 409 requires near-real-time reporting of all material events, whether internal or external, to investors and the appropriate regulatory bodies. This can be accomplished by using a single, enterprise-wide document management system that can issue appropriate "alerts," and that has the notifications and workflow functions configured according to the design of the compliance-based business processes. Such a system ensures that all relevant information is relayed almost immediately to top management (CEO and CFO), the compliance committee, and the advisors, with minimum delay or latency. The capabilities of DMS allow the compliance advisors to make a recommendation (within the stipulated time frame) linked to each alert and send on the reports to the executives with the appropriate recommendations. The executives can then decide whether a matter merits disclosure under the compliance requirements, based on recommendations of their compliance committee or advisors.

Section 802

Sarbanes-Oxley establishes criminal penalties for knowing alteration, destruction, or concealment of records, as well as other activities such as introduction of false records, that might impede or influence an ongoing or potential investigation by a federal agency. This means that a company should hold all documents in a secure system where absolutely no one in the company can alter them once they are finalized. Also, this provision necessitates a formal document retention and destruction policy that is strictly adhered to (and can in fact be proven to have been adhered to) and that ensures that no document potentially required by any investigating agency is destroyed or deleted.

Further, Sarbanes-Oxley requires that as soon as the company comes to know about a potential investigation, all documents pertaining or possibly germane to that investigation are immediately ordered indestructible or unalterable by anyone, including the company executives. This makes it important to have a feature that creates and accepts alerts from the legal department about any ongoing or upcoming investigations; such an alert should trigger immediate vaulting of all related documents and information. This feature will ensure compliance with Section 802, thereby avoiding a potential prison term, a large monetary fine, and, of course, loss of credibility.

This Sarbanes-Oxley section has a strong bearing on a company's records or document management policy. The company must develop a suitable document management policy and adhere to it in a timely and rigorous manner. If this is not done, the company will be exposed to severe costs and damages in terms of providing documents to hostile parties in pretrial discovery, (the legal process of providing all relevant documents to the opposing party in a lawsuit). It also exposes the company to accusations that it has illegally hidden or destroyed relevant documents, even if done at a later stage and before any legal proceedings are begun against the company itself (as was the case with Arthur Andersen's Enron-related documents).

Document management systems provide several benefits to a company. Because an IT system is a business process frozen in a particular software and hardware implementation, the DMS proves that the particular business process is being consciously and diligently adhered to. In the worst case, it at least proves that the spirit of compliance is being observed. Whether the compliance requirements are being followed in form can be found out from the results of the particular system, and also by auditing at various stages of the business process.

The capability to follow an audit trail on all documents created or processed through the DMS is essential in executing compliance activities and also in proving compliance at a later time. The capability to create workflows automatically creates auditable process paths. The DMS also makes it possible to access any documents at any point in time with relative ease, because it acts as a centralized repository of documents (both structured and unstructured). All publicly disclosed documents can be locked in their final form as images and thus cannot be tampered with later on. These images can be stored and deleted according to the schedules of various regulatory and compliance edicts. Documents and information intended for limited consumption at the top management level can also be strictly screened, and internal controls on these can be enforced rigorously. At the appropriate time, the documents can be published.

Section 806

For compliance with this whistleblower section of the Act, it is important that a DMS logs all whistleblower communications, absolutely securely, in a manner such that no unauthorized personnel can access them. The system must also store all such communications.

An indirect requirement for the enterprise DMS is for the storage of documents related to enterprise compliance policies, including updates and amendments; the company's internal control policies; and other documents of a similar nature that could help in demonstrating the compliance process. The company needs to make policies about the following aspects of documents:

- Creation
- Approval
- Publishing
- Retention
- Access
- Distribution
- Life cycle

These policies will assist in implementing the conflicting requirements of (1) document retention for compliance purposes and (2) document deletion for reducing the cost of document retention and improving operational efficiency. The initial step is to define a document retention policy. The second step is to survey the company's existing DMS. The third step is to create a proper DMS that:

- Has a centralized repository of documents.
- Has a structured and hierarchical architecture.
- Has security and access control.

DOCUMENT SECURITY

Enterprise security is an important topic relating to Sarbanes-Oxley, which has implications for the overall enterprise technology ecosystem security. If unauthorized access is possible on any part of the system, especially by those related to or having an effect on financial data, then compliance with Sections 302 and 404 will be difficult. If the anonymity of the whistleblower system is threatened, Section 301 compliance is compromised. Section 409 violations may also be expected if security hampers detection of material events at the required management levels. In short, security of the enterprise technology ecosystem is a fundamental issue in compliance with Sarbanes-Oxley.

Several technologies are available to ensure enterprise security. However, it should be remembered that the people part is one of the weakest links in the security value chain. Hence, user training is a must. Another general principle is to *make human-error security violations difficult through automation and configuration of security systems*. For example, the system can be configured to avoid having people:

- Delete files unintentionally.
- Send files to an unintended audience by mistake.
- Gain physical access to unauthorized systems unintentionally.

Policies, procedures, and processes for security are extremely important. Here again, a general principle is recommended: *Do not make security procedures so complicated, difficult to adapt to, and time-consuming that people find ways to bypass them in daily operations*. For example, it defeats the purpose of requiring passwords if they must be so lengthy or so difficult to remember that people write them down.

The following sections discuss some of the crucial security technologies for Sarbanes-Oxley.

Hierarchical Access Control System

An excellent implementation framework for a hierarchical access control system is role-based access control (RBAC). RBAC makes it easier and more cost-effective for the enterprise to enforce its security procedures.

RBAC requires that the security architecture of the technology systems be based on the organization architecture. Access is provided to particular roles in the organization based on the responsibilities that have been assigned to these roles. Access rights are restricted to the minimum resources required to fulfill that role and its responsibilities. Once the access rights for each role have been defined, individual users are assigned more specific tasks.

This makes it easier to focus on defining the organizational architecture and operations carefully and then following up with the RBAC definitions, instead of trying to configure each individual user's access rights. In the latter case, if the role of a particular user changes, his or her access rights must be changed for each and every system. In RBAC, that individual is assigned a new role or set of roles, and the system automatically makes all the associated changes for restricting access to the systems required by the old roles and providing access to the systems required by the new roles. Simply by changing a user's position in the organizational architecture, RBAC allows the new access controls to be implemented.

Further, any change in the business processes, operations, or organizational structure can be easily implemented by reflecting them in the RBAC. All that is needed thereafter is to attach individuals to their new roles in the new structure and processes.

If an individual leaves the organization, removing him or her from the organization structure closes all assigned security access. A new person who joins the organization in the same role can be assigned all the access rights to the same systems by associating him or her with the appropriate location in the organization structure.

Authentication Management

Authentication management means identifying users correctly before granting them access. How will a CFO be identified, for example? User names and passwords are the most basic means of authentication. Other means that employ biometrics (e.g., fingerprint, retinal scans, etc.) can be used for authentication access to the most sensitive data. There are other methods in between these two extremes, such as smart cards or other hardware devices that are in the possession of the appropriate individual, and digital certificates stored on particular computers, physical access to which is heavily guarded and provided only to the appropriate user.

To a large extent, these systems, in combination with proper documentation, will both ensure proper operation of internal controls and provide proof of proper implementation of internal controls for Section 404.

Audit Control System.   Audit control systems keep a log of all access and modification events on all systems by:

- Other systems.
- Application processes.
- Users.

They can follow and audit the trail of any event or process throughout the enterprise technology ecosystem.

Encryption System. These systems are useful in security at the most fundamental of the data and document levels. Encryption is helpful in safeguarding the data or documents: Even if someone gains physical access to the data, it is in an encrypted format, and can be decrypted only by the appropriate person bearing the decryption key. If the encryption algorithm uses a sufficiently large number of bits (e.g., 64, 128, or more), it becomes practically impossible to decrypt information without the key.

Vulnerability Audit Systems. Periodic and ongoing audits of security vulnerability using the appropriate software systems, in combination with manual audits carried out by qualified personnel or consultants, provide yet more documentary proof of good internal controls. They also raise confidence as to financial accuracy.

Vulnerability systems are based on a thorough knowledge of security loopholes in the enterprise technology ecosystem. Known weaknesses are identified and marked to be addressed. Generally, certain specific configurations or other systems can be put in place to cover the vulnerabilities.

Intrusion Detection (Firewalls and Antivirus System). Again, intrusion detection is not a direct requirement for Sarbanes-Oxley compliance, but it is important for demonstrating that internal controls are in place and that they are secure and safe. It will also prevent some occurrences of data inaccuracy.

Security Policy and Its Enforcement and Documentation. The security policy, and the enforcement and documentation of that policy, will be important from the standpoint of providing documentary proof of internal controls. This policy will likely be the most important segment of the security infrastructure. Security technologies can function and be used properly only by defining a good security policy, documenting it, and enforcing it. Training on the security policy and the security systems, for proper and maximum usage of the security systems, and ongoing audits by a security committee, to ensure adherence to the policy, will be critical.

ISO 17799 and ISO 1335

- ISO 1335: **Information Technology.** Guidelines for the management of IT security.
- ISO 17799: **Information Technology.** Code of practice for information security management.

A Computer Security Institute and FBI joint survey[2] reported that in 30 percent of the responding companies, security breaches were from internal systems; in 77 percent of the responding companies, employees were the hackers. The COSO Framework defined by the Treadway Commission clearly states that auditors must consider IT as part of the internal control during an audit. Hence, security breaches or vulnerability of the IT systems become part of the weakness in the internal control system.[3]

Security must be implemented throughout the information value chain. The ERP system stores data in databases; the databases must be secure. This data then goes into an analytics or reporting system, which is then made into a report and stored on a file server; all these components of the information value chain must be secure. The interfaces among the various elements of the information value chain also have to be secure.

Finally, reports and most other value-added information usually resides in office productivity tools, such as word processors, spreadsheets, and e-mails exchanged between top management and the board. These systems have to be especially secure, as there is a high likelihood of security laxity at this level.

ISO 17799 and Separation of Duties. One of the tenets underlying the provisions of Sarbanes-Oxley is separation of duties. This applies over an entire organization, and thus includes IT policies as well. Many companies have policies in place covering separation of duties, but Sarbanes-Oxley has forced companies to review all their financial system practices to an unprecedented degree.

Controlling access to key corporate applications is fast becoming a security and governance issue for many organizations. A focus on separation of duties reduces risk by providing internal control over access to functions. Even information down to the field level may have to be controlled to obtain true separation of duties.

An example of an area where companies may find problems with separation of duties is the use of spreadsheets. Spreadsheets tend to be programmed by their users, have the data entered by the same user, and be operated by that user. Beyond that, the company usually has no standards for use of spreadsheets, though it should regulate change management, version control, and release management. Put all of this together and you have a high-risk area for fraud.

With increased reliance on IT systems to control user access, data flow, reporting systems, and third-party access, it is becoming imperative that companies review their practices and comply with some industry standards to maintain the integrity of their businesses. ISO 17799 is a comprehensive set of controls comprising best practices in information security that, when adopted and followed, can help a company achieve reasonable assurance that its security measures are adequately protecting the business. It is essentially an internationally recognized, generic standard for information security.

The ISO 17799 standard is made up of 10 domains:

1. Security policy.
2. System access control.
3. Communications and operations management.
4. System development and maintenance.
5. Physical and environmental security.
6. Compliance.
7. Personnel security.
8. Security organization.
9. Asset classification and control.
10. Business continuity management.

Within each section are detailed statements that constitute the standard itself. Overall, 127 best security practices are detailed under these 10 domains.

ISO 17799 includes statements on separation of duties as related to IT security under two domains: "Communications and Operations Management" and "System Access Control."

Communications and Operations Management. Under the communications and operations domain, the ISO 17799 standard requires separation of duties. From an IT standpoint, this means that development and test environments are separated to reduce opportunities for unauthorized modification or misuse of information and services. The person testing an application should not be able to make changes to the underlying code. Keeping a log of changes will help ensure that any changes made can be audited as needed.

Also, development and testing environments should be separated from operational environments. Rules for the migration of software from development to operational status should be defined and documented. This will ensure that the person moving an application to the operational environment cannot make any changes to the application, thus reducing the chance for fraud. Operation logs should be maintained and available for regular independent audit.

Following the ISO 17799 standard controls will help a company ensure that a malicious employee cannot make unauthorized changes that could be used for fraudulent purposes to the system. Rights and duties should be separately assigned to different individuals so that no individual has the power to divert business or transactions in a fraudulent manner.

System Access Control.   Access to data and systems is potentially problematic under the new rules of Sarbanes-Oxley. Automation has often been used to make access to data and systems easier. Now companies are facing the problem of making sure that only the people who need access are getting access. Even if a company has passed an initial Sarbanes-Oxley audit, it may be wise to go back and look at access controls again, as well as who really has access to what data and what systems.

Under the system access control domain of ISO 17799, privilege management and review of user access rights are required. *Privilege management* requires that the allocation and use of privileges be restricted and controlled. Users should have direct access only to the services that they have been specifically authorized to use. Management is also required to conduct a formal process, at regular intervals, to review users' access rights.

Separation in networks can also be utilized to protect company data from employees who may have malicious intent. By separating groups of information services, users, and information systems, a company can restrict individual users to only the pieces of information they require to do their jobs. Also, by restricting access to only the networks that contain the information the user needs, and not allowing access to other parts of the corporate network, user access to information is controlled.

Access control requires enforced authentication for all users and applications, thereby ensuring the integrity of network authentication services. Such a system means that unauthorized users—including system administrators with super-user privileges—cannot view financial information. Within a database system, for example, one individual may be able to create tables and views, while another individual is given the ability to assign the permissions that enable individual users to execute queries.

If a company follows the ISO 17799 standards, no individual user should be able to access all of the IT systems involved in financial transactions, because knowledge of the full path of transactions through the system makes it easier for this knowledgeable person to commit fraud.

Separation of duties is an important requirement for corporate governance. Some level of separation of duties should be mandatory at all companies, because self-monitoring introduces the possibility of no monitoring. ISO 17799 is an excellent source for discovering what aspects of security should to be verified during a Sarbanes-Oxley audit. Although many companies have achieved ISO 17799 certification, this may not be practical for other organizations; nevertheless, they should look to the ISO 17799 standard for guidance. At a minimum, policies and procedures should be in place to address physical security, intrusion detection and prevention, error/incident logging, antivirus functions, remote access, configuration (e.g., networks, servers, installation of new software), authentication/access controls, and regular vulnerability assessment.

Storage, Disaster Recovery, and Continuity Planning

Storage is the fundamental requirement for the safekeeping of all the data and documents of an enterprise (i.e., enterprise information). Proper storage, and its management, security, and safety, are important issues. Today, organizations are literally generating terabytes of data each week. Combined with the requirement to store auditor-relevant documents (such as internal control documentation, internal audit documents, and so forth) safely for seven years, the company's storage requirements are expected to go up even further. Given these conditions, choosing the right storage technology and architecture is important.

Hardware technologies such as RAID (redundant array of inexpensive disks) are much better than JBODs (just a bunch of disks), because RAID provides some fault tolerance at the disk level itself. Choosing the architecture to use these in, such as a network attached storage (NAS) or a storage area network (SAN), is still very difficult, but it is expected that most organizations will have several NAS servers in place soon. If the enterprise is very large and is looking at a long-term solution for its storage problems, SAN architecture might be the way to go. Existing NAS devices, in which an investment has already been made, can be integrated into the SAN architecture.

Both these architectures are designed to ease the pressure on the network, as well as centralize the enterprise information. Although NAS is a good solution at the workgroup or department level, SAN is the solution for long-term, enterprise-level storage requirements.

Again, Sarbanes-Oxley contains no direct requirement to install SAN or NAS, but the acquisition of these will be essential because the information retention dictated by Sarbanes-Oxley sections definitely requires large amounts of storage capacity. Further, the requirements of internal controls and real-time notification of material events dictate storage systems from which data can be retrieved and processed efficiently.

Disaster recovery is important because a company must prove that all appropriate documents have been retained and are available to investigating agencies; hence, disaster recovery is part of what safeguards the organization against Section 802 violations. Further, a disaster recovery policy shows that several potential material events have already been considered and taken care of. The bottom line is that all documents must be kept safe for the required seven-year period and for any agency investigations that might need them.

Business continuity planning will be more important from an operational viewpoint than from a Sarbanes-Oxley requirements perspective. Nevertheless, it makes good business sense to do the proper planning and have a policy or procedure in place.

COMMUNICATION AND NETWORKING

A good communication and networking system is important for providing a solid communications infrastructure between the operational and executive management. Specifically for Sarbanes-Oxley purposes, this system must supply information in real time about material events. Further, the whistleblower requirements of Section 301 mandate an anonymous and secure communication system. The internal controls requirement of Section 404 and the financial accuracy requirements of Section 302 also require a secure communication system, because many important commands and controls are implemented through e-mail and messaging systems and important financial information travels through these communication channels.

Enterprise Integration: Data Integrity and Multiple Systems

For Sarbanes-Oxley compliance, the sections on reporting significant events, together with those on accurate and timely financial and other data, reveal a critical need to bring all the data together. The need for auditable internal controls also requires that all the data be integrated, work across various business processes, and be traceable. Sections 302, 404, and 409 thus call for a massive enterprise integration effort.

Financial accuracy demands a highly integrated enterprise. If the information from the trio of core transactional systems (i.e., ERP, SCM, CRM) and other supporting functional automation systems is not integrated, the financial data will remain inaccurate, and large amounts of resources will be required to reconcile the differing, though overlapping, data from the various sources.

Such data remains open to distortion, loss, and corruption. Further, it becomes easy to prove the inadequacy of internal controls. All the places where data comes out of the transaction systems and is then entered into the financial reporting systems is a point of vulnerability, because of both unintentional human errors and intentional mischief. The possibility of providing real-time reports of material events, as required under Section 409, is extremely low with a non-integrated enterprise.

Fortunately, several integration technologies are available today. The CIO will have to choose the appropriate one based on the specific requirements and constraints of the organization. The main technologies are:

- Enterprise application integration.
- Web services.
- Middleware.
- Business process integration.
- Data integration.[4]

It is challenging to choose the right technology from this array. In fact, chances are that all these technologies already exist in the organization—and that compounds the problem.

Enterprise application integration (EAI) is a reliable technology; Web services (or, more generally, service-oriented architectures) are the integration tools of the future. Hence, a company will probably want to adopt a combination of both these technologies.

Once all the data from an application is converted into XML, it becomes much easier to make that data accessible and available to other applications. These applications can then use the data to generate whatever reports are required for regulatory purposes.

EAI legacy tools that are available in the organization, combined with service-oriented architecture based on Web services and XML-based data storage, are recommended for enabling Sarbanes-Oxley compliance and better business practices.

Current Enterprise Technology Ecosystem: What Does It Deliver? It is important first to audit the capabilities of the existing or current technology ecosystem. The audit has to be done from the perspective of compliance with Sarbanes-Oxley. A few CIOs might realize that they are already close to compliance; they just need to gain a clear understanding of what the Sarbanes-Oxley rules require and then configure a few functions in the key technology systems to achieve compliance.

Most CIOs, however, will need to perform a detailed study from the ecosystem perspective, to evaluate the overall system for compliance. If the overall system seems healthy and can cope with compliance (ideally, this would be the case), then the next step is to identify

EXHIBIT 14.1   Questions

Questions	Remarks
Do your transactional systems share data between them?	
How many major transactional systems (ERP, SCM, CRM, etc.) exist in your organization?	
Are all of these on a single database platform? If yes, is it the same version?	
If no, are they integrated with each other?	
Are all of these on the same or similar operating system platform? If yes, is it the same version?	
What other minor transactional systems exist in the organization?	
What legacy systems are being used in the organization?	
What reporting systems are being used in the organization?	
What analysis tools exist?	
What business intelligence or knowledge management tools exist?	
Can an unauthorized person or software or IT user or any other entity gain access to the financial information of the company?	
Is there a possibility of data loss?	
Is the organization's IT infrastructure dependent on few important people, or is it more process driven? What happens if these people leave their jobs, get sick, or for some reason are not available to the enterprise for an extended period? Will the IT function keep working reasonably well with the help of other staff?	
Are documents stored properly? Can they be retrieved on demand? Can these documents be stored for the long term (at least seven years)? Are they safe from fire, floods, earthquakes, terrorist attacks, and other higher or lower forms of risk to their existence?	
How close to real-time is the information delivery at the organization? Can material events or operational risks be detected and reported as early as two days from the occurrence?	
Can you certify that your financial reporting is accurate?	
Can you certify that the internal controls are in place to prevent intentional or unintentional distortion of financial data?	

parts of the system that could potentially lead to noncompliance. Most of the effort for compliance should be focused on these parts:

- What is wrong with these parts or species or components?
- Can they be reconfigured to manage compliance?
- Can they be supported by some manual systems to achieve compliance?
- Can these systems be supported by some new utilities?
- Is a fundamental redesign of the business process called for?
- Should a new IT system be brought in to replace these parts?

Is Your IT Infrastructure Sarbanes-Oxley Compliant?   Do a self-evaluation using the checklist in Exhibit 14.1. This checklist will give you a feel for the kind of IT infrastructure it will take to achieve Sarbanes-Oxley compliance. It might seem that throwing a whole lot of technology at the problem can produce Sarbanes-Oxley compliance, but in reality, nothing could be further from the truth. It is the stated position in this book that *80 percent of companies already have 80 percent of the technology required to achieve Sarbanes-Oxley compliance.*

What is required is not more technology per se, but effective use of the existing technology, with the goal of aligning it with the requirements of Sarbanes-Oxley. In general, a company will probably be able to supplement its existing technology with only minor technology buys.

ENDNOTES

1. *http://www.gartner.com/resources/113800/113864/113864.pdf*
2. *http://www.gocsi.com/forms/fbi/csi_fbi_survey.jhtml* (accessed 11-28-05).
3. The U.S. General Accounting Office guidelines for auditors for internal control audits are available at *http://www.gao.gov/special .pubs/ai12.19.6.pdf* (accessed 11-28-05).
4. There are several more with only slight differences, and it becomes difficult to distinguish the offerings except by chronology and the original platform design time (i.e., when an offering was first introduced).

CHAPTER 15

The Process

One of the key ingredients for success in a Sarbanes-Oxley compliance effort is *process*. Process gives us a step-by-step, structured approach to implementation.

INTRODUCTION TO THE PROCESS

SOCKET Vision

Immediate. The initial goal is foolproof implementation of Sarbanes-Oxley Compliant Key Enterprise Technologies (SOCKET) across the organization. Any change in the SOCKET ecosystem should be arrived at via a structured approach, without affecting the Sarbanes-Oxley compliance status of the system.

Long-Term. A longer-term goal is to achieve strategic enterprise goals through proper encapsulation of key business processes in the SOCKET ecosystem.

SOCKET Strategy

To address Sarbanes-Oxley compliance across the organization, the SOCKET strategy has to be carefully created, keeping in mind that *80 percent of companies already have 80 percent of the technology they need to achieve Sarbanes-Oxley compliance*. Strategy creation is best done by leveraging the existing body of knowledge on Sarbanes-Oxley from consultants, publications, and other learning channels.

More focus should be dedicated to long-term strategy than to short-term or corrective approaches. Remember that compliance with Sarbanes-Oxley makes good business sense, as the requirements dictate the use of business practices that lead to an efficient and self-aware organization.

Team Definition

A full-time, dedicated team is required for the success of a Sarbanes-Oxley compliance project. Roles, responsibilities, authority, and deliverables should be clearly defined.

Appointment of a CCO and a SOCC

A top executive—namely, a Chief Compliance Officer (CCO)[1]—who has clout with the management council and the board of directors leads the compliance team. This executive (let us call him or her the Sarbanes-Oxley Champion) is the one person in charge of Sarbanes-Oxley implementation across the organization overall. She or he reports directly to the CEO and takes help and guidance from the CFO and the finance team.

The Sarbanes-Oxley Champion heads a high-powered Sarbanes-Oxley compliance committee (SOCC), which includes the COO, location heads, corporate heads, and so on. A high-level team of senior Sarbanes-Oxley consultants[2] assists the SOCC. The external Sarbanes-Oxley consulting team consists of technology consultants, business process consultants, risk-management consultants, internal controls consultants, legal consultants, and Sarbanes-Oxley audit specialists.

The CIO, who is also the SOCKET head, supports the Sarbanes-Oxley Champion (that is, the CCO). The COO (or vice president of operations or equivalent), who understands middle management and has enough clout at the operational level, supports the CIO. They are in turn supported by the corporate IT head (such as a vice president of IT operations or the IT manager who reports to the CIO).

The corporate IT head works with a highly qualified team consisting of experts in functional/business analysis, technology, applications, information, hardware, networking, and so on. They are supported by a dedicated IT development team and consultants, as well as hardware, networking, and database experts working at various locations and managing the IT infrastructure.

The corporate IT head is supported at different locations by an IT location[3] head; we will refer to this latter person as the SOCKET location coordinator (SLC). The corporate IT head is supported by SLC1, SLC2, SLC3, and so on, depending on the number of locations the company has. Each SLC is supported by SOCKET sublocation[4] coordinators (SSLCs) who are part of the location and who actively support the business. The SOCKET team consists of an audit team and an implementation team. Each team has distinct roles, and they work collaboratively for the success of SOCKET.

SOCKET Audit Team

The SOCKET audit team consists of experts who understand the domain of IT and who have a thorough understanding of business operations, function, business process, and financial and legal regulations. The team ideally consists of professionals who have worked in the company's functional areas and have handled the key business processes.

The main function of this group is to conduct audits of all key business processes and of the enterprise technology ecosystem across the organization. After the implementation, it conducts audits of all the work done by the SOCKET implementation team. After implementation, this team also is responsible for conducting internal audits at regular intervals and obtaining feedback at the operational levels. It is responsible for closing all noncompliance reports (NCRs) and ensuring that the gap analysis, risk control plan, and internal control projects are delivering as required. This team uses the SLC to oversee and the SSLC to conduct the internal audits at all locations. The team works closely with the Sarbanes-Oxley compliance committee and SOCKET implementation team. See Exhibit 15.1 (downloadable at *www.sarbanesoxleyguide.com*).

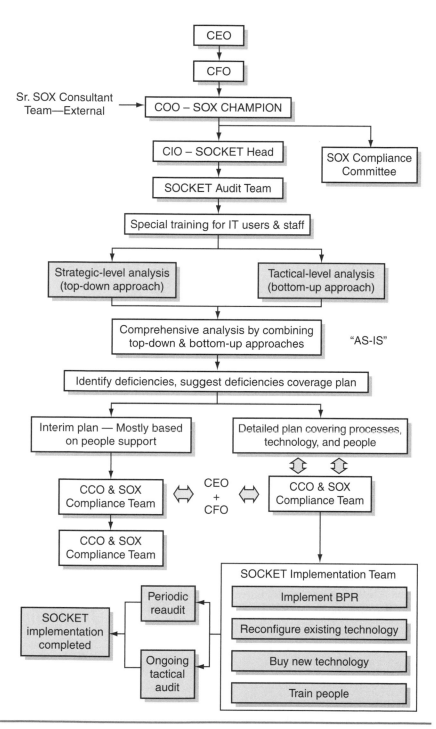

EXHIBIT 15.1 Hierarchy

SOCKET Implementation Team

The SOCKET implementation team consists of experts in IT: system and architecture analysis, databases, enterprise and transactions applications, integration tools, software development, hardware, and networking, among others. Their main function is to provide IT solutions; that is, to develop, configure, align, integrate, and customize business process and other systems for Sarbanes-Oxley compliance.

They are supported at the company's various locations by an IT location head, referred to as the SOCKET location coordinator (SLC).[5] The corporate IT head is supported by SLC1, SLC2, SLC3, and so on, depending on the number of locations in the company. Each SLC is supported by SOCKET sublocation coordinators (SSLCs), who are part of the location and are actively supporting the business.

External Consulting Team

The CIO and SOCKET heads work closely with three to five (depending on the requirement and the size of the organization) external Sarbanes-Oxley consultants per location. These consultants should be experts in information technology, business process integration, risk control analysis, internal controls, and Sarbanes-Oxley audits. See Exhibit 15.2.

Awareness and Training

Before initiating Sarbanes-Oxley compliance efforts, all the team members should undergo detailed and extensive education (i.e., an advanced level of understanding beyond mere training) on Sarbanes-Oxley. All top- and mid-level management should also undergo training and workshops on Sarbanes-Oxley.

"As-Is" Analysis

After this, the organization should undergo an "as-is" analysis audit, carried out by the SOCKET audit team, to help in benchmarking

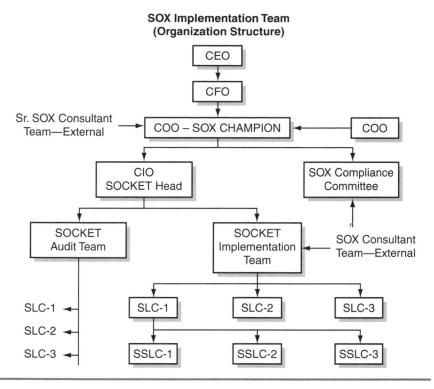

EXHIBIT 15.2   Sarbanes-Oxley Implementation Team

against each section and area for Sarbanes-Oxley compliance. The company can use external consultants to assist the SOCKET audit team for this analysis. The objective is to get a clear picture of the status of the organization vis-à-vis Sarbanes-Oxley compliance.

STRATEGIC (TOP-DOWN) APPROACH

Strategic-level analysis looks at the organization overall. It takes a "from the top down" approach for identification of gaps and shortcomings in the overall SOCKET ecosystem. The PCAOB, in it's May 16, 2005 Policy Statement (Release NO. 2005-009) recommends the following;

> . . . *Use a top-down approach that begins with company-level controls, to identify for further testing only those accounts and*

processes that are, in fact, relevant to internal control over financial reporting, and use the risk assessment required by the standard to eliminate from further consideration those accounts that have only a remote likelihood of containing a material misstatement. (PCAOB Release No. 2005-009, May 16, 2005, p 2).

SOCKET Ecosystem Audit

Here are the steps for the preliminary study to be carried out on the entire organization:

1. List the key business processes (BP) of the company (BP1, BP2, BP3, etc.).
2. For each business process, make a list of the software applications (APP) that are utilized to automate the whole or a part of the business process (APP1, APP2, APP3, etc.).
3. For each software application, make a list of the sub-business processes (SBP) it automates (SBP1, SBP2, SBP3, etc.).
4. Scan the list of SBPs and put them in a sequence that recreates the complete automated key business process.
5. Mark out the applications that span more than one key business process.
6. Using this list, start checking the SBP sequence to see how information is transferred across the interface from one application (automating a particular SBP) to another (automating the successive SBP).
7. Verify and validate the data that is transferred across each interface. Does what enters the information creation point of the business process remain consistent with what comes out? Is there data loss during the travel of information across the SBP application sequence?
8. Most important, ask: Are all financial data accurate, consistent, and validated?
9. Ask: Are adequate internal controls in place across all the applications and interfaces?

Following the initial study outlined in these steps, a more specific and detailed study should be carried out. Extensive study of the entire organization is done with the help of internal and external audit teams. Audits are conducted in following areas:

Business Process Audit
- Identify and list the key business processes.
- Break down each business process into subprocesses.
- How do various business processes relate to each other?
- Benchmark your business processes against industry standards.
- Is there a plan for adapting the business processes, IT, and so forth of acquired or merged companies after the acquisition or merger?
- Determine localization and linguistic issues.

Information Audit
- Map the information value chain.
- Identify points of information creation (e.g., order taking, payment or purchase).
- Is the appropriate information captured at the point of creation? What method is used to capture this information? Have the appropriate forms been designed? (Information might come in different media: paper forms, e-mails, web sites, databases, fax, telephone, and so on.)
- Investigate:
  - Storing and archiving of information.
  - Retrieval and display of information.
  - Information distribution.
  - Analysis, reporting, and visualization.
  - Inferences and decisions.

Application Audit
- List all software applications.
- Identify points of information creation for each application; that is, all input forms for each application. Do these forms allow the capture of relevant information per the information audit?
- What method is used to capture information from different media (i.e., handwritten or printed forms, e-mails, faxes, web-based forms, etc.)?
- Is all the data being captured through the applications? Are all the fields in the forms mapped to the fields in the applications? Are

all the fields in the form being captured? Are there missing fields either in the application or in the form?

- What databases are used for storing various pieces of information?
- What is the sequence of applications automating the information value chain for each business process?
- Can the data be transferred from one application to the next? Is this done via a common database, interlinking software, or other integration mechanisms, or is it done through spreadsheet files or manual rekeying?
- Data validation: Is the data generated at the creation point the same as the data that arrives after traveling through the sequence of applications?
- Can the data be stored and retrieved easily?
- Which is the master ERP, or the master application, for each business process?
- Is there a master application for all business processes? Does this application provide reports to the CEO/CFO? Is the reporting real-time? If not, how much is it delayed?

Technology Audit

- List the technology elements supporting these processes and sub-processes.
- Identify and list the software applications supporting these processes.
- List the hardware systems supporting these processes.
- List the networking systems.
- List the databases.
- Assess:
  - Speed.
  - Architecture.
  - Storage capacity.
  - Performance.
  - Scalability.
  - Backup.
  - Disaster recovery, failover.
  - Business continuity planning.
  - Web-enablement.
- Identify legacy systems.
- Are there systems or parts that might fail eventually?

- Are there systems or parts no longer supported by the manufacturer/supplier?
- Is there an IT vision document? Does it align with the company's strategic vision?
- Is the existing IT infrastructure aligned with the IT vision?
- Change management processes: If a new application or technology is introduced or an old one is retired, or if any modification takes place, is there a mechanism to notify the appropriate authorities about it and evaluate the effect of the change on Sarbanes-Oxley compliance?
- Are there systems to alert the IT heads if any unauthorized software or technology is introduced?
- Are there identification techniques for applications and technology?
- Is there a proper inventory of the IT systems?
- Is there a phaseout mechanism for the IT systems?
- Is the total cost of ownership (TCO) and return on investment (ROI) of all the major systems tracked and benchmarked with industry standards and against the TCO and ROI promised at the time of purchase/acquisition?

A key question the audit committee asks during this audit pertains to data integrity, and hence, financial data accuracy and internal controls. Also relevant is the speed with which information travels across the enterprise through various applications and systems, and related information security issues. Detailed documentation of the strategic-level analysis is completed and submitted to the CIO-SOCKET head. This document covers the status, action plan, recommendations, and so forth.

TACTICAL (BOTTOM-UP) APPROACH

Tactical-level analysis looks into operational aspects across the organizations. It takes a bottom-up approach for identification of gaps and shortcomings in the overall SOCKET ecosystem. The tactical approach uncovers gaps, which are more operational in nature from the user's point of view. For this, a noncompliance report (NCR) form is designed to assist in capturing any tactical or operational gap. See Exhibit 15.3 (for a downloadable form, go to *www.SarbanesOx-*

SOCKET Non-Compliance Report (NCR)

SOCKET:	Date:	NCR No.:
SOCKET Avenues H/w Sys. S/w App. S/w N/w Database People Process		
SOCKET Location: Sub Location:	SLC:	SSLC:
Step 1: Define Noncompliance	Step 2: Observation	
SECTION:		
	Step 3: Analysis	
	Step 4: Plan	
Name & Signature of Auditee: *Internal Auditor:*		
Objective Measure for		
Desired situation		
Actual situation	*Don't forget to implement and verify the effectiveness of interim containment corrections*	
Step 5: What action taken? Role played?	By Whom?	Step 6: Result achieved and verified?
Step 7: New Action	NCR Evaluation	
	Proactive action: 1 Root cause eliminated: 1 Near-nil investment made: 1	
Business Process Document Update:	*NC closing date:* *Signature of Auditor:*	
	Signature of CCO:	
Remarks:		

EXHIBIT 15.3 SOCKET Noncompliance Report

leyGuide.com). This is also called a *problem-solving form*, because it helps auditors document and understand the problem or noncompliance area; it also helps them formulate a PDCA (Plan-Do-Check-Act) analysis for problem solving and achieving compliance.

Any employee who feels that the systems are not working per requirements can submit a report to the tactical audit team and fill out an NCR form. To encourage employees to discover and analyze gaps, a suitable reward or incentive may be created. This can both accelerate the audit and implementation process and heighten the awareness of Sarbanes-Oxley across the organization. A detailed document is prepared at the end of the tactical audit and findings, suggestions, and an action plan are submitted.

MONITORING THE AUDIT TEAM

At the corporate level, the SOCKET audit team is monitored by the Sarbanes-Oxley compliance committee. After the training phase, and on a periodic and ongoing basis, the Sarbanes-Oxley compliance committee will conduct audits throughout the organization to ensure that the SOCKET audit team is carrying out its mandate in a systematic and thorough manner. The Sarbanes-Oxley compliance committee may develop a checklist for conducting its audits; a sample is given in Exhibit 15.4.

Comprehensive Analysis

The CIO goes through the strategic-level analysis and tactical-level analysis documents. A comprehensive detailed report is jointly prepared, to give a clear picture of the organization's status. Based on this, and with the help of Sarbanes-Oxley consultants, a gap analysis is done with respect to Sarbanes-Oxley compliance. Also, risk control areas and internal control systems should be identified at this stage, and two reports prepared:

1. **Interim Compliance Plan.** This report, which is corrective in nature, focuses on the immediate steps to be taken for controlling risk and making temporary arrangements for Sarbanes-Oxley compliance. This will involve mostly solutions related to the allocation of manpower (people support).

   This report is submitted to the CCO or Sarbanes-Oxley Champion. She or he will analyze the report findings and sug-

EXHIBIT 15.4   Points to Be Audited

Seq. No.	Point to Be Audited	Remarks of the Auditor
1	Is there sufficient evidence that all the auditees have gone through the SOCKET guidebook?	
2	Is there sufficient evidence that all the auditees have gone through and understood the major sections and implications of Sarbanes-Oxley?	
3	Is there sufficient evidence that all the auditees have gone through and understood the roles of the CEO, CFO, CIO, CCO, and Sarbanes-Oxley audit and implementation teams?	
4	Is there sufficient and documentary evidence that the IT team has given regular reports on any major changes or additions to the systems, if those changes might affect Sarbanes-Oxley compliance?	
5	Is there sufficient and documentary evidence that all the auditees have conducted compliance meetings regularly with the IT and users staff?	
6	Is there sufficient and documentary evidence that the auditees have invited the top-level Sarbanes-Oxley compliance committee for periodic SOCKET presentations?	
7	Is there documentary evidence to prove that the compliance meetings have been recorded, and progress tracked, by the SOCKET team?	
8	Is there sufficient and documentary evidence that the SOCKET team has identified, communicated, and maintained the records of SOCKET training?	

Seq. No.	Point to Be Audited	Remarks of the Auditor
9	Is there sufficient evidence that the SOCKET location coordinators have analyzed the periodic compliance reports about any new IT system or changes to the existing systems?	
10	Is there evidence that an analysis was done of SOCKET noncompliance reports that have come through IT staff/users?	
11	Was an analysis done by the SOCKET location coordinators to determine whether the implementation of SOCKET has resulted in cultural and attitudinal change in the organization?	

gested project plan, with the help of Sarbanes-Oxley consultants and the Sarbanes-Oxley compliance team. After the interim compliance plan is finalized, the CEO and CFO give the go-ahead.

2. **"To Be": Implementing a Sarbanes-Oxley–Compliant Framework Process.** The Sarbanes-Oxley gap analysis is now focused on the business processes. All business processes are carefully analyzed for each gap and internal control. Process flow diagrams are drawn for detailed analysis.

Technology. Technological aspects are looked into in detail. Data flow and input-output diagrams are drawn for each interface and application. Specific technological requirements are carefully analyzed.

People. Personnel and staff aspects are analyzed; special skills requirements are investigated.

Total Cost of Compliance. Total cost of compliance is calculated taking into account process, technology, and people. Cash flow, internal rate of return, and other related calculations are done for financial justification.

This is one of the most crucial steps in SOCKET implementation. All the inputs related to process, technology, and people are understood. Each gap, risk control area, and internal control systems area is analyzed in detail, and for each identified initiative a detailed project plan is made. For each project, requirements of resources, time frame, deliverables, budget, and control measures are worked out. (For more details, download the SOCKET TCC calculator spreadsheet from *www.sarbanesoxleyguide.com*)

A detailed "To Be" document, in the form of a project report, is created and submitted to the CCO. The Sarbanes-Oxley compliance team, along with any Sarbanes-Oxley consultants, analyzes these reports in detail. Each project is analyzed and discussed with the CIO and the SOCKET team. After several iterations and deliberations, a final list of projects is drawn up.

The CCO makes a final presentation to the CFO and the CEO. A comprehensive strategy is created for each project. The Sarbanes-Oxley compliance team is given the responsibility for project management of the entire project. After final approval from the CEO, the SOCKET implementation team takes responsibility for implementing the project.

IMPLEMENTATION PROCESS: REENGINEERING FOR SARBANES-OXLEY COMPLIANCE

Guided by the "To Be" report, the SOCKET implementation team reengineers the key business processes, with the help of external consultants. The reengineered business process should be implemented, as far as possible, by reconfiguring existing technology. If existing technologies cannot support the reengineered business process, new technology is investigated for that purpose.

Technology

Before any technological changes are implemented, it is imperative that a survey of existing technology be conducted, as well as a needs analysis for new technology.

Existing Technology. All the process charts, manuals, and other relevant documentation (such as engineering change management and system upgrade management) are assembled and understood. The reengineered business process is mapped to various configurations of the existing technology until a suitable reconfigured technology ecosystem design with minimal gaps is reached. The remaining gaps in the new ecosystem and the reengineered business processes are identified to be filled in by new technology.

New Technology. The precise specifications for the new technology are defined, keeping in view the long-term implications. Various vendors and products are identified to fill this new technology need. If a commercial, off-the-shelf product is not available, suitable vendors or an in-house team is identified to find or make a suitable project. Appropriate data migration and change management are carried out during the changeover from the old business process and ecosystem to the new ecosystem.

People: Training

The IT users are trained on the reengineered technology ecosystem. IT maintenance teams are retrained and reconfigured, if necessary, and new roles and responsibilities are assigned for various parts of the new ecosystem.

Audit: Post-Implementation

Once the technology has been introduced and the people have been trained, the crucial next step is to audit the effectiveness of the changes made.

Strategic. The SOCKET audit team carries out an audit similar to the one it did during the "as-is" analysis phase at a strategic level. Benchmarking is conducted against various relevant sections of Sarbanes-Oxley. Further, specific recommendations made by the audit team in the "To Be" document are checked for implementation in the new ecosystem. The tactical audit supplements this work.

Tactical. The tactical audit is carried out using the NCR forms and a limited-time incentive scheme that encourages employees to bring to the notice of the audit team any discrepancies between Sarbanes-Oxley requirements and the reengineered business processes. At the end of the incentive period, all the NCRs are reviewed and the results used to supplement the strategic audit. The tactical audit NCRs are reviewed, and NCR closing procedures are continued on an ongoing basis throughout the lifetime of the organization.

Ongoing Monitoring of Process and Technology

The whole implementation process is organic; as such, it must change and evolve continuously. Therefore, an effective system is required for monitoring and evaluating the process.

Strategic. Strategic audits are carried out on a periodic basis; for example, quarterly, semiannually, or annually.

Tactical. Tactical audits are carried out on an ongoing basis, with short incentive periods in between, to keep employee interest alive. Continued monitoring of the processes ensures compliance with SOCKET throughout the lifetime of the organization.

Continuous Alignment with Business and Governance Goals. During the periodic strategic audits, questions related to business and IT alignments are also asked. After one annual compliance cycle has been completed successfully, more time will be available for the audit team to focus on aligning the ecosystem with the strategic goals of the enterprise.

BEYOND SARBANES-OXLEY: FROM SOCKET TO SUCCESS ECOSYSTEM

It is expected that the insight gained from the SOCKET implementation, business process reengineering, and ecosystem reconfiguration will help not only in compliance with the Sarbanes-Oxley Act, but also in better corporate governance, more efficient business operations, better alignment of the business and IT goals, and sustained competitive advantage of the enterprise. SOCKET provides a road map for a Sarbanes-Oxley–compliant architecture that gives the enterprise-user a sustained competitive advantage. The SOCKET system is designed to be easy to follow and comprehensive; following it will ensure that the business moves beyond simply complying with Sarbanes-Oxley to capitalizing on the incredible opportunities that will result as a byproduct of compliance.

CONCLUSIONS

In summary, the Sarbanes-Oxley Act is intended to ensure good corporate governance. The various sections of the Act are, essentially, aimed at mandating the best practices for running large companies.

Surveys have shown that most CEOs and CFOs have regarded these same practices as ideals for some time, but never had the time or the wherewithal to implement them fully. Now is a good time to implement these ideals and to comply with Sarbanes-Oxley at the same time. For the CIO, this is an opportunity to use the Sarbanes-Oxley compliance mandate as a springboard to unleash a vision of a more efficient, effective, and expeditious technology-enabled enterprise.

Exhibit 15.5 briefly reviews the most important sections of the Act.

EXHIBIT 15.5 Business Processes and Technologies Affected

Sections	Business Process	Technology Impacted
Sec. 302	Financial Reporting	ERP, SCM, CRM, MIS, Reporting Software, Enterprise Integration, ETL, Data Warehousing, Business Intelligence
Sec. 404	Internal Controls	ERP, SCM, CRM, Enterprise Security, Secure Enterprise Integration, Business Process Mgmt, Workflow
Sec. 409	Reporting "Material Events"	ERP, CRM, SCM, EAI, Business Activity Monitoring, Executive Dashboards, Business Performance Monitoring, Operational Intelligence
Sec. 103	Document and Records Management	Document Imaging and Records Management System, Knowledge Management
Sec. 301	Whistleblower Provision	Secure Communication System, Workflow and Document Management

ENDNOTES

1. The CCO will usually be a person, with a legal and financial background, who has an understanding of enterprise functioning at the broad or big-picture level and also at the detail level. She or he should have the appropriate authority within the company, and the CEO, CFO, and CIO should be accessible to her or him. The key personnel in the enterprise should also believe in her or his capability and expertise. The CCO can be either a consultant or a homegrown officer with a long history in the organization.
2. Preferably external Sarbanes-Oxley specialist consultants, so that objectivity and authority are maintained.
3. *Location* refers to the geographic location of a business unit.
4. *Sublocation* refers to specific departments or workgroups within each location or business unit.
5. Note that the SLC and SSLC of the implementation team are different from the SLC and SSLC of the audit team, to avoid role conflict.

Sarbanes-Oxley Implementation Plan: Developing an Internal Control System for Compliance (Focusing on Sections 302 and 404)

An effective internal control system is integral to the ability to comply with Sarbanes-Oxley. An internal control system is what will reduce the likelihood of noncompliance and alert the company to breaches, failures, or weaknesses in the system that must be addressed. Internal controls as preventive and detective measures are the front line for ensuring that the regulatory requirements are being met, and thus much thought and consideration must be put into developing and maintaining those controls. The following is a guide for achieving just that.

EIGHT-STEP PROCESS TO SOX COMPLIANCE

An internal control system that meets the requirements of Sarbanes-Oxley can be developed by following an eight-step process. When a compliance plan is structured in this way, the journey to compliance is easy, and the system is easily implemented and followed. The eight steps are:

1. Establish a compliance committee.
2. Assess risk.
3. Set reporting objectives.
4. Prepare a formal implementation plan.

5. Communicate the ongoing procedures.
6. Provide training.
7. Document processes and risk management.
8. Perform continuous evaluation.

PROJECT MANAGER'S STEPS TO SUCCESSFUL COMPLETION

Each of the eight steps in the compliance plan involves distinct processes. The following is a list of the critical elements in each step.

1. Establish a compliance committee.
   Who?

COMPLIANCE COMMITTEE	
Mandatory Members:	
Position	**Name**
CEO	
CFO	
Major Business Unit Heads:	
Additional—Recommended Members:	
Functional Areas—Executives:	
Finance	
IT	
Legal	
Internal Audit	

Member characteristics include:

■ Committed to Sarbanes-Oxley compliance
■ Capable of taking a company-wide perspective regarding:
  ● Risk identification
  ● Suggested solutions

What?

The compliance committee focuses on:

■ Communicating program objectives and initiatives
■ Managing the overall process and activities
■ Providing training, assessment resources, and tools as necessary
■ Engaging the various departments or business units to identify risks and solutions
■ Keeping the goals of the committee visible and compelling

2. Assess risk.
  ■ Identify the corporation's appetite for risk as defined by the board.
    ● Identify the types and scope of risks that the organization is facing as defined.
      ■ Review the board's risk guidelines.
      ■ Review the communication process for the risk guidelines.
    ● Identify the enterprise-wide risks within the organization. The number and types of risks will vary by type of business and other factors. The general categories that should be reviewed for risks include:
    ● Financial risks—for example, the risk of financial loss from investing in new acquisition or currency losses from exchange-rate fluctuations affecting international operations.
    ● Human capital risk—for example, the risk of not having qualified staff because of past deemphasis on college recruiting, or the risk of losing key staff members because of a below-market compensation program.
    ● Legal and regulatory risks—for example, operating in a highly regulated industry, such as nuclear power, or merely operating "on the edge."
    ● Strategic risks—for example, growth through aggressive acquisitions, or operating too conservatively and letting competitors pass the organization by.

- Operational risks—for example, a lack of documented processes, or failure to act quickly because of strong, centralized administrative controls.
- Technological risks—for example, failure to upgrade and modernize systems, or systems privacy or security penetration violations.
- Quantify the magnitude and potential impact of each risk.
- Create a risk portfolio to identify the interrelationships among the various risks.
- Develop the enterprise risk management (ERM) framework.

3. Set reporting objectives. The overall objective is to create a system that ensures internal control compliance.

    What?

- Determine likelihood of risks and errors.
- Define decision rules and reporting objectives to address risks. How do we ensure that the internal control system is effective? The controls must be
  - Preventive (stop)
  - Detective (catch)
  - Corrective (fix)

    What areas of the operation require control objectives?

    Assess and set objectives for internal control in the following areas:

    A. Personnel Controls
    - Separation of duties
    - Careful hiring, assignment of duties, training, and supervision
    - Performance reviews

    B. System and Resource Controls
    - Physical controls—access to hardware components of system
    - Logistics controls—access and authorization to use system
    - System controls—document order, internal validity, checks and balances

    C. Strategic Planning Controls
    - Establishing steering committees
    - Identifying opportunities provided by enterprise ERP systems

- Evaluating and balancing the level of skills and outside resources required to complete IT projects satisfactorily
- Evaluating automated systems for internal control

D. Business/Transactions Service Controls

- Policies and procedures
- Document validation and matching
- Transaction detail calculation
- Account summary comparison
- Periodic ledger reconciliations
- Help and incident reporting and support
- Management reports

4. Prepare a formal implementation plan (transition plan to move from project stage to ongoing, day-to-day internal control operations).

What steps are involved in transitioning from the project stage to the ongoing, day-to-day operations for an internal control system?

- Define the key controls and tasks and their start and end dates.
- Allocate ownership of each control task to a specific employee.
- Provide a mechanism for access to appropriate information and resources for each control task.
- Establish various chains and lines of command.
- Establish a direct and systematic reporting process through those lines of command.
- Define individual roles and responsibilities within the organization.
- Communicate individual roles and responsibilities to ensure organization-wide understanding and respect.

What factors affect the proper execution of internal control methods?

- Employee execution of the internal controls depends on information being:
  - Identified:
    - Proper form
  - Captured:
    - A reasonable time frame
  - Exchanged
- Accountability for each control activity depends on the methods used to

- Record:
  - Transactions
- Process:
  - Events
- Summarize:
  - Conditions
- Report

5. Communicate the ongoing procedures.
   - It is imperative that messages regarding Sarbanes-Oxley compliance emphasize the *"why"* associated with the changes.
   - New procedures must be presented clearly and effectively.
   - Focus on:
     - Understanding
       - Collaboration
     - Acceptance
       - Set a cultural "tone"
     - Observance

6. Provide training.
   - Compliance committee will lead this process and will provide the resources employees need to function successfully in the new environment.
   - Training may consist of both internal and external components, depending on what type of system is put in place.
   - Focus on internal policies, procedures, and practices to ensure that each is being performed correctly, including:
     - Classifying and recording authorized transactions in the proper period.
     - Making operational and financial disclosures.
     - Protecting company assets from improper, unauthorized use.
   - Potential changes: Job roles and responsibilities of some employees will change. The human resources department should take appropriate measures (e.g., compensation review) to eliminate any potential staff dissatisfaction.

7. Document processes and risk management.

   The CEO and CFO will have to certify that the internal control systems of the corporation are sufficient and that they have been monitored within 90 days of the report being filed. A company must maintain "evidential matter," including documentation, to prove that the internal control system is effective.

What does this mean?

- The controls must be documented diligently.
- All systems require detailed descriptions and analysis—clear enough that any audit of that system can be conducted easily and efficiently.
- Risks must be documented:
  - To provide reasons and a resource for why the controls were put in place.
  - To assist in the identification of new or changing sources of risk.

8. Perform continuous evaluation. Continuous evaluation and modification of internal controls are musts.

   Who? It is management's responsibility to establish and maintain controls, and to ensure that they operate as intended or are modified as appropriate.

   - Maintenance and monitoring of the internal controls depend on
     - Detection of deviation
     - Timeliness of response

     What is the process for detection of noncompliance?
   - Initially, a reactive process can work for early detection, analysis, and resolution of problems.
     - With experience, the process should be formalized.
     - Action against violations of the internal controls should be swift and just. Actions can include disciplinary and corrective actions to help reinforce established codes of practice.

PROJECT MANAGER'S POCKET-BOOK PROJECT PLAN

Section 404 Compliance Review Work Breakdown Structure[1]

Plan, Scope, and Assess Sarbanes-Oxley Project

1. Assemble project team, including sponsor and other review team members. Review team members should include representatives from
   - Finance
   - Internal Audit

- IT
- Legal
- Human Resources

2. Define project objectives and assess where the organization is with regard to Sarbanes-Oxley compliance.

  - Determine the scope of the review. Will it cover controls other than financial ones?
  - Determine which business units will be covered.
  - Review results from any previous Section 404 or internal audit reviews requiring follow-up.
  - Establish project time line. Be sure to allow time for external auditing and review.
  - Develop guidelines for assessing risk management.
    - Develop the ERM framework following the COSO guidelines:
      - Develop internal ERM environment. Management is responsible for establishing the foundation of attitudes toward the organization's appetite for risk, for all members of the organization, as a set of guidelines.
      - Set strategic and risk objectives in support of management's choice as to how the organization will seek to enhance value. These should involve some overall risk-related objectives.
      - Develop processes to implement the ERM framework successfully and to identify events that may affect (either positively or negatively) the risk-related strategies.
      - Develop plans to respond to the various risk challenges that were identified in the risk assessments.
      - Identify various responses to risk options and consider their effect on event likelihood and impact, in relation to the organization's response for risk. (This is a management task.)
      - Undertake control activities, as defined in the policies and procedures to ensure that appropriate risk responses are executed, throughout all levels and functions within the organization, including approvals, authorizations, performance reviews, safety and security issues, and appropriate segregation of duties.

- Develop an information and communication plan that identifies, captures, and communicates risk-related information in a form that allows appropriate members of the organization to carry out their responsibilities, as well as flowing throughout the organization at all levels and to external parties such as customers, vendors, regulators, and shareholders.
- Develop ongoing risk monitoring procedures to monitor the ERM program and the quality of its performance over time.
- Review planned objectives with the CFO and the audit committee.

3. Create a project plan that covers in detail the internal processes that are to be reviewed.

Identify and Document Key Processes and Controls

1. Establish a review approach for each process/system included in the review.
   - Identify financial reporting processes.
   - Identify key systems and supporting systems.
   - Review existing documentation.
   - Define nature and types of possible errors and omissions.
   - Define nature, size, and composition of transactions to be reviewed.
   - Determine volume, size, complexity, and homogeneity of individual transactions processed.
   - Establish guidelines for materiality and error significance.
   - Understand process transaction susceptibility to error or omission.
2. Review approach and timing with external auditors.

Evaluate Control Design, Operational Effectiveness

1. Establish standards for review of documentation and project progress reporting.
2. Complete preliminary reviews for each identified process or system. Apply:

- Committee of Sponsoring Organizations of the Treadway Commissions (COSO) framework.
- Control Objectives for Information and Related Technology (CobiT) framework.
- Sarbanes-Oxley Compliance Key Enterprise Technology (SOCKET) methodology to evaluate:
  - Operational audits.
  - Business processes.
  - Controls.

Identify and Remediate Deficiencies/Weaknesses

1. Follow up and resolve any items requiring investigation.
   - A *material weakness* is "a reportable condition in which the design or operation of one or more of the internal control components does not reduce[,] to a relatively low level, the risk of misstatements caused by errors or fraud in amounts that would be material in relation to the financial statements being audited may occur and not be detected within a timely period by employees in the normal course of performing their assigned functions."
   - The deficiencies/weaknesses are assessed by:
     - Testing.
     - Determining the significance of the weakness.
     - Determining the effects on financial reporting.
2. Consolidate review work and prepare a preliminary 404 report.

Establish Ongoing Audit/Monitoring Procedures

1. Build in a continuous review process.
   Continuous monitoring of the internal control system is crucial for Sarbanes-Oxley compliance. The purpose of monitoring is to determine whether internal controls are adequately designed, properly executed, and effective. How?
   - Techniques for monitoring include:
     - Spot checks of transactions.
     - Basic sampling techniques.
   - When monitoring internal control performance, be sure to review:

- Self-assessments
- Peer reviews
- Internal audits
- To evaluate operating effectiveness, further study and follow-up are needed when tolerances are exceeded.
  - Check the level of tolerances used
  - Check the frequency of the analysis
  - Review supporting documentation for:
    - Evidence of follow-up action
    - Corrective action, such as changes in policy
- Establish an audit committee.
- Develop a whistleblower program.
- Initiate an internal management control process.
- Enhance financial disclosure as appropriate.
- Develop a process for continuous evaluation of the internal control processes.

2. Build in sustainability.

   The criteria for ensuring sustainability include:
   - Strong internal control process
   - Continuous management support
   - Continuous evaluation

3. Review 404 report results with the CFO and release the report.

Standard Framework for Sarbanes-Oxley Implementation Projects. The most effective implementation of a Sarbanes-Oxley compliance initiative will involve the COSO and COBIT frameworks, and a methodology such as SOCKET:

1. **COSO** (Committee of Sponsoring Organizations, a group of professional auditing organizations).
   - The SOCKET methodology has to be supplemented by the COSO Integrated Framework for achieving Sarbanes-Oxley compliance.
   - There are three main objectives for determining which internal controls are to be applied:
     1. Efficiency and effectiveness of operations
     2. Financial reporting reliability
     3. Regulatory compliance

- For each of these objectives, five components of internal controls are evaluated at the unit level (functional) and the activity level (business process):
  1. *Control environment.* Corporate control culture and consciousness.
  2. *Risk assessment.* Assessment of risk factors for each objective.
  3. *Control activities.* Corporate policies, procedures, and processes that ensure the span of management control throughout the enterprise.
  4. *Information and communication.* Implementation of key business processes for efficient capture, storage, and distribution of relevant information required for efficient operations.
  5. *Monitoring.* Ongoing or periodic internal control assessment processes.
2. **SOCKET** (Sarbanes-Oxley Compliance Key Enterprise Technology).
   - The SOCKET methodology was designed in view of the fact that 80 percent of companies already have 80 percent of the technology they need to achieve Sarbanes-Oxley compliance.
   - It assists and enables the CIO to:
     - Visualize the enterprise IT infrastructure holistically.
     - Gain insight into that infrastructure's interaction and relationship to Sarbanes-Oxley and the key, financially relevant business processes.
   - It is a business ecosystem that defines the fundamental requirements of the enterprise technology ecosystem. It captures how the people, processes, technology, and systems all work together. See Exhibit A.1.
   - General principles for achieving a SOCKET ecosystem include:
     - Centralized (or centrally accessible) data repository.
     - Centralized (or centrally accessible) document repository.
     - Pervasive logical and physical security infrastructure.
     - Pervasive enterprise hierarchical access control to IT and information assets.
     - Access to information assets and IT to personnel restricted to the required domain of their responsibilities.

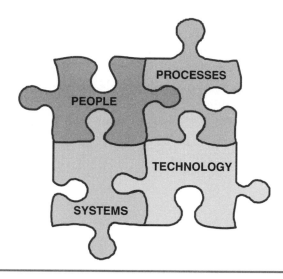

EXHIBIT A.1   Interrelationship of People, Processes, Technology, and Systems

- Secure and accurate mechanisms for the transfer of data, documents, and other information assets from one layer or species of technology to another.
- Enterprise-wide business continuity plans and disaster recovery procedures for the enterprise technology ecosystem.
3. **CobiT.** See later sections of this appendix.

Transactional Systems.   The three categories of enterprise software that will most effectively enable the success of the ecosystem are:

1. Enterprise resource planning (ERP). An enterprise-wide transactional system capturing the key business process data at the point of generation.
2. Customer relationship management (CRM). Provides automation for the front end or demand side of the enterprise.
3. Supply chain management (SCM). Provides automation for the front end or demand side of the enterprise.

Analytical and Reporting Systems (to Meet Requirements of Sections 302 and 404)

- Once the centralized data repository is in place, another strategy is to obtain a reporting tool that has good features for transformation and visualization. An example is the online analytical processing (OLAP) tools.
- The reporting system should be configured and tuned to track potential threats and assist executives in understanding whether an occurrence or condition is a "material event."

Data Warehousing

- A data warehouse provides a centralized data repository that can consolidate the data islands spread across the enterprise ecosystem in various transactional and other functional automation systems.
- It is critical that users be well trained and made aware of the importance of accurate data entry, and that a monitoring and control system be put in place to enforce good data-entry quality.
- Data mining can reveal new patterns and correlations between sets of data that might not seem to have any direct relationship to each other. It can be a useful tool for internal auditors for forensic accounting. It can also potentially alert the enterprise to material events by detecting unforeseen patterns.

Knowledge Management: Document and Records Management

Records management will become a priority issue for many CIOs in the coming years. Why?

- Section 302 requires a system to be in place that will make the CEO and CFO confident that all the disclosures the company makes are accurate and authentic.
  - As proof supporting the final company financials, as filed or reported, it is important to archive all e-mails, spreadsheets, instant messages, and other communications and documents that led to a final certified filing by the CEO and CFO.

- For Section 404 compliance, all e-mails and attached documents should be archived for the purpose of proving that the internal controls are appropriate and effective. Ideally, a workflow module will provide added assurance that the internal controls are being implemented.

- Section 103 requires auditors to store documents for seven years. The company should replicate that documentation and retention to guard against any discrepancy, miscommunication, or mismanagement.

- Section 409 requires near-real-time reporting of all material events. This can be accomplished by using a single, enterprise-wide document management system with appropriate alerts, and with notifications and workflow configured according to the design of the compliance-based business processes.

- Section 802 requires that all documents be held in a secure system where no one in the company can alter them once they are finalized. It calls for a formal document retention and destruction policy which is strictly adhered to and which ensures that no document that any investigating agency might require is destroyed or deleted. It is important to have a feature that creates and accepts alerts from the company's legal department about any ongoing or potential investigations; these alerts should trigger immediate information vaulting of all pertinent or related documents.

A document management system will provide several benefits relating to Sarbanes-Oxley compliance:

- Proving that the particular business process is being consciously and diligently adhered to.

- Providing the capability to follow an audit trail on all documents created or processed; this is useful in executing compliance activities and also in proving compliance at a later stage.

- Providing access to any documents at any point in time.

- Acting as a centralized repository of documents (both structured and unstructured). All publicly disclosed documents can be locked in final form as images that cannot be tampered with later on.

- Providing a secure and confidential log of all whistleblower communications.

Policies. The company needs to make policies about the following aspects of documents:

- Creation
- Approvals
- Publishing
- Retention
- Access
- Distribution
- Life cycle

Security. The "people" part is one of the weakest links in the security value chain.

- Make human-error security violations difficult through automation and configuration of security systems.
- Do not make security procedures so complicated, difficult to adapt to, and time-consuming that people find ways to bypass them in daily operations.

Hierarchical Access Control System. Hierarchical access control systems, such as role-based access control (RBAC), require that the security architecture of the technology system be based on the organization architecture.

- Access is provided to particular roles in the organization based on the responsibilities they have been assigned.
- Access rights are restricted to the minimum resources required to fulfill a role and its responsibilities.

Authentication Management

- User names and passwords are the most basic means of authentication.
- Audit control systems keep a log of all access and modification events on all systems.

- Encryption systems safeguard data or documents. Even if someone gains physical access to the data, it is in an encrypted format that can be decrypted only by the appropriate person bearing the encryption key.
- Vulnerability audit systems permit periodic and ongoing audits of security vulnerability, using the appropriate software systems, and through manual audits carried out by qualified personnel or consultants. This provides another documentary proof of good internal controls and provides confidence as to financial accuracy.

Other

- Intrusion detection
- Firewalls and antivirus systems
- Security policy, and policy enforcement and documentation
- ISO 17799 and ISO 1335
- Storage, disaster recovery, and continuity planning

Communication and Networking

- A good communication and networking system is important for providing a solid communications infrastructure between the operational and executive management, and to supply information in real time about material events.
- Enterprise integration technologies support massive enterprise integration efforts. Some examples include:
  - Enterprise application integration
  - Web services
  - Middleware (XML)
  - Business process integration
  - Data integration

STRATEGIC VERSUS TACTICAL ANALYSIS

The SOCKET methodology includes both a strategic and a tactical level of analysis. The strategic analysis looks at the organization from the top down and helps to identify needs and weaknesses from a holistic, organization-wide perspective. The tactical analysis starts at the operational level and goes from the bottom up, looking for areas where improvements are needed. The synthesis of these two types of analysis is what makes SOCKET so powerful. Exhibit A.2 is a representation of the SOCKET methodology; Exhibit A.3 delineates a method for monitoring the SOCKET audit team; Exhibit A.4 is a graphic representation of the hierarchy in which the SOCKET implementation team operates.

CobiT[2]

The CobiT framework provides guidance for the IT controls that must be established and integrated to achieve financial reporting and disclosure objectives. The IT controls should consider the overall governance framework in supporting the quality and integrity of information.

The CobiT objectives include (see also Appendix E and F):

- Plan and organize
- Acquire and implement
- Deliver and support
- Monitor and evaluate

Plan and Scope

Though there may be many IT systems operating within an organization, only those that are associated with a significant account or related business process need be considered for compliance purposes. The scope of the program generally includes the following processes and controls:

- Controls over initiating, recording, processing, and reporting significant accounts and disclosures and related assertions embodied in the financial statements.
- Controls over the selection and application of accounting policies that are in conformity with generally accepted accounting principles.

EXHIBIT A.2 Strategic Analysis, Tactical Analysis

Strategic Analysis

HOW?

The steps to carrying out the preliminary study of the organization include:

1. List the key business processes of the company.
2. For each business process, list the software applications that are utilized to automate the whole or a part of the business process.
3. For each software application, list the subbusiness processes (SBP) it automates.
4. Scan the list of SBPs and put the SBPs in a sequence that recreates the completed, automated key business process.
5. Mark out applications that span more than one key business process.
6. Start checking the SBP sequence to see how information is transferred across the interface from one application (automating a particular SBP) to another (automating the successive SBP).
7. Verify and validate the data that gets transferred across each interface.
   - Does what enters the information creation point of the business process remain consistent with what comes out?
   - Is there data loss during the travel of information across the SBP application process?
   - Most important: Are the financial data accurate, consistent, and validated?
   - Are adequate internal controls in place across all the applications and interfaces?

Extensive study of the organization is done with the help of internal and external auditors. The audits are conducted in the following areas:
- Business process
- Information
- Application
- Technology
  When reviewing the audit documentation, the audit committee will assess:
- Data integrity
  - Financial data accuracy
  - Internal controls
- Speed of information travel across the enterprise
- Information security issues

Detailed documentation of the strategic-level analysis is made and submitted to the CIO-SOCKET head.

Tactical Analysis

HOW?

The purpose of this approach is to uncover gaps and shortcomings of an operational nature from the user's point of view.
- A noncompliance report (NCR) is completed that captures the tactical or operational "gap". See Exhibit A.3; a copy of the form is downloadable at *www.SarbanesOxleyGuide.com.*
- To encourage employees to fill and analyze the "Gap," a suitable reward or incentive may be created.

EXHIBIT A.3   Monitoring the Audit: SOCKET Audit Team

Monitoring The Audit: SOCKET Audit Team

The SOCKET audit team is monitored by the Sarbanes-Oxley compliance committee at the corporate level. This is done on a periodic and ongoing basis.

Comprehensive Analysis:

- The CIO goes through the strategic- and tactical-level analysis documents.
- An "As-Is" report is jointly prepared.
- A gap analysis with respect to Sarbanes-Oxley compliance is prepared.
- Risk control areas and internal control systems need to be identified.
- From this analysis, two reports are prepared:
  - An *interim compliance plan* that focuses on the immediate steps to be taken for controlling the risk and temporary arrangements for Sarbanes-Oxley compliance.
  - A *"To Be" report* on implementing a Sarbanes-Oxley–compliant framework. At this point, a detailed project plan is developed, detailing the processes, technology, people, and total cost of compliance required to address each gap, risk control area, and internal control system.
- The COO or CCO makes a final presentation to the CFO and CEO.
- Once approved, the SOCKET implementation team takes responsibility for implementing the project.

SOCKET Implementation Completed

Implementation

- The SOCKET implementation team reengineers the key business processes with the help of external consultants.

Technology

- Existing technology:
  - All the process charts, manuals, and other relevant documentation are assembled and understood.
  - The reengineered business process is mapped to various configurations of the existing technology until a suitable reconfigured technology ecosystem design with minimal gaps is reached.
  - The remaining gaps in the new ecosystem and the reengineered business processes are identified to be filled in by new technology.
- New Technology:
  - Define precise specifications required for the new technology.
  - Identify and evaluate potential products and vendors.
- Transition to new technology with appropriate data migration and change management.

People: Training

- IT Users.
- IT maintenance team.

Audit: Postimplementation

Strategic

- Audit the "To Be" documentation against the implementation of the new ecosystem.

Tactical

- Use the noncompliance report form to document the findings.
- Bring to notice any discrepancies between Sarbanes-Oxley requirements and the reengineered business processes.
- Results supplement the strategic audit.
- NCR closing procedures are continued on an ongoing basis throughout the lifetime of the organization.

Ongoing Monitoring Of Process And Technology

- *Strategic.* Strategic audits are carried out on a periodic basis; for example, quarterly, semiannually, or annually.
- *Tactical.* Tactical audits are carried out on an ongoing basis to ensure compliance throughout the lifetime of the organization.
- *Continuous Alignment with Business and Governance Goals.* During the periodic strategic audits, review the alignment of the ecosystem with the strategic goals of the enterprise.

- Antifraud programs and controls.
- Controls, including IT general controls, on which other controls depend.
- Controls over significant nonroutine and nonsystematic transactions, such as accounts involving judgments and estimates.
- Controls over the period-end financial reporting process, including controls over procedures used to enter transaction totals into the general ledger; and to record recurring and nonrecurring adjustments to the financial statements (e.g., consolidating adjustments, report combinations and reclassifications).

Factors to be considered when determining whether a system should be reviewed and tested include:

- Does it process large volumes of transactions?
- Does it process large-dollar-value items?
- Is it used to process complex transactions?
- Is it used to support highly sensitive financial data repositories?

SOCKET IMPLEMENTATION TEAM

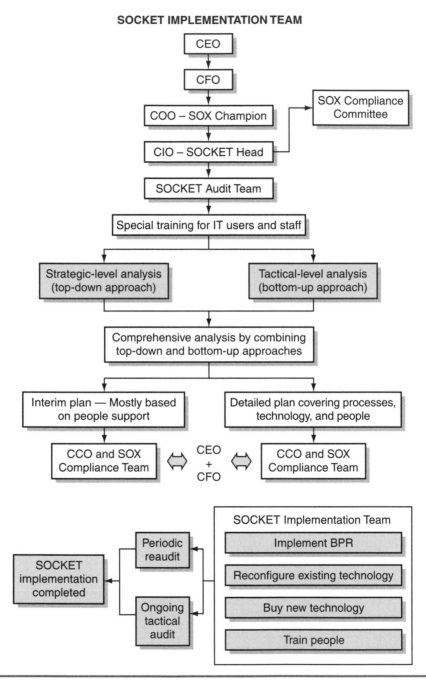

EXHIBIT A.4   SOCKET Implementation Team

Which locations or business units should be included? Consider:

- The extent of dependence on IT at the various locations or business units.
- The degree of consistency in processes and procedures with other locations or business units. Where processes and procedures are unique, organizations may need to consider these locations separately and ensure that overall control objectives are met.
- The organization's assessment of risk related to the location or business unit.

Perform Risk Assessment

Risk assessment requires two perspectives:

1. Impact—reflects the effects of events.
2. Probability or likelihood—reflects the potential for events to occur.

Identify Significant Account/Controls

Identify significant accounts that could have a material impact on the financial reporting and disclosure process. Identify application controls relevant to the identified significant accounts.

Document Control Design

Documentation takes many forms, including paper, electronic files, and other media; and can include a variety of information, such as policy manuals, process models, flowcharts, job descriptions, documents, and forms. The form and extent of documentation will vary depending on the size, nature, and complexity of the company. Management should discuss the proposed extent and detail of the documentation with the external auditors early in the process. Documentation should be prepared—at both the entity level and the activity level—regarding the objectives that the controls are designed to achieve in supporting the organization's internal control over financial reporting and disclosure controls and procedures.

Evaluate Control Design

IT must evaluate the ability of its control program to reduce IT risk to an acceptable level. It requires that control attributes, including preventive, detective, automated, and manual attributes, be considered when designing an approach to effectively address risks.

ENDNOTES

1. This section is based on Robert R. Moeller, *Sarbanes-Oxley and the New Internal Auditing Rules* (Hoboken, N.J.: John Wiley & Sons, 2004), exhibit 5.1.
2. This section is based on IT Governance Institute, "IT Control Objectives for Sarbanes-Oxley," Information Audit and Control Association (ISACA).

Project to Process: Making the House a Home

Companies that deal with large projects, such as construction, often differentiate *projects* from *programs* by noting that projects have a definite beginning and a definite end, whereas programs have a definite beginning, but no definite end. Sarbanes-Oxley compliance is a requirement that companies will have to deal with indefinitely, so it should not be considered a one-time-only project. Companies that have gone through the process of ensuring Sarbanes-Oxley compliance now have the choice of making it an annual project, or of setting up their systems, processes, and controls in such a way that they automatically provide continuous and sustained compliance.

Some of the lessons learned in becoming compliant include the need to work smarter rather than harder, and the opportunity to exploit technology so as to enable better governance, fewer risks, and tighter controls. Given the expense of going throughout the company to check for full compliance and just "get the job done," most companies recognize the need, and the opportunity, to improve their functional operations so that compliance becomes a natural byproduct of good governance.

Many companies have already found that by striving for good governance, the cost and pain of compliance with the letter of the law can be transformed into an impetus to promote the spirit of good governance, resulting in a favorable return on investment (ROI). They have found that good governance, adding value to corporate endeavors, and ROI are not mutually exclusive, but can, and should be, complementary. These organizations are using initial Sarbanes-Oxley compliance results as a blueprint for an ongoing, proactive process of continuous improvement. For the best payoff, compliance should be transformed from a project to an ongoing process.

The Sarbanes-Oxley regulations are only the minimum requirements for financial information transparency, accuracy of reporting,
and timeliness of actionable information. When they set a corporate
goal of achieving the corporate objectives efficiently, effectively, and
reliably, companies realize that they must strengthen their current
processes and systems, and implement needed new ones. Achieving
Sarbanes-Oxley compliance has enabled companies to identify the
processes that should be changed or that should be added. By
approaching the necessary process improvements in a proactive light,
rather than in a regulation-reactive fashion, a company can realize the
synergistic benefits of collaborative and integrated approaches.

THE NEED

These first few years under Sarbanes-Oxley have revealed the need for
many, if not most, companies to ensure that controls are built into all
systems, rather than being applied periodically by outside functions.
Many of the areas needing attention share certain characteristics,
which can be generalized across several areas of responsibility.

One such characteristic is change. All systems and processes have
to be prepared for change, both from external stakeholders (such as
regulatory agencies and shareholders) and from internal stakeholders,
who receive changes from the various processes either in the input
they receive or the output they send to receivers. Predicting the next
regulatory change is like predicting next week's weather: dubious and
highly prone to error. For an organization to deal effectively with
change, each and every process within the organization must be able
and prepared to change.

The requirements of Sarbanes-Oxley itself drive some of a company's most acute needs to incorporate continuous processes into the
compliance effort. Several parts of the Act require ongoing actions
and thus ongoing reviews of compliance. The sections requiring continuous processing include the following.

- Section 302 requires that the CEO and the CFO make certain certifications each quarter and annually. They must certify that the
  company's reports contain no untrue statements; that the company's financial position is fairly presented in all material aspects;

that responsibility has been assigned for the design and maintenance of internal controls, and that these procedures are in place; and that financial information is surfaced through disclosure controls. They must also submit a deficiencies report if they find a lack of controls that could adversely affect the reports.

- Section 403 requires that companies with web sites be prepared to post, within a specified time, a statement regarding major changes in ownership of stock. This section mandates near-immediate, online reporting by the company.

- Section 404 requires annual certification by the CEO and CFO as to the presence of effective internal controls, in addition to an assessment of those internal controls. This assessment must be accompanied every year by the independent auditors' attestation report.

- Section 408 requires the company to expect a full review by the SEC every three years. Managers will need to be prepared to demonstrate the actions the company has taken to ensure compliance.

- Section 409 requires rapid disclosure of material changes in financial condition and operations, again thereby necessitating real-time reporting to management.

- Section 802 requires that all business records be saved for "not less than five years"; the term "business records," as used in the Act includes electronic records and messages. This section also creates a need to constantly handle relevant digital and hard-copy archiving of e-mails, records, and correspondence.

After the passage of Sarbanes-Oxley, the SEC issued new rules stating that auditors need to retain relevant records of audits and reviews for seven years, whether or not they support the auditor's final conclusions. This essentially mandates the continuous processing or retention of relevant data.

Not only does the Sarbanes-Oxley Act require a great deal of continuous processing, but several aspects of the general business environment also require it. The factors and issues that initially spurred adoption of Sarbanes-Oxley are still present, and the need for controls still has to be dealt with on a continuing basis. Sarbanes-Oxley defines the required controls, but the impetus for its imposition of the controls remains.

Investor confidence was one of the most urgent issues leading to the passage of the Sarbanes-Oxley Act. That lack of confidence still exists, and management needs to know how to address it. Companies that focus on transparency to address this issue, rather than doing only the minimum to comply, are finding that they are experiencing a marketing advantage from it. Because equity investors are more concerned than ever with corporate governance, companies that have improved their corporate governance are viewed more favorably by the investor community. The same is true for certain service providers, such as insurance companies and banks.

Insurance companies and credit-granting service companies are going to give better rates to the companies whose information they can understand and compare openly via benchmarking. This equates to better terms and conditions for capital and services for the company that is focusing on good governance, which in turn appeals to external stakeholders above and beyond the requirements of compliance. With the high cost of capital today, this can be a sizeable advantage. Any company that is involved in due diligence and possesses consistent reporting with built-in controls will receive advantages that a less transparent company would not.

Another big advantage to sustained compliance can be found in the United States Sentencing Commission (USSC) guidelines. In 2004, the USSC issued revised guidelines for determining the severity of the sentence a company would receive if a court were to hold that fraud or other criminal conduct had arisen from an organization's operations. Being able to demonstrate that one's company has a compliance program in place, and that the program is effective, can drastically reduce such a sentence—by up to 95 percent. If a company has an effective compliance program in place, a court can easily find that a criminal act was the result of aberrant behavior rather than the natural product of a lax environment. The seven high-level USSC guidelines are:

1. "Standards and procedures to prevent and detect criminal conduct."
2. "Clearly assigned responsibility at all levels (including senior management), adequate resources, and clear lines of program authority." This includes assigning ownership of the compliance program to a specific individual.

3. "Personnel screening related to program goals," including background checks on all senior-level managers.
4. "Training at all levels" on an ongoing basis for all employees, including the board.
5. "Auditing, monitoring, and evaluating program effectiveness coupled with nonretaliatory internal reporting systems." This refers to whistleblowing systems like that required by Sarbanes-Oxley.
6. "Incentives and discipline to promote compliance." This requires a company to have processes for handling and resolving compliance issues.
7. "Reasonable steps to respond to and prevent further similar offenses upon detection of a violation." This includes the responsibility to change the compliance program, using an iterative process, to ensure that unwanted actions do not recur.

From a risk management viewpoint, the opportunity to reduce a potential liability by up to 95 percent in itself provides ample justification for establishing an ethics compliance program.

IT compliance, and especially IT risk, are other fundamental reasons to throw away the bandages and perform triage—and then perform invasive surgery if necessary. Smaller companies with homegrown applications, and even larger companies that have based much of their financial processes on Excel or some other spreadsheet package, will have problems. Many times these processes are not documented, or the documentation is not maintained.

Spreadsheet applications are often a problem because they are not process-driven. They are defined by their relationships, which determine their formulas and algorithms, but all activity happens at once: when either the "Return" key or the F9 key is hit. Spreadsheets thus do not reveal their inputs, nor do they show where their outputs become the inputs for another function. Furthermore, spreadsheets that have certain parameters embedded in their formulas are almost impossible to put through control tests or to verify.

Large companies with complex enterprise resource planning (ERP) processes face a myriad of compliance issues if they have developed their own code for certain processes. In a benchmark test of more than 60 enterprises across Europe in 2003 to 2005, ERP users were shown to be using less than 50 percent of the vendor software capabilities.[1] Often, the vendor software included modules that simply were not being utilized, and often the companies had developed modules through custom-coding to replace or augment the vendor software. Such custom-coding may be done by company employees, or by outside consultants such as the ERP vendor's partners.

The frequent patching of vendor software has made vouching for system integrity a crapshoot at best. Application erosion occurs when the percentage of vendor software being used regularly drops and the percentage of custom code increases. It is important that the level of application erosion be tracked, for both ROI and compliance reasons. The benchmark study recommended that each company develop a matrix such as that as depicted in Exhibit B.1.

The company should then identify how much of its currently installed software is included in each of the matrix squares. Unused vendor software should be included as a cost for ROI purposes, as it represents costs not only for the software, but also for training, documentation, and annual maintenance fees—all of which are paid for but not used. The custom-coded software should also be identified, both for ROI purposes (with design, coding, testing, documenting, and training costs) and for compliance purposes.

It is not enough for a company to rely on the ERP vendor to vouch for compliance without a thorough analysis of all its custom-coded software. Every custom module has touch points where it interfaces with the ERP software. Vendor compliance cannot be assured when these touch points exist. The additional costs associated with custom-coding, as well as the ROI costs of unused vendor software, will often produce different analysis results than an ROI analysis that looks only at direct costs.

The risk management provisions of Sarbanes-Oxley also address a great and ongoing need with regard to information technology infrastructure. The needs for disaster recovery planning (DRP) and

EXHIBIT B.1   Vendor Software Analysis Matrix

	Currently Used	Currently Unused
Vendor Software		
Custom Code Software		

business continuity (BC) within the IT organization are immense. These plans are necessary not only for Sarbanes-Oxley, but also for good governance. It just makes good business sense to have such plans formalized as part of the overall corporate contingency planning program. In addition, these programs have to be constantly revisited for compliance purposes, so, whenever possible, their associated controls should be automated.

Another reason why companies should incorporate compliance into their normal processing is to minimize the costs of external audits. Sarbanes-Oxley explicitly states that auditors must perform walkthroughs of major classes of transactions and agree to the process flows. The auditor must assess the design and effectiveness of controls, including those on the various application programs and the IT general controls. The auditor is not allowed to follow the processes up to a system and then pick up the trail at the output side; an intimate knowledge of the logic and flow of internal processes is necessary. Considering that Sarbanes-Oxley now requires that a company change its auditor from time to time, the need to have the required level of documentation constantly updated mandates that the processes be maintained in an ongoing manner.

Finally, the need for Sarbanes-Oxley compliance to be proceduralized is heightened by the need for companies to be in compliance with the rules and regulations of an increasing number of other regulatory bodies and standards organizations. For example, every company that falls under the domain of Sarbanes-Oxley needs to coordinate its compliance with the rulings from the PCAOB. Thus, many companies that have already achieved compliance, or are trying to come into compliance, are doing so for a variety of reasons other than just to satisfy Sarbanes-Oxley requirements.

Entire matrix grids can and should be developed for the groups with which a company wishes to maintain compliance, in addition to Sarbanes-Oxley. Some of these other standards and bodies include ISO 15489, on records management; IS 17799, on security standards; USO 9000 (series), on quality; ISO 14001, OHSAS 18001, HIPPA, and BS 7799-2, on environmental issues; CobiT and BS 7799, on information security; the FDA, WEEE, and RoHS, on product risk management; and SA 8000, on supply chain risk management. All of these standards are process-driven, so they should be incorporated in an integrated manner with Sarbanes-Oxley process requirements.

The compliance cycle for Sarbanes-Oxley, and other standards if they exist, includes a constant approach to compliance. This approach must be formalized to establish a process cycle of (1) determining the new scopes and domains; (2) identifying new processes and changes in existing processes for documentation and training; (3) creating controls, and then testing and validating these controls for the processes; and (4) analyzing, reporting, and documenting the control results and taking appropriate follow-up measures. A company cannot possibly expect to maintain compliance, on an ongoing basis, with regard to one or more process-oriented standards or regulatory bodies, if it does not do so in a planned way.

THE HOUSE

In this section, we describe how to build a house—but keep in mind that our purpose here is not just to build a house. Rather, we describe how to build a *home*, which will provide shelter from the risks of external factors and will comply with pertinent local ordinances through effective and efficient application of the "house rules." We include the modern conveniences available today for the betterment of the entire community of people living in this home. Though we provide a blueprint describing the foundation, the structure, and the roof, each company must provide the skilled craftspeople to actually create this sustainable home.

The main structure of this house consists of three focuses: (1) governance, (2) risk management, and (3) compliance. All three of these focuses are supported by the foundation of an IT focus. The overarching roof is a collaborative culture that permeates the entire internal and external organization. See Exhibit B.2 for a graphical depiction of this relationship. The collaborative culture focus is responsible for the effectiveness of the other four focuses and how they integrate and work together. If these four focuses do not work together, the house will likely either not be constructed at all, or will be in constant need of repair.

Although most buildings are constructed beginning with the foundation and working up to the roof, we describe this house starting with the roof and then working our way down to the foundation.

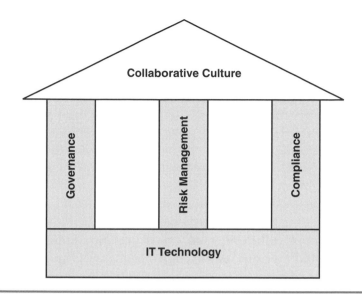

EXHIBIT B.2 The House

The Roof: Collaborative Culture

The term *culture* can have several meanings. In one sense, it can refer to the culture of a society, which is usually delineated by the traditions, customs, mores, values, arts, and behaviors of that society over a long time period. Other meanings include a training of the mind, or the social manners of a person within his or her society. Another definition is the deliberate growing of an organism in a controlled environment, such as the cultures grown in a biology laboratory.

In relation to *corporate culture*, several of these definitions could be applied, but the most pertinent is the development of an organism in a controlled environment. Every corporation has a culture, whether or not it is formally acknowledged. One result of Sarbanes-Oxley is that top-level management has been deliberately tasked with creating a corporate culture that includes an ethical domain. This is expressly stated in the Act. However, Sarbanes-Oxley also requires several other aspects of corporate culture: a culture of controls, a culture of processes, a culture of risk management, and a culture of compliance.

On a meta-level, each company has to develop a collaborative culture. Collaboration requires that policies be based on the consideration of all stakeholders in an endeavor. The first requirement in a collaborative arena is the identification of who the stakeholders are. Corporate stakeholders, for the purposes of Sarbanes-Oxley, include both internal and external stakeholders. The primary external stakeholders are the corporate shareholders and, by proxy perhaps, the SEC. The corporation must constantly base its decisions concerning practices, policies, mission statements, value statements, and even strategy on these stakeholders. The real mission of Sarbanes-Oxley was to make financial reports more transparent and reliable—for the shareholders.

Other external stakeholders that have become a focus of attention are external auditors and the PCAOB. Sarbanes-Oxley defines the relationship of an organization with its external auditors. What used to be standard operating procedures between the two may now be illegal. It used to be that the external consultants owned the internal consultants (or at least their functions) in a relationship that could only be graphically illustrated as a Klein bottle, where the outside is part of the inside and the inside is part of the outside. Today, there is a definite distinction. The roles of the external consultant are described with reference to top management, the audit committee, and the internal auditors.

Internal stakeholders include the board, the audit committee, top-level management, the CEO and CFO (who are specifically named in Sarbanes-Oxley), the internal audit department, process owners, process workers, support organizations such as IT, financial department workers, and anyone else who needs to be informed of and instructed on the corporate ethics program and the whistleblower program. Management needs to take all of these internal stakeholders into consideration when designing programs, processes, systems, and controls and when setting policies and issuing directives.

A collaborative culture can be developed only by top-level management, because it must permeate the entire organization internally as well as the outer reaches of the company's influences. This will require a paradigm shift for many corporations, from a culture of competition and control to one of collaboration. Many companies are used to operating under the belief that information equates to control, and thus controlling information became a tool for controlling stakeholders. Many internal stakeholders felt that they had to compete for control: IT might compete with finance, internal auditing might compete with the external auditors, and the CFO might compete with the audit committee or the CIO. The winner of each competition was the group that wrested control of an area away from another. In these companies' cultures, most groups and employees felt that responsibility required complete control.

In a collaborative paradigm, the key words are *cooperation* and *coordination*, rather than *competition* and *control*. Areas of responsibility are managed by teams or groups rather than individuals or a single group. For teams to operate effectively and efficiently, they must cooperate. A team leader may be appointed, but that person will not necessarily be the leader because of position or rank; rather, he or she will be able to lead because of his or her skill in team building for that particular effort. That team leader will be more of a facilitator or coordinator than a manager or controller. Similarly, the other team members will have to approach their task with a cooperative attitude, agreeing to work with the team leader and with each of the other team members. This is the only way to get these responsible functions performed by people with the proper skill sets.

Because control functions cross so many boundaries in their scope, collaborative efforts are necessary to perform them; no one group will have the expertise or knowledge to do the effort justice. The IT group needs to work with other groups to suggest and provide appropriate IT enabling tools. The process owners need to be represented to provide their wisdom and insight into the logic and logistics of the processes. The internal audit group needs to be represented because its goals will differ from those of the process owners.

In a collaborative environment, the team members themselves will come from a variety of backgrounds and will bring their own particular skills and needs to the table. Nevertheless, the needs of other stakeholders will be acknowledged and considered, even if those stakeholders are not personally represented on the team. Upper management, as it considers its mission statements, vision, strategy, and so forth, will have to consider all of the company's stakeholders, external and internal. The collaborative culture of top-level management will be reflected and carried through to other levels, so that the many efforts undertaken throughout the corporation are accomplished as a collaborative team—whether or not those efforts pertain to Sarbanes-Oxley. This culture should permeate the entire organization and become the way of life for all employees.

A collaborative culture is an integral part of each of the components of the sustaining structure: governance, risk management, compliance, and especially IT.

Structure of the House

Governance.   Compliance with Sarbanes-Oxley provides an opportunity to exercise good governance. *Governance* can be defined as the process whereby the corporation's board of directors establishes the objectives for the organization and oversees progress toward these objectives. Given that repeatability leads to reliability and sustainability, the board should mandate that processes be critically engineered, assigned to responsible process owners, integrated economically with other processes, and designed for change.

Good governance sets the corporate goals and then assures that all processes are designed to attain those goals both efficiently and effectively, so that the company is a good steward of its stockholders' resources. A process may be efficient, but if it does not help attain the corporate goals, it is ineffective and a waste of resources. If a process is effective but not efficient, it also is a waste of resources. Sarbanes-Oxley compliance assures that a company is a good steward of shareholder resources: Specifically, it mandates that good governance expects and requires from process owners processes that are both efficient and effective.

Just as a governor on an automobile is used to control the speed of the drive shaft, good governance of a company is used to control both the speed and the direction of an organization's progress. A fast-moving car going in the wrong direction has speed, but it is out of control. Similarly, the board will set the bounds for the functions to be performed by the company as a whole, as well as the bounds for compliance.

Risk management is not the same as risk avoidance. There will always be elements of risk in any corporate endeavor. The risk process owners are responsible for intelligently determining what those risks are, but it is the governors of the corporation that will make the decision as to which risks to accept and which to avoid or remediate. In this way, the board sets the bounds for the risks inherent in such functions as compliance, risk management, informational integrity, and even ethical obligations.

An aspect of good governance that reveals the true corporate culture is the provision of necessary and desirable tools such as best practices. Good governors do not lay out demands and expectations without providing the means to meet them. If sustainable compliance is one of the goals of the company's governing body, that body must be willing to provide the tools and resources necessary for sustaining compliance. These resources may include personnel, IT technologies, and productivity tools.

The tone of governance is set by what the governors are prepared to offer along with their demands. If the board does not increase the number of internal consultants over what the company had before Sarbanes-Oxley, it cannot expect to get any more internal control processing than it did before. The same is true of training. Good governance includes the recognition that if people are going to have different roles, or roles requiring certain skill levels, they must be given training. For example, the board should ensure that there are people in the organization with skills in root-cause analysis. The quality of the sustaining program will be measured by to the training offered to the various internal stakeholders.

Good governance also includes exhibiting and demonstrating a collaborative corporate culture with regard to change. If the culture is to accept and even embrace change, the governors must allow the internal stakeholders to do so. Governance will be collaborative if it can recognize the need for change as described by the various process owners or even process workers. Management must not feel that it is the sole arbiter of what change is necessary and when. Certainly, a scope and boundaries must be set for change management, but those decisions should be based on the input that only a collaborative environment will provide.

Because the entire functional operations of the company are now being defined in terms of processes, good governance requires that these processes be owned by responsible individuals; that is, the business process owners. The culture of empowerment, especially as to process owners, has to be reinforced by good governance under which owners or leaders know their responsibilities and also their authority. They need to be responsible for identifying the controls in their processes, and also for testing their processes. They need to be responsible for analysis of the tests, and also for the appropriate responses to test results. The governing body must not try to micromanage the process, but must operate collaboratively and work with the process owners as a team.

Just as good governance requires that process owners be responsible for their processes, good governance also requires that process performance be measured and communicated up the channels. Management has the responsibility to monitor process performance and to analyze the results, to determine if performance is acceptable as is or if some form of remediation is required. Good governance also requires that this monitoring cycle be completed and performed in a timely manner, so that any necessary remediation can be performed before adverse effects are felt. This is all done in collaboration not only with the process owners, but also with the risk management and compliance teams.

Any process that is measured is measured to determine possible actions; this logically indicates an associated risk. Thus, although governance is one of the pillars of the structure, it must work collaboratively with the other pillars, risk management and compliance. Also, the means by which monitoring is done may very well take the collaborative efforts of IT. This is especially true of any processes that Sarbanes-Oxley requires for real-time monitoring. Monitoring of processes is done not only for management's benefit, but also so that management can pass on information to the company's external stakeholders—either directly or indirectly, either immediately or later.

Another aspect of good governance directly addressed by Sarbanes-Oxley is segregation of duties. Segregation of duties is required as a control means to ensure that a person does not have access to assets as well as the recording of assets, or other dual roles whereby it would be easy to perpetrate or perpetuate fraud without being discovered. It is the role of the governing management to define what roles are permitted to be held by one individual, and what roles are not allowed if the individual has already been assigned a conflicting role. Often a company will not be large enough to avoid all overlaps of critical functions, so it will need a set of compensating controls. These will be exceptions to the normal segregation-of-duties rules set out by management, as will the compensating measures. Compensation controls that exhibit good governance include some of the following:

- Audit trails (easily trackable).
- Reconciliations (preferably performed by the end user or the customer of the information).
- Exception reporting (made to and reviewed by supervisory-level personnel).
- Transaction logs (using both automatic or electronic forms, and manual forms, such as handwritten logs).
- Independent and frequent reviews (such as those performed by the internal controls department).

Again, management needs to work with the process owners, internal controls, and other stakeholders to set the policies regarding segregation of duties and the respective compensation controls. Good governance requires that top-level management be intimately aware of all business processes. Sarbanes-Oxley requires the CEO and CFO to sign off on the controls that are a part of all of the processes. This level of engagement requires a collaborative effort, one that will exhibit and promote the established corporate culture. This is one of the pillars necessary to ensure that Sarbanes-Oxley compliance migrates from being merely a project to an ongoing house process.

Risk Management.   As noted earlier, risk management is not the same as risk avoidance. It is a given that risks will be associated with many efforts, and that many of these risks will be assumed and accepted. In its 2004 publication, *Enterprise Risk Management: Integrated Framework*, the Committee of Sponsoring Organizations of the Treadway Commission (COSO) began its Executive Summary with the following definition:

> *The underlying premise of enterprise risk management is that every entity exists to provide value for its stakeholders. All entities face uncertainty and the challenge for management is to determine how much uncertainty to accept as it strives to grow stakeholder value. Uncertainty presents both risk and opportunity, with the potential to erode or enhance value. Enterprise risk management enables management to effectively deal with uncertainty and associated risk and opportunity, enhancing the capacity to build value.*
> *Enterprise risk management is a process, effected by an entity's board of directors, management and other personnel, applied in strategy setting and across the enterprise, designed to identify poten-*

tial events that may affect the entity, and manage risk to be within its risk appetite, to provide reasonable assurance regarding the achievement of entity objectives.

From this we see that enterprise risk management (ERM) is a collaborative effort involving the board, top-level management, and others such as business process owners, IT, and risk management specialists. We also see that it is a collaborative effort, in that it "exists to provide value for its stakeholders," (in this case, the shareholders). Risk is important to Sarbanes-Oxley compliance because it is used often as a basis for the controls that are applied to all the processes. Each company needs to develop a risk intelligence system, an iterative, ongoing process consisting of four stages: (1) identify/enhance, (2) inform, (3) control, and (4) evaluate.

A scenario or occurrence must be identified as a risk before any action can be taken. Risks may be identified as being strategic, operational, financial, or legal. *Strategic risks* are risks that a company's long- or short-range strategies will not achieve their intended objectives. For example, a long-range goal may be to acquire certain competitive smaller companies; there may be a strategic risk that another competitor will acquire them first.

Operational risks may cause the company's objectives not to be met as effectively or efficiently as desired. For example, operational dashboards may include certain metrics of operational efficiencies; there is an operational risk that they may not meet the desired rates. *Financial risks* include changes in cost, or expense, or income projections. For example, there is a financial risk that the actual cost of goods sold may exceed the budgeted cost of goods sold that was projected last year. *Legal* or *regulatory risks* include the chance that compliance requirements and/or regulations may change suddenly. Legal risks also include the possibility that adverse litigation will occur and result in either litigation expenses, which will affect the corporate goals even the company is judged not guilty, or legal fines or penalties.

Once risks have been identified, an educational effort must be undertaken to inform the various stakeholders of those risks. They must be identified to top-level management, if substantial in nature, and/or to the business process owners, and/or to the process workers, and/or sometimes to external stakeholders. General risks must be communicated to everyone in the organization. Sarbanes-Oxley requires that each company establish a whistleblower program and that this process be communicated to everyone in the organization. The same is true of the ethics program. The type of risk, the level of risk, and the scope of the risk scenario will determine the extent of the educational effort.

Once risks have been identified as being associated with specific processes, controls must be set in place to alert the necessary people. These controls may block an action that would increase the risk, or they may be designed to detect certain actions or levels of performance that indicate an increased risk. Controls, which are often monitoring tools set up as responses to strategic and financial risks, are usually the responsibility of management. Assuming that some intelligence logic has been built into the system, however, some controls may by themselves eliminate some legal and operational risks.

Management usually handles the evaluation function of the risk cycle. Managers will need to evaluate the results of the controls that have been used to identify risks that have crossed a threshold. This threshold may be binary, indicating that something has been done or not done; or may be analog, in that a predetermined threshold that has been entered into the system has been crossed. Executive Dashboards are examples of these kinds of risks, which are monitored for subjective analysis by management. Managers are then responsible for making the risk responses, decisions, and actions.

Social risks are those created by the conduct of people, either inside or outside the organization. These include conduct that could lead to civil liability; conduct that could lead to regulatory infraction; conduct that could cause economic loss or damage to the company's reputation; or conduct that violates the organization's policies and procedures (which are not necessarily mandated by outside agencies).

An entirely different type of risk is associated with IT than with the rest of the organization. Internal IT risks include the possibility of disruption in the information processing systems; there are employee risks associated with lack of training or motivation, change in jobs or roles, or change in management responsibilities. External risk factors include technological developments, new or changed regulations or legislation, and, of course, natural calamities. Often an IT department has a special subset of risk management called vulnerability management, which is responsible for discovering, evaluating, and fixing vulnerabilities of the IT systems.

Sarbanes-Oxley lists explicitly what must be protected in terms of risk. These are the financial controls, including transaction processing and corporate financial records, systems, and reports. Sarbanes-Oxley is also explicit about what to protect against: accidental data contamination and intentional, malicious activities (both internal and external). What Sarbanes-Oxley is not explicit about is *how* to protect these elements. That is why the risk management team must work with management, the compliance teams, the process owners, IT, and others to develop the best strategy for that company's risk management system.

The corporate culture is displayed in the risk management focus. Just like individuals, some corporations will be very risk averse, whereas others will almost be risk embracing. A look at the companies that suffered during the dot-com bust will reveal a broad spectrum of risk management, all reflecting corporate culture.

Compliance.   The third pillar of the sustainable home is compliance. *Compliance* is the acceptance of an external organization's rules of governance in such a way that those rules become intertwined with one's own, internal rules of governance. A breach of an external rule becomes viewed as if it were a breach of an internal rule. Individuals as well as groups must comply with the rules of Sarbanes-Oxley if the organization overall is going to be considered in compliance by the SEC.

Sarbanes-Oxley compliance management begins by defining and promoting the compliance objectives; identifying the legal and other risks that can impede compliance; establishing the internal rules, structures, resources, policies, procedures, and other factors necessary to obtain compliance; and then establishing a compliance program to integrate these into the business process systems of the organization.

The Open Compliance and Ethics Group (OCEG), a not-for-profit organization, was established to help organizations "align their governance, compliance, and risk management activities"[2] to promote better business performance and integrity. OCEG was formed by a multi-industry, multidisciplinary coalition because the member entities felt a need to integrate the "principles of effective governance, compliance, risk management, and integrity into the practice of everyday business."

Realizing that many companies need to be concerned with compliance not only with Sarbanes-Oxley, but also with perhaps a myriad of other standards, OCEG developed guidelines as a model for multiple compliances. Its OCEG framework is free to download, analyze, and use. This guideline addresses the full life cycle of a compliance program, including planning, implementing, managing, evaluating, and improving integrated compliance programs.

Compliance programs often migrate through stages; the first stage usually aims to discover process needs and shortcomings. The next stage sets out to meet these needs and fix the shortcomings. The third stage is to grow a continuous improvement culture. Prioritization and scheduling are important ways of determining the course of this focus. A company may also want to establish its compliance program in the context of a maturity model, recognizing that a compliance program will not be able to perform all of the advanced functions while it is still going through the initial stages.

Compliance programs are a collaborative effort that receive their directives from management, but then work with the risk management focuses, the IT focus, the business process owners, and the individual process owners. Together, all these participants determine what risks exist that would lead to undesired results, and decide how to prevent or minimize the effects of those risks so as to continue to be in compliance with a standard or set of rules (whether external or internal).

One of the chief responsibilities of the compliance focus is to establish a response process. This response process analyzes the responses to control alerts and determines what action should be taken. These actions may be performed automatically, through a workflow program that IT has established, or may be performed by individuals. The compliance focus will need a special level of intimacy and knowledge about the outside organization's standards, so special training will be necessary for this focus.

The compliance focus is concerned with mapping requirements from the outside standard to the company's business processes. This group is responsible for working out with others what controls (such as required documentation) should be established. It is responsible for determining the criteria for judging whether existing documentation meets the required standards. It is also responsible for determining the appropriate remediation for any level of documentation that does not meet the requirements. This is the response process of the compliance focus. This group will be responsible for performing the follow-up to determine when anything originally judged to be in noncompliance can be rejudged. As part of the response process, areas that are found to be in noncompliance must be reported to the various levels of management, as well as to the leaders of the compliance focus.

The effectiveness of the compliance focus will largely be the product of the corporate culture. If the corporate governors say that corporate compliance is a high priority, and the culture tends to back up this statement, then the compliance effort can expect to receive the cooperation it needs. However, if the corporate culture says that "cash is king" and everything else is secondary, the compliance focus may have problems convincing the various other business areas of the need to supply the necessary resources. The compliance focus will not have the resources to carry out its mandate on its own, so it will need the cooperation of many other areas. If the company's culture is one of collaboration, cooperation can be expected. If competition and control of resources is a chief paradigm of the culture, compliance will consistently remain a project that has to be performed each quarter and each year, without the benefit of process.

Foundation of the House: IT

The foundation of the sustaining home that underlies all the other functions, and actually supports all of them, is IT. Just as there must be a focus for the pillars of governance, risk management, and compliance, there must be a special focus for IT. It is extremely important that IT use a collaborative approach, as it will almost always be working with other stakeholders. Sometimes an IT person will be the team leader, and other times IT folk will serve as team members with a different team leader. Regardless of its leadership or membership role, if IT approaches efforts with an attitude of competition (as in resources) or of control (of the process functions or controls), the whole house will fall down.

When dealing with IT and sustainable compliance, one must separately address two domains: IT as an open system supporting the various business processes, and IT as a closed system independent of the business processes. As an open system, IT provides the technology and the infrastructure for the functional operations of the business processes. This creates a need for controls to include the technology and network topology for general computing, such as client/server platforms; applications controls, such as validation; business process controls, such as the contracts-to-cash process chain in an ERP environment; transaction controls, such as contract data entry; and financial account balance controls, such as balance sheet, income statement (sales), inventory, and purchases. Needless to say, IT must work very closely with the compliance focus, as well as the business process owners, to provide the level of service required.

Closed-system IT must view itself as its own processes with its own process owners, and work in an ongoing way to determine risks as well as the controls necessary for compliance. The chief objectives of such an introspective analysis include:

- Developing and enforcing formal policies and procedures to deal with system security.
- Establishing a change management system with its own change control board (CCB).
- Insisting on segregation of duties so that developers are not also responsible for production runs.
- Developing a set of internal controls, as well as the templates and automation processes for these controls.
- Working closely with the risk management focus to identify the risks attendant to its infrastructure and operations.
- Developing a documentation program that includes training, manuals, version control, and audit history.

IT will need to work with the governance focus in determining what IT technology tools will enable the latter to govern effectively. This may include installing dashboard and portal technologies and their applications. IT will also have to work closely with the business process owners to determine what applications and technologies would enable them to perform their responsibilities efficiently and effectively. This may include making available intranet applications such as training and documentation resources; workflow technology; documentation management systems; collaborative tools such as instant messaging or work suites that include meetings, voice, multimedia, and so on; and internal and external means of information transmission such as XBRL.

IT will also have to work with the compliance focus as it works with the business processes in certifying compliance with outside standards. IT will be a leading force in the integration of financial processes and internal control and their monitoring and reporting. By working together with internal controls, IT can provide the technology for control monitoring, testing, evaluation, reporting, and documentation. In order to move from a project mentality to a process approach, IT may want to consider developing applications that use analytics and continuous monitoring systems.

There will be times when the demands of compliance will not fit with the needs of any particular business process. E-mail is a good example. For business process purposes, a good e-mail system is one that transmits messages reliably and maybe ties in with some collaborative functions such as personal calendars. Compliance requires the archiving of e-mail messages. This function does not pertain to any business process, yet it is a need that the IT area must address. Another example is an electronic archival system that is needed for compliance purposes. Although not a requirement for many business processes, once this archiving system has been installed and implemented, it may be found to provide a definite benefit for many of the processes; thus, it becomes a matter of good governance to require that level of control—especially if it is done right. If IT is considered an enabling tool, it can be used to reduce costs, complexities, and even risk.

When evaluating the IT area as a closed system for compliance purposes, the IT area may want to consider using standard maturity models such as Capability Maturity Model Integrated (CMMI). This is part of Carnegie Mellon's Software Engineering Institute (SEI) and focuses on process improvements. It deals with the various development and delivery life cycles (product life cycles, project life cycles, etc.) that many IT groups already use. These complement the Sarbanes-Oxley requirements of project management, requirements management, metrics, quality, and configuration management.

IT needs to work with the risk management focus again for the IT technology and applications used throughout the organization and also for itself. Often when a risk is identified, it can be controlled through IT applications before it becomes a reality, or it can be monitored and reported after it crosses a predetermined threshold.

One of the biggest risk scenarios that risk management will face will be the IT practices relating to a disaster recovery plan and/or business continuity. The risks of having to relocate the physical IT sites, or of using backup systems, either hot (already up and running) or cold (having to be configured and set up before use); the risks of having the necessary operators at these other sites; and the need for the network to be duplicated from these other sites, with all the security measures intact, is daunting, to say the least. Nevertheless, incidents such as 9/11 and natural disasters such as hurricanes have shown that these risks are real and must be addressed, no matter how daunting or complex they are.

Another model is the Information Technology Infrastructure Library (ITIL), which has become popular in Europe and is becoming increasingly popular in the United States. ITIL is an integrated set of best practices with common definitions and terminology. ITIL covers areas such as change management, release management, problem management, and incident management. ITIL divides IT services into two domains: service support and service delivery. Service support includes the best practices of those disciplines that enable IT services to be provided effectively and efficiently. Service delivery refers to the management of the IT services themselves. It includes a number of management best practices to ensure that IT services are actually provided according to the agreement between the IT provider and the customer stakeholder.

One of the more popular models for IT compliance is the CobiT/COSO cube. CobiT (Control Objectives for Information and related Technology) is an accepted reference tool dealing with IT controls. The CobiT framework, which deals primarily with IT, is used widely by IT management and internal and external auditors. The tool is published jointly by the IT Governance Institute (ITGI) and the Information Systems Audit and Control Association (ISACA). CobiT defines 34 high-level IT control objectives. For an overview of CobiT, see Appendix E and F.

The COSO Framework is explicitly recommended for Sarbanes-Oxley compliance by both the Public Company Accounting Oversight Board (PCAOB) and the SEC. COSO's framework consists of five components, and requires competency in all five areas to achieve an integrated control program. These components, which deal specifically with controls within the business processes, are control environment, risk assessment, control activities, information and communication, and monitoring.

Because COSO deals with controls of business processes, and CobiT deals with IT controls, and because Sarbanes-Oxley insists that the control objectives for the financial processes include IT controls, these two models have been mapped onto a cube. The five COSO components constitute five layers of the face of the cube. Four CobiT objectives are then mapped across the top plane of the cube. Some cubes label the third dimension, the depth, to show the various business units. The four CobiT objectives used in this model are: plan and organize; acquire and implement; deliver and support; and monitor and evaluate. By viewing the controls of each COSO component in the light of the four CobiT objectives, a very detailed control environment plan can be laid out in a way that will help to assure compliance with Sarbanes-Oxley.

DEMYSTIFYING THE SARBANES-OXLEY, SEC, PCAOB, COSO, AND COBIT RELATIONSHIP

If you had to pick one word to describe the relationship of the Sarbanes-Oxley Act, the SEC, the PCAOB, COSO, and CobiT, it would be *hierarchical*. Although it is not a true hierarchy, the image does fit the reality well. If you picture a reverse pyramid, with the Sarbanes-Oxley Act at the top and CobiT at the bottom, you will have a pretty good understanding of how these entities interrelate. See Exhibit B.3.

So what is wrong with this picture? It's simple . . . literally! The actual relationships are a little more complicated. The Sarbanes-Oxley Act essentially tells publicly traded companies what they cannot do, but not what to do to attain or prove compliance. The Act mandated the creation of the PCAOB, which to a degree does give direction, but only on a high level. The SEC acts as the enforcer of the legislation. It oversees the PCAOB and has the ability to override any decisions or penalties that the PCAOB makes or imposes.

COSO, which has been around since the 1990s, is simply a methodology of best business practices. All Sarbanes-Oxley did was make best business practices mandatory instead of optional. It is not

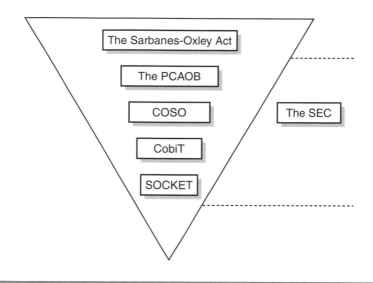

EXHIBIT B.3   Interrelationship of the Sarbanes-Oxley Act, the SEC, the PCAOB, COSO, and CobiT

mandated that companies use the COSO Integrated Framework, but that framework is a proven commodity. The Big 4 accounting firms have adopted this methodology in an effort to comply, and it has been accepted by the PCAOB. It is fair to say that it has become the de facto methodology for Sarbanes-Oxley compliance on the business side.

That brings us to CobiT. CobiT does for IT processes what COSO does for business processes. Neither the assessment of internal controls over financial reporting, nor Sarbanes-Oxley compliance, is complete without both.

According to the ITGI, CobiT is "100 percent compliant with ISO17799 and maps to many other related standards." ITGI also asserts that "CobiT is a way to bridge the communication gap between IT functions, the business and auditors, by providing a common approach, understandable by all." Truly, the common perception in the IT world is that CobiT picks up where COSO leaves off.

IT should be included in the corporate culture of continuous improvement. Whenever any of the internal stakeholders consider how to improve their processes, IT should be involved. As we have seen, IT should be included in all collaborative efforts of the three pillars: (1) governance, (2) risk management, and (3) compliance. The corporate culture will determine how proactive the IT focus is or how reactive it is forced to be. If the culture is truly one of continuous improvement, IT will have the opportunity to be a strong team player, working along with the other teams and providing the necessary enabling technology and applications.

THE HOUSE BECOMES THE HOME

With the foundation of IT technology and applications, and the three structural pillars of governance, risk management, and compliance, all under the roof of the corporate collaborative culture, we now have the makings of a home for the foreseeable future. Compliance should not be a major construction project that occurs every quarter or every year. It should not be a checklist of things to do or confirm just to say that they have been done. Compliance should not be an isolated exercise by an isolated group. Compliance with Sarbanes-Oxley should be integrated with compliance with other standards, and should be integrated within the framework of functional operations and business processes throughout the organization as an effort to perform continuous improvement.

As noted earlier, the most important element is the roof, the collaborative culture of the organization. If the culture is one of team building and teamwork, the transition from project to process will be much easier. Without such a culture, it will be difficult, if not impossible. The culture must also firmly support the approach of constant improvement. Without this approach, it will be too easy for the process to be assigned a lower priority, and then be forced always to respond reactively rather than proactively.

This collaborative culture must permeate the governance focus, as these people will be setting the scope and boundaries of the effort. All directives and policies must be made with the consideration it must also permeate the risk management focus, as that group determines the risks that are embedded in the company's processes. The compliance focus must also approach its tasks in a collaborative fashion as it works to map outside standards to the internal processes. The IT focus is not only the foundation for the whole endeavor, but it is also the infrastructure that radiates up through the three pillars, because it provides the technology and the applications that will make viable each of the three focuses' efforts to transform a compliance project into an integrated process for attaining corporate objectives in an effective and efficient manner.

ENDNOTES

1. *http://www.benchmark-express* and *http://www.cimaglobal.com/cps/role/xchg/s1D-OAAAC564-FBGB7B58/live/root.xsl/6382_7789.htm* (last accessed January 2006)
2. *http://www.oceg.org*

Enterprise Project Management and the Sarbanes-Oxley Compliance Project

Enterprise-wide project management, though infinitely more intricate, follows the same methodology as a locally implemented project. The nine knowledge areas and five process groups defined by the Project Management Institute's Project Management Framework apply to all projects, large and small. Sarbanes-Oxley compliance projects are no exception.

There are six steps to Sarbanes-Oxley compliance. These six steps map to the nine knowledge areas delineated in Exhibit C.1.

GLOBALIZATION

Corporate globalization has created an environment in which the alignment of resources and business activities with strategic objectives cannot be effectively managed using a stand-alone approach. Site-specific projects have given way to enterprise project management (EPM), whereby organizations manage their processes and procedures as projects. This has provided greater flexibility and quicker response to risks and opportunities. Key components in the EPM effort have been Project Portfolio Management, a creation of the Project Management Office; and the availability of software solutions that can integrate portfolio management, enterprise resource management (ERM), and supply chain management (SCM).

The EPM approach enables a once slow-to-react global corporation to attain new agility in identifying, prioritizing, and investing in projects that align with its corporate strategy. Mandatory projects such as Sarbanes-Oxley compliance do not require identification or prioritization. However, because of the horrendously high costs of Sarbanes-Oxley projects, and the importance of completing them correctly and on time, the EPM approach emerges as the most cost-effective one.

Many companies today are not only multilocational, but also international. Proper resource allocation and communications are two of their greatest challenges. How do you get the number of people who are qualified for a particular role to the desired locations in time to complete an audit? How do you schedule meetings across different time zones?

These are merely two questions of probably thousands that must be answered. The only way to get this accomplished is by using an extremely organized approach that can, at any time, let you know how many resources with what skill sets are available. You will need a calendar with which you can schedule meetings (conference calls, video conferencing, Internet communications, etc.) and take into account the different time zones involved. Status reporting must be done in a timely fashion.

RISK MANAGEMENT

In addition to the logistical and global communications challenges, risk management must be carefully considered. Risk identification, on the local level as well as on a global basis, comprises three basic variables: known risks, known unknowns, and unknown unknowns. The difference is that, on a global basis, the risks from unknown unknowns are much greater, because of logistical issues and cultural issues. Of the two, cultural issues can present the greatest challenge and the greatest amount of unknown unknowns.

Risk identification and mitigation of unknowns in a localized Sarbanes-Oxley compliance effort can come to seem fairly tame once you have completed one or two engagements. In contrast, the unknowns in a global Sarbanes-Oxley compliance project can really be, well, unknown! Consider the difference in local customs in the United States when going from east to west, or north to south, or urban to rural. Imagine what differences there are from global region to global region, or country to country. Aside from local customs, there are language differences, religious differences, and more. The point is that unless you have a management team that is intimately familiar with the culture, ethnicity, religious customs, and language of the specific locale, the only tool you have to identify the unknown risks is your imagination—a truly scary thought! In situations like this, communication can be the key factor in successfully completing a Sarbanes-Oxley compliance project. The team in the field must be relied on to identify potential risks as they present themselves and communicate them to management in a timely enough fashion that controls can be put in place.

So far we have considered logistical, cultural, religious, and ethnic differences from the unknown-unknowns point of view. What about the known unknowns, such as competing compliance issues? Laws change from country to country and region to region. One of the main concerns of opponents of the Sarbanes-Oxley Act is the buy-in from foreign markets. The fear has always been that foreign interest in the U.S. market will drop because of the expense involved in becoming Sarbanes-Oxley compliant. If they are to satisfy the PCAOB, foreign companies will have to follow the same stringent regulation as U.S. companies. How will this play out when U.S. companies try to implement Sarbanes-Oxley compliance projects in foreign countries?

It is clear that the EPM team will have to be comprised of a diverse group of subject-matter experts—experts in local laws as well as the languages and customs of the region in which the compliance project is taking place. Where does one find a "dream team" such as this? The answer is in the company's ERP package.

It is well known that the ERP package is essential in assessing a company's internal controls over financial reporting. From an enterprise portfolio management perspective, it is also an excellent tool for identifying the best internal resources: the people who have the required skill sets for the roles and responsibilities needed for an enterprise-wide compliance project.

So far we have discussed risk management in general. There is, however, another risk factor to be discussed: the fact that different industries come with their own inherent risks. Companies that deal in merchandise and commodities will incur more and different risks than companies that deal only in information. Manufacturing companies, for example, have inventory and supply chain management issues added to their potential risk factors. Supply chain management (SCM) is just as important as ERP for these companies when it comes to assessing internal controls over their financial reporting.

There are software packages that will help manage an enterprise-wide project, from a project management point of view; such packages usually use the Internet as a centralized project management database. Naturally, the cost of this software package must be included in the compliance budget. Also, to be useful and successful, it will have to be integrated with the company's SCM and ERP packages.

PMBOK®

Project Management

1. Integration Management
2. Scope Management
3. Time Management
4. Cost Management
5. Quality Management
6. HR Management
7. Communications Mgmt.
8. Risk Management
9. Procurement Mgmt.

SOXPM™

1. Plan, Scope and Assess Sarbanes-Oxley Project
2. Identify and Document Key Processes, Controls
3. Evaluate Control Design, Operational Effectiveness
4. Identify and Remediate Deficiencies/Weaknesses
5. Establish Ongoing Audit/ Monitoring Procedures
6. Build-in Sustainability

EXHIBIT C.1   Sarbanes-Oxley Project Management "PMBOK® is a registered trademark of the Project Management Institute (*www.pmi.org*)"

Enterprise Risk Management— Integrated Framework[1]

EXECUTIVE SUMMARY

The underlying premise of enterprise risk management is that every entity exists to provide value for its stakeholders. All entities face uncertainty, and the challenge for management is to determine how much uncertainty to accept as it strives to grow stakeholder value. Uncertainty presents both risk and opportunity, with the potential to erode or enhance value. Enterprise risk management enables management to effectively deal with uncertainty and associated risk and opportunity, enhancing the capacity to build value.

Value is maximized when management sets strategy and objectives to strike an optimal balance between growth and return goals and related risks, and efficiently and effectively deploys resources in pursuit of the entity's objectives. Enterprise risk management encompasses:

- *Aligning risk appetite and strategy*—Management considers the entity's risk appetite in evaluating strategic alternatives, setting related objectives, and developing mechanisms to manage related risks.
- *Enhancing risk response decisions*—Enterprise risk management provides the rigor to identify and select among alternative risk responses—risk avoidance, reduction, sharing, and acceptance.
- *Reducing operational surprises and losses*—Entities gain enhanced capability to identify potential events and establish responses, reducing surprises and associated costs or losses.
- *Identifying and managing multiple and cross-enterprise risks*— Every enterprise faces a myriad of risks affecting different parts of the organization, and enterprise risk management facilitates effec-

tive response to the interrelated impacts, and integrated responses to multiple risks.

- *Seizing opportunities*—By considering a full range of potential events, management is positioned to identify and proactively realize opportunities.
- *Improving deployment of capital*—Obtaining robust risk information allows management to effectively assess overall capital needs and enhance capital allocation.

These capabilities inherent in enterprise risk management help management achieve the entity's performance and profitability targets and prevent loss of resources. Enterprise risk management helps ensure effective reporting and compliance with laws and regulations, and helps avoid damage to the entity's reputation and associated consequences. In sum, enterprise risk management helps an entity get to where it wants to go and avoid pitfalls and surprises along the way.

Events—Risks and Opportunities

Events can have negative impact, positive impact, or both. Events with a negative impact represent risks, which can prevent value creation or erode existing value. Events with positive impact may offset negative impacts or represent opportunities. Opportunities are the possibility that an event will occur and positively affect the achievement of objectives, supporting value creation or preservation. Management channels opportunities back to its strategy or objective-setting processes, formulating plans to seize the opportunities.

Enterprise Risk Management Defined

Enterprise risk management deals with risks and opportunities affecting value creation or preservation, defined as follows:

> *Enterprise risk management is a process, effected by an entity's board of directors, management and other personnel, applied in strategy setting and across the enterprise, designed to identify potential events that may affect the entity, and manage risk to be within its risk appetite, to provide reasonable assurance regarding the achievement of entity objectives.*

The definition reflects certain fundamental concepts. Enterprise risk management is:

- A process, ongoing and flowing through an entity
- Effected by people at every level of an organization
- Applied in strategy setting
- Applied across the enterprise, at every level and unit, and includes taking an entity-level portfolio view of risk
- Designed to identify potential events that, if they occur, will affect the entity and to manage risk within its risk appetite
- Able to provide reasonable assurance to an entity's management and board of directors
- Geared to achievement of objectives in one or more separate but overlapping categories

This definition is purposefully broad. It captures key concepts fundamental to how companies and other organizations manage risk, providing a basis for application across organizations, industries, and sectors. It focuses directly on achievement of objectives established by a particular entity and provides a basis for defining enterprise risk management effectiveness.

Achievement of Objectives

Within the context of an entity's established mission or vision, management establishes strategic objectives, selects strategy, and sets aligned objectives cascading through the enterprise. This enterprise risk management framework is geared to achieving an entity's objectives, set forth in four categories:

- *Strategic*—high-level goals, aligned with and supporting its mission
- *Operations*—effective and efficient use of its resources
- *Reporting*—reliability of reporting
- *Compliance*—compliance with applicable laws and regulations.

This categorization of entity objectives allows a focus on separate aspects of enterprise risk management. These distinct but overlapping categories—a particular objective can fall into more than one category—address different entity needs and may be the direct responsibility of different executives. This categorization also allows distinctions between what can be expected from each category of objectives. Another category, safeguarding of resources, used by some entities, also is described.

Because objectives relating to reliability of reporting and compliance with laws and regulations are within the entity's control, enterprise risk management can be expected to provide reasonable assurance of achieving those objectives. Achievement of strategic objectives and operations objectives, however, is subject to external events not always within the entity's control; accordingly, for these objectives, enterprise risk management can provide reasonable assurance that management, and the board in its oversight role, are made aware, in a timely manner, of the extent to which the entity is moving toward achievement of the objectives.

Components of Enterprise Risk Management

Enterprise risk management consists of eight interrelated components. These are derived from the way management runs an enterprise and are integrated with the management process. These components are:

- *Internal Environment*—The internal environment encompasses the tone of an organization, and sets the basis for how risk is viewed and addressed by an entity's people, including risk management philosophy and risk appetite, integrity and ethical values, and the environment in which they operate.
- *Objective Setting*—Objectives must exist before management can identify potential events affecting their achievement. Enterprise risk management ensures that management has in place a process to set objectives and that the chosen objectives support and align with the entity's mission and are consistent with its risk appetite.
- *Event Identification*—Internal and external events affecting achievement of an entity's objectives must be identified, distinguishing between risks and opportunities. Opportunities are channeled back to management's strategy or objective-setting processes.
- *Risk Assessment*—Risks are analyzed, considering likelihood and impact, as a basis for determining how they should be managed. Risks are assessed on an inherent and a residual basis.

- *Risk Response*—Management selects risk responses—avoiding, accepting, reducing, or sharing risk—developing a set of actions to align risks with the entity's risk tolerances and risk appetite.
- *Control Activities*—Policies and procedures are established and implemented to help ensure the risk responses are effectively carried out.
- *Information and Communication*—Relevant information is identified, captured, and communicated in a form and timeframe that enable people to carry out their responsibilities. Effective communication also occurs in a broader sense, flowing down, across, and up the entity.
- *Monitoring*—The entirety of enterprise risk management is monitored and modifications made as necessary. Monitoring is accomplished through ongoing management activities, separate evaluations, or both.

Enterprise risk management is not strictly a serial process, where one component affects only the next. It is a multidirectional, iterative process in which almost any component can and does influence another.

Relationship of Objectives and Components

There is a direct relationship between objectives, which are what an entity strives to achieve, and enterprise risk management components, which represent what is needed to achieve them. The relationship is depicted in a three-dimensional matrix, in the form of a cube (see Exhibit D.1).

The four objectives categories—strategic, operations, reporting, and compliance—are represented by the vertical columns, the eight components by horizontal rows, and an entity's units by the third dimension. This depiction portrays the ability to focus on the entirety of an entity's enterprise risk management, or by objectives category, component, entity unit, or any subset thereof.

Effectiveness

Determining whether an entity's enterprise risk management is "effective" is a judgment resulting from an assessment of whether the eight components are present and functioning effectively. Thus, the com-

EXHIBIT D.1 Relationship of Objectives and Components in a Three-Dimensional Matrix.

ponents are also criteria for effective enterprise risk management. For the components to be present and functioning properly there can be no material weaknesses, and risk needs to have been brought within the entity's risk appetite.

When enterprise risk management is determined to be effective in each of the four categories of objectives, respectively, the board of directors and management have reasonable assurance that they understand the extent to which the entity's strategic and operations objectives are being achieved, and that the entity's reporting is reliable and applicable laws and regulations are being complied with.

The eight components will not function identically in every entity. Application in small and mid-size entities, for example, may be less formal and less structured. Nonetheless, small entities still can have effective enterprise risk management, as long as each of the components is present and functioning properly.

Limitations

While enterprise risk management provides important benefits, limitations exist. In addition to factors discussed above, limitations result from the realities that human judgment in decision making can be faulty, decisions on responding to risk and establishing controls need to consider the relative costs and benefits, breakdowns can occur because of human failures such as simple errors or mistakes, controls can be circumvented by collusion of two or more people, and management has the ability to override enterprise risk management decisions. These limitations preclude a board and management from having absolute assurance as to achievement of the entity's objectives.

Encompasses Internal Control

Internal control is an integral part of enterprise risk management. This enterprise risk management framework encompasses internal control, forming a more robust conceptualization and tool for management. Internal control is defined and described in *Internal Control—Integrated Framework*. Because that framework has stood the test of time and is the basis for existing rules, regulations, and laws, that document remains in place as the definition of and framework for internal control. While only portions of the text of *Internal Control—Integrated Framework* are reproduced in this framework, the entirety of that framework is incorporated by reference into this one.

Roles and Responsibilities

Everyone in an entity has some responsibility for enterprise risk management. The chief executive officer is ultimately responsible and should assume ownership. Other managers support the entity's risk management philosophy, promote compliance with its risk appetite, and manage risks within their spheres of responsibility consistent with risk tolerances. A risk officer, financial officer, internal auditor, and others usually have key support responsibilities. Other entity personnel are responsible for executing enterprise risk management in accordance with established directives and protocols. The board of directors provides important oversight to enterprise risk management, and is aware of and concurs with the entity's risk appetite. A number of external parties, such as customers, vendors, business partners, external auditors, regulators, and financial analysts often provide information useful in effecting enterprise risk management, but they are not responsible for the effectiveness of, nor are they a part of, the entity's enterprise risk management.

Organization of This Report

This report is in two volumes. The first volume contains the *Framework* as well as this *Executive Summary*. The *Framework* defines enterprise risk management and describes principles and concepts, providing direction for all levels of management in businesses and other organizations to use in evaluating and enhancing the effectiveness of enterprise risk management. This *Executive Summary* is a high-level overview directed to chief executives, other senior executives, board members, and regulators. The second volume, *Application Techniques*, provides illustrations of techniques useful in applying elements of the framework.

Use of This Report

Suggested actions that might be taken as a result of this report depend on position and role of the parties involved:

- *Board of Directors*—The board should discuss with senior management the state of the entity's enterprise risk management and provide oversight as needed. The board should ensure it is apprised of the most significant risks, along with actions management is taking and how it is ensuring effective enterprise risk management. The board should consider seeking input from internal auditors, external auditors, and others.
- *Senior Management*—This study suggests that the chief executive assess the organization's enterprise risk management capabilities. In one approach, the chief executive brings together business unit heads and key functional staff to discuss an initial assessment of enterprise risk management capabilities and effectiveness. Whatever its form, an initial assessment should determine whether there is a need for, and how to proceed with, a broader, more in-depth evaluation.
- *Other Entity Personnel*—Managers and other personnel should consider how they are conducting their responsibilities in light of

this framework and discuss with more-senior personnel ideas for strengthening enterprise risk management. Internal auditors should consider the breadth of their focus on enterprise risk management.

- *Regulators*—This framework can promote a shared view of enterprise risk management, including what it can do and its limitations. Regulators may refer to this framework in establishing expectations, whether by rule or guidance or in conducting examinations, for entities they oversee.

- *Professional Organizations*—Rule-making and other professional organizations providing guidance on financial management, auditing, and related topics should consider their standards and guidance in light of this framework. To the extent diversity in concepts and terminology is eliminated, all parties benefit.

- *Educators*—This framework might be the subject of academic research and analysis, to see where future enhancements can be made. With the presumption that this report becomes accepted as a common ground for understanding, its concepts and terms should find their way into university curricula.

With this foundation for mutual understanding, all parties will be able to speak a common language and communicate more effectively. Business executives will be positioned to assess their company's enterprise risk management process against a standard, and strengthen the process and move their enterprise toward established goals. Future research can be leveraged off an established base. Legislators and regulators will be able to gain an increased understanding of enterprise risk management, including its benefits and limitations. With all parties utilizing a common enterprise risk management framework, these benefits will be realized.

ENDNOTE

1. Committee of Sponsoring Organizations of the Treadway Commission, *Enterprise Risk Management-Integrated Framework* (September 2004). Reprinted with permission. Copyright © 2004 by the Committee of Sponsoring Organizations of the Treadway Commission. Reproduced with permission from the AICPA acting as authorized copyright administrator for COSO.

COBIT 3 Executive Summary

Includes excerpts from the Cobit Executive Summary.
Source: © 1996, 1998, 2000 IT Governance Institute (ITGI).
All rights reserved.

EXECUTIVE OVERVIEW

Critically important to the survival and success of an organisation is effective management of information and related Information Technology (IT). In this global information society—where information travels through cyberspace without the constraints of time, distance and speed—this criticality arises from the:

- Increasing dependence on information and the systems that deliver this information
- Increasing vulnerabilities and a wide spectrum of threats, such as cyber threats and information warfare
- Scale and cost of the current and future investments in information and information systems
- Potential for technologies to dramatically change organisations and business practices, create new opportunities and reduce costs

For many organisations, information and the technology that supports it represent the organisation's most valuable assets. Moreover, in today's very competitive and rapidly changing business environment, management has heightened expectations regarding IT delivery functions: management requires increased quality, functionality and ease of use; decreased delivery time; and continuously improving service levels—while demanding that this be accomplished at lower costs.

Many organisations recognise the potential benefits that technology can yield. Successful organisations, however, understand and manage the risks associated with implementing new technologies.

There are numerous changes in IT and its operating environment that emphasise the need to better manage IT-related risks. Dependence on electronic information and IT systems is essential to support critical business processes. In addition, the regulatory environment is mandating stricter control over information. This, in turn, is driven by increasing disclosures of information system disasters and increasing electronic fraud. The management of IT-related risks is now being understood as a key part of enterprise governance.

Within enterprise governance, IT governance is becoming more and more prominent, and is defined as a structure of relationships and processes to direct and control the enterprise in order to achieve the enterprise's goals by adding value while balancing risk versus return over IT and its processes. IT governance is integral to the success of enterprise governance by assuring efficient and effective measurable improvements in related enterprise processes. IT governance provides the structure that links IT processes, IT resources and information to enterprise strategies and objectives. Furthermore, IT governance integrates and institutionalises good (or best) practices of planning and organising,

acquiring and implementing, delivering and supporting, and monitoring IT performance to ensure that the enterprise's information and related technology support its business objectives. IT governance thus enables the enterprise to take full advantage of its information, thereby maximising benefits, capitalising on opportunities and gaining competitive advantage.

IT GOVERNANCE

A structure of relationships and processes to direct and control the enterprise in order to achieve the enterprise's goals by adding value while balancing risk versus return over IT and its processes.

Organisations must satisfy the quality, fiduciary and security requirements for their information, as for all assets. Management must also optimise the use of available resources, including data, application systems, technology, facilities and people. To discharge these responsibilities, as well as to achieve its objectives, management must understand the status of its own IT systems and decide what security and control they should provide.

Control Objectives for Information and related Technology (COBIT), now in its 3rd edition, helps meet the multiple needs of management by bridging the gaps between business risks, control needs and technical issues. It provides good practices across a domain and process framework and presents activities in a manageable and logical structure. COBIT's "good practices" means consensus of the experts—they will help optimise information investments and will provide a measure to be judged against when things do go wrong.

Management must ensure that an internal control system or framework is in place which supports the business processes, makes it clear how each individual control activity satisfies the information requirements and impacts the IT resources. Impact on IT resources is highlighted in the COBIT *Framework* together with the business requirements for effectiveness, efficiency, confidentiality, integrity, availability, compliance and reliability of information that need to be satisfied. Control, which includes policies, organisational structures, practices and procedures, is management's responsibility. Management, through its enterprise governance, must ensure that due diligence is exercised by all individuals involved in the management, use, design, development, maintenance or operation of information systems. An IT control objective is a statement of the desired result or purpose to be achieved by implementing control procedures within a particular IT activity.

Business orientation is the main theme of COBIT. It is designed to be employed not only by users and auditors, but also, and more importantly, as comprehensive guidance for management and business process owners. Increasingly, business practice involves the full empowerment of business process owners so they have total responsibility for all aspects of the business process. In particular, this includes providing adequate controls.

The COBIT *Framework* provides a tool for the business process owner that facilitates the discharge of this responsibility. The *Framework* starts from a simple and pragmatic premise:

In order to provide the information that the organisation needs to achieve its objectives, IT resources need to be managed by a set of naturally grouped processes.

The *Framework* continues with a set of 34 high-level *Control Objectives*, one for each of the IT processes, grouped into four domains: planning and organisation, acquisition and implementation, delivery and support, and monitoring. This structure covers all aspects of information and the technology that supports it. By addressing these 34 high-level control objectives, the business process owner can ensure that an adequate control system is provided for the IT environment.

IT governance guidance is also provided in the COBIT *Framework*. IT governance provides the structure that links IT processes, IT resources and information to enterprise strategies and objectives. IT governance integrates optimal ways of planning and organising, acquiring and implementing, delivering and supporting, and monitoring IT performance. IT governance enables the enterprise to take full advantage of its information, thereby maximising benefits, capitalising on opportunities and gaining competitive advantage.

In addition, corresponding to each of the 34 high-level control objectives is an *Audit Guideline* to enable the review of IT processes against COBIT's 318 recommended detailed control objectives to provide management assurance and/or advice for improvement.

The *Management Guidelines*, COBIT's most recent development, further enhances and enables enterprise management to deal more effectively with the needs and requirements of IT governance. The guidelines are action oriented and generic and provide management direction for getting the enterprise's information and related processes under control, for monitoring achievement of organisational goals, for monitoring performance within each IT process and for benchmarking organisational achievement.

Specifically, COBIT provides **Maturity Models** for control over IT processes, so that management can map where the organisation is today, where it stands in relation to the best-in-class in its industry and to international standards and where the organisation wants to be; **Critical Success Factors**, which define the most important management-oriented implementation guidelines to achieve control over and within its IT processes; **Key Goal Indicators**, which define measures that tell management—after the fact—whether an IT process has achieved its business requirements; and **Key Performance Indicators**, which are lead indicators that define measures of how well the IT process is performing in enabling the goal to be reached.

> COBIT's *Management Guidelines* are generic and action oriented for the purpose of answering the following types of management questions: How far should we go, and is the cost justified by the benefit? What are the indicators of good performance? What are the critical success factors? What are the risks of not achieving our objectives? What do others do? How do we measure and compare?

COBIT also contains an *Implementation Tool Set* that provides lessons learned from those organisations that quickly and successfully applied COBIT in their work environments. It has two particularly useful tools—Management Awareness Diagnostic and IT Control Diagnostic—to assist in analysing an organisation's IT control environment.

Over the next few years, the management of organisations will need to demonstrably attain increased levels of security and control. COBIT is a tool that allows managers to bridge the gap with respect to control requirements, technical issues and business risks and communicate that level of control to stakeholders. COBIT enables the development of clear policy and good practice for IT control throughout organisations, worldwide. **Thus, COBIT is designed to be the breakthrough IT governance tool that helps in understanding and managing the risks and benefits associated with information and related IT.**

COBIT IT PROCESSES DEFINED WITHIN THE FOUR DOMAINS

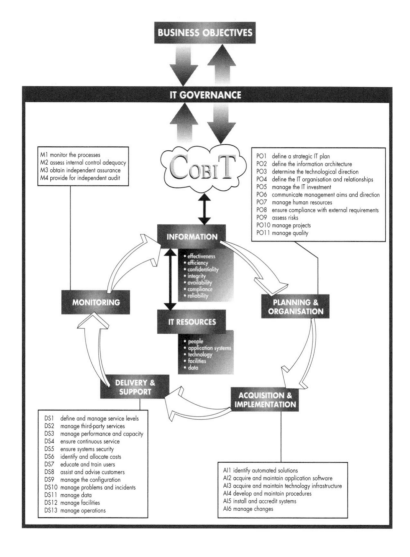

Source: © 1996, 1998, 2000 IT Governance Institute (ITGI). All rights reserved.

THE COBIT FRAMEWORK

THE NEED FOR CONTROL IN INFORMATION TECHNOLOGY

In recent years, it has become increasingly evident that there is a need for a reference framework for security and control in IT. Successful organisations require an appreciation for and a basic understanding of the risks and constraints of IT at all levels within the enterprise in order to achieve effective direction and adequate controls.

MANAGEMENT has to decide what to reasonably invest for security and control in IT and how to balance risk and control investment in an often unpredictable IT environment. While information systems security and control help manage risks, they do not eliminate them. In addition, the exact level of risk can never be known since there is always some degree of uncertainty. Ultimately, management must decide on the level of risk it is willing to accept. Judging what level can be tolerated, particularly when weighted against the cost, can be a difficult management decision. Therefore, management clearly needs a framework of generally accepted IT security and control practices to benchmark the existing and planned IT environment.

There is an increasing need for **USERS** of IT services to be assured, through accreditation and audit of IT services provided by internal or third parties, that adequate security and control exists. At present, however, the implementation of good IT controls in information systems, be they commercial, non-profit or governmental, is hampered by confusion. The confusion arises from the different evaluation methods such as ITSEC, TCSEC, ISO 9000 evaluations, emerging COSO internal control evaluations, etc. As a result, users need a general foundation to be established as a first step.

Frequently, **AUDITORS** have taken the lead in such international standardisation efforts because they are continuously confronted with the need to substantiate their opinion on internal control to management. Without a framework, this is an exceedingly difficult task. Furthermore, auditors are increasingly being called on by management to proactively consult and advise on IT security and control-related matters.

THE BUSINESS ENVIRONMENT: COMPETITION, CHANGE AND COST

Global competition is here. Organisations are restructuring to streamline operations and simultaneously take advantage of the advances in IT to improve their competitive position. Business re-engineering, right-sizing, outsourcing, empowerment, flattened organisations and distributed processing are all changes that impact the way that business and governmental organisations operate. These changes are having, and will continue to have, profound implications for the management and operational control structures within organisations worldwide.

Emphasis on attaining competitive advantage and cost-efficiency implies an ever-increasing reliance on technology as a major component in the strategy of most organisations. Automating organisational functions is, by its very nature, dictating the incorporation of more powerful control mechanisms into computers and networks, both hardware-based and software-based. Furthermore, the fundamental structural characteristics of these controls are evolving at the same rate and in the same "leap frog" manner as the underlying computing and networking technologies are evolving.

Within the framework of accelerated change, if managers, information systems specialists and auditors are indeed going to be able to effectively fulfil their roles, their skills must evolve as rapidly as the technology and the environment. One must understand the technology of controls involved and its changing nature if one is to exercise reasonable and prudent judgments in evaluating control practices found in typical business or governmental organisations.

EMERGENCE OF ENTERPRISE AND IT GOVERNANCE

To achieve success in this information economy, enterprise governance and IT governance can no longer be considered separate and distinct disciplines. Effective enterprise governance focuses individual and group expertise and experience where it can be most productive, monitors and measures performance and provides assurance to critical issues. IT, long considered solely an enabler of an enterprise's strategy, must now be regarded as an integral part of that strategy.

IT governance provides the structure that links IT processes, IT resources, and information to enterprise strategies and objectives. IT governance integrates and institutionalises optimal ways of planning and organising, acquiring and implementing, delivering and supporting, and monitoring IT performance. IT governance is integral to the success of enterprise governance by assuring efficient and effective measurable improvements in related enterprise processes. IT governance enables the enterprise to take full advantage of its information, thereby maximising benefits, capitalising on opportunities and gaining competitive advantage.

Looking at the interplay of enterprise and IT governance processes in more detail, enterprise governance, the system by which entities are directed and controlled, drives and sets IT governance. At the same time, IT should provide critical input to, and constitute an important component of, strategic plans. IT may in fact influence strategic opportunities outlined by the enterprise.

Enterprise activities require information from IT activities in order to meet business objectives. Successful organisations ensure interdependence between their

strategic planning and their IT activities. IT must be aligned with and enable the enterprise to take full advantage of its information, thereby maximising benefits, capitalising on opportunities and gaining a competitive advantage.

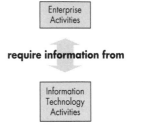

Enterprises are governed by generally accepted good (or best) practices, to ensure that the enterprise is achieving its goals–the assurance of which is guaranteed by certain controls. From these objectives flows the organisation's direction, which dictates certain enterprise activities, using the enterprise's resources. The results of the enterprise activities are measured and reported on, providing input to the constant revision and maintenance of the controls, beginning the cycle again.

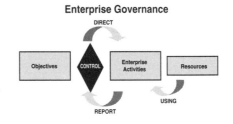

THE COBIT FRAMEWORK, *continued*

IT also is governed by good (or best) practices, to ensure that the enterprise's information and related technology support its business objectives, its resources are used responsibly and its risks are managed appropriately. These practices form a basis for direction of IT activities, which can be characterised as planning and organising, acquiring and implementing, delivering and supporting, and monitoring, for the dual purposes of managing risks (to gain security, reliability and compliance) and realising benefits (increasing effectiveness and efficiency). Reports are issued on the outcomes of IT activities, which are measured against the various practices and controls, and the cycle begins again.

IT Governance

In order to ensure that management reaches its business objectives, it must direct and manage IT activities to reach an effective balance between managing risks and realising benefits. To accomplish this, management needs to identify the most important activities to be performed, measure progress towards achieving goals and determine how well the IT processes are performing. In addition, it needs the ability to evaluate the organisation's maturity level against industry best practices and international standards. **To support these management needs, the COBIT *Management Guidelines* have identified specific Critical Success Factors, Key Goal Indicators, Key Performance Indicators and an associated Maturity Model for IT governance, as presented in Appendix 1.**

RESPONSE TO THE NEED

In view of these ongoing changes, the development of this framework for control objectives for IT, along with continued applied research in IT controls based on this framework, are cornerstones for effective progress in the field of information and related technology controls.

On the one hand, we have witnessed the development and publication of overall business control models like COSO (Committee of Sponsoring Organisations of the Treadway Commission—*Internal Control-Integrated Framework*, 1992) in the US, Cadbury in the UK, CoCo in Canada and King in South Africa. On the other hand,

an important number of more focused control models are in existence at the level of IT. Good examples of the latter category are the Security Code of Conduct from DTI (Department of Trade and Industry, UK), Information Technology Control Guidelines from CICA (Canadian Institute of Chartered Accountants, Canada), and the Security Handbook from NIST (National Institute of Standards and Technology, US). However, these focused control models do not provide a comprehensive and usable control model over IT in support of business processes. The purpose of COBIT is to bridge this gap by providing a foundation that is closely linked to business objectives while focusing on IT.

(Most closely related to CoBiT is the recently published *AICPA/CICA SysTrust™ Principles and Criteria for Systems Reliability.* SysTrust is an authoritative issuance of both the Assurance Services Executive Committee in the United States and the Assurance Services Development Board in Canada, based in part on the CoBiT *Control Objectives.* SysTrust is designed to increase the comfort of management, customers and business partners with the systems that support a business or a particular activity. The SysTrust service entails the public accountant providing an assurance service in which he or she evaluates and tests whether a system is reliable when measured against four essential principles: availability, security, integrity and maintainability.)

A focus on the business requirements for controls in IT and the application of emerging control models and related international standards evolved the original Information Systems Audit and Control Foundation's *Control Objectives* from an auditor's tool to CoBiT, a management tool. Further, the development of IT *Management Guidelines* has taken CoBiT to the next level–providing management with Key Goal Indicators (KGIs), Key Performance Indicators (KPIs), Critical Success Factors (CSFs) and Maturity Models so that it can assess its IT environment and make choices for control implementation and control improvements over the organisation's information and related technology.

Hence, the main objective of the CoBiT project is the development of clear policies and good practices for security and control in IT for worldwide endorsement by commercial, governmental and professional organisations. It is the goal of the project to develop these control objectives primarily from the business objectives and needs perspective. (This is compliant with the COSO perspective, which is first and foremost a management framework for internal controls.) Subsequently, control objectives have been developed from the audit objectives (certification of financial information, certification of internal control measures, efficiency and effectiveness, etc.) perspective.

AUDIENCE: MANAGEMENT, USERS AND AUDITORS

CoBiT is designed to be used by three distinct audiences.

MANAGEMENT:
to help them balance risk and control investment in an often unpredictable IT environment.

USERS:
to obtain assurance on the security and controls of IT services provided by internal or third parties.

AUDITORS:
to substantiate their opinions and/or provide advice to management on internal controls.

BUSINESS OBJECTIVES ORIENTATION

CoBiT is aimed at addressing business objectives. The control objectives make a clear and distinct link to business objectives in order to support significant use outside the audit community. Control objectives are defined in a process-oriented manner following the principle of business re-engineering. At identified domains and processes, a high-level control objective is identified and rationale provided to document the link to the business objectives. In addition, considerations and guidelines are provided to define and implement the IT control objective.

The classification of domains where high-level control objectives apply (domains and processes), an indication of the business requirements for information in that domain, as well as the IT resources primarily impacted by the control objectives, together form the CoBiT *Framework.* The *Framework* is based on the research activities that have identified 34 high-level control objectives and 318 detailed control objectives. The *Framework* was exposed to the IT industry and the audit profession to allow an opportunity for review, challenge and comment. The insights gained have been appropriately incorporated.

THE COBIT FRAMEWORK, *continued*

GENERAL DEFINITIONS

For the purpose of this project, the following definitions are provided. "Control" is adapted from the COSO Report (*Internal Control—Integrated Framework*, Committee of Sponsoring Organisations of the Treadway Commission, 1992) and "IT Control Objective" is adapted from the SAC Report (*Systems Auditability and Control Report*, The Institute of Internal Auditors Research Foundation, 1991 and 1994).

Control is defined as	the policies, procedures, practices and organisational structures designed to provide reasonable assurance that business objectives will be achieved and that undesired events will be prevented or detected and corrected.
IT Control Objective is defined as	a statement of the desired result or purpose to be achieved by implementing control procedures in a particular IT activity.
IT Governance is defined as	a structure of relationships and processes to direct and control the enterprise in order to achieve the enterprise's goals by adding value while balancing risk versus return over IT and its processes.

The diagram below illustrates CobiT's basic concept: in order to provide the information that the organisation needs to achieve its objectives, IT governance must be exercised by the organisation to ensure that IT resources are managed by a set of naturally grouped IT processes.

COBIT IT PROCESSES DEFINED WITHIN THE FOUR DOMAINS

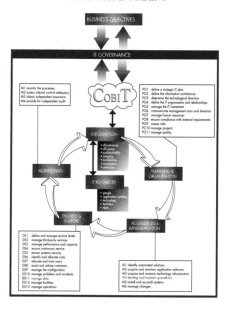

IT GOVERNANCE MANAGEMENT GUIDELINE

The following Management Guideline and Maturity Model identify the Critical Success Factors (CSFs), Key Goal Indicators (KGIs), Key Performance Indicators (KPIs) and Maturity Model for **IT governance.** First, IT governance is defined, articulating the business need. Next, the information criteria related to IT governance are identified. The business need is measured by the KGIs and enabled by a control statement, leveraged by all the IT resources. The achievement of the enabling control statement is measured by the KPIs, which consider the CSFs. The Maturity Model is used to evaluate an organisation's level of achievement of IT governance—from Non-existent (the lowest level) to Initial/Ad Hoc, to Repeatable but Intuitive, to Defined Process, to Managed and Measurable, to Optimised (the highest level). To achieve the Optimised maturity level for IT governance, an organisation must be at least at the Optimised level for the Monitoring domain and at least at the Managed and Measurable level for all other domains.

(See the COBIT *Management Guidelines* for a thorough discussion of the use of these tools.)

IT GOVERNANCE MANAGEMENT GUIDELINE

Governance over information technology and its processes with the business goal of adding value, while balancing risk versus return

ensures delivery of information to the business that addresses the required Information Criteria and is measured by Key Goal Indicators

> is enabled by *creating and maintaining a system of process and control excellence appropriate for the business that directs and monitors the business value delivery of IT*

considers Critical Success Factors that leverage all IT Resources and is measured by Key Performance Indicators

Information Criteria	IT Resources
effectiveness	people
efficiency	applications
confidentiality	technology
integrity	facilities
availability	data
compliance	
reliability	

Key Goal Indicators

- Enhanced performance and cost management
- Improved return on major IT investments
- Improved time to market
- Increased quality, innovation and risk management
- Appropriately integrated and standardised business processes
- Reaching new and satisfying existing customers
- Availability of appropriate bandwidth, computing power and IT delivery mechanisms
- Meeting requirements and expectations of the customer of the process on budget and on time
- Adherence to laws, regulations, industry standards and contractual commitments
- Transparency on risk taking and adherence to the agreed organisational risk profile
- Benchmarking comparisons of IT governance maturity
- Creation of new service delivery channels

Critical Success Factors

- IT governance activities are integrated into the enterprise governance process and leadership behaviours
- IT governance focuses on the enterprise goals, strategic initiatives, the use of technology to enhance the business and on the availability of sufficient resources and capabilities to keep up with the business demands
- IT governance activities are defined with a clear purpose, documented and implemented, based on enterprise needs and with unambiguous accountabilities
- Management practices are implemented to increase efficient and optimal use of resources and increase the effectiveness of IT processes
- Organisational practices are established to enable: sound oversight; a control environment/culture; risk assessment as standard practice; degree of adherence to established standards; monitoring and follow up of control deficiencies and risks
- Control practices are defined to avoid breakdowns in internal control and oversight
- There is integration and smooth interoperability of the more complex IT processes such as problem, change and configuration management
- An audit committee is established to appoint and oversee an independent auditor, focusing on IT when driving audit plans, and review the results of audits and third-party reviews.

Key Performance Indicators

- Improved cost-efficiency of IT processes (costs vs. deliverables)
- Increased number of IT action plans for process improvement initiatives
- Increased utilisation of IT infrastructure
- Increased satisfaction of stakeholders (survey and number of complaints)
- Improved staff productivity (number of deliverables) and morale (survey)
- Increased availability of knowledge and information for managing the enterprise
- Increased linkage between IT and enterprise governance
- Improved performance as measured by IT balanced scorecards

IT Governance Maturity Model

Governance over information technology and its processes with the business goal of adding value, while balancing risk versus return

0   **Non-existent** There is a complete lack of any recognisable IT governance process. The organisation has not even recognised that there is an issue to be addressed and hence there is no communication about the issue.

1   **Initial /Ad Hoc** There is evidence that the organisation has recognised that IT governance issues exist and need to be addressed. There are, however, no standardised processes, but instead there are ad hoc approaches applied on an individual or case-by-case basis. Management's approach is chaotic and there is only sporadic, non-consistent communication on issues and approaches to address them. There may be some acknowledgement of capturing the value of IT in outcome-oriented performance of related enterprise processes. There is no standard assessment process. IT monitoring is only implemented reactively to an incident that has caused some loss or embarrassment to the organisation.

2   **Repeatable but Intuitive** There is global awareness of IT governance issues. IT governance activities and performance indicators are under development, which include IT planning, delivery and monitoring processes. As part of this effort, IT governance activities are formally established into the organisation's change management process, with active senior management involvement and oversight. Selected IT processes are identified for improving and/or controlling core enterprise processes and are effectively planned and monitored as investments, and are derived within the context of a defined IT architectural framework. Management has identified basic IT governance measurements and assessment methods and techniques, however, the process has not been adopted across the organisation. There is no formal training and communication on governance standards and responsibilities are left to the individual. Individuals drive the governance processes within various IT projects and processes. Limited governance tools are chosen and

implemented for gathering governance metrics, but may not be used to their full capacity due to a lack of expertise in their functionality.

3   **Defined Process** The need to act with respect to IT governance is understood and accepted. A baseline set of IT governance indicators is developed, where linkages between outcome measures and performance drivers are defined, documented and integrated into strategic and operational planning and monitoring processes. Procedures have been standardised, documented and implemented. Management has communicated standardised procedures and informal training is established. Performance indicators over all IT governance activities are being recorded and tracked, leading to enterprise-wide improvements. Although measurable, procedures are not sophisticated, but are the formalisation of existing practices. Tools are standardised, using currently available techniques. IT Balanced Business Scorecard ideas are being adopted by the organization. It is, however, left to the individual to get training, to follow the standards and to apply them. Root cause analysis is only occasionally applied. Most processes are monitored against some (baseline) metrics, but any deviation, while mostly being acted upon by individual initiative, would unlikely be detected by management. Nevertheless, overall accountability of key process performance is clear and management is rewarded based on key performance measures.

4   **Managed and Measurable** There is full understanding of IT governance issues at all levels, supported by formal training. There is a clear understanding of who the customer is and responsibilities are defined and monitored through service level agreements. Responsibilities are clear and process ownership is established. IT processes are aligned with the business and with the IT strategy. Improvement in IT processes is based primarily upon a quantitative understanding and it is possible to monitor and measure compliance with procedures and process metrics. All process stakeholders are aware of risks, the importance of IT and the opportunities it can offer. Management has defined tolerances under which processes must operate. Action is taken in many, but not all cases where processes appear not to be working effectively or efficiently. Processes are occasionally improved and best internal practices are enforced. Root cause analysis is being standardised. Continuous improvement is beginning to be addressed. There is limited, primarily tactical, use of technology, based on mature techniques and enforced standard tools. There is involvement of all required internal domain experts. IT governance evolves into an enterprise-wide process. IT governance activities are becoming integrated with the enterprise governance process.

Optimised There is advanced and forward-looking understanding of IT governance issues and solutions. Training and communication is supported by leading-edge concepts and techniques. Processes have been refined to a level of external best practice, based on results of continuous improvement and maturity modeling with other organisations. The implementation of these policies has led to an organisation, people and processes that are quick to adapt and fully support IT

governance requirements. All problems and deviations are root cause analysed and efficient action is expediently identified and initiated. IT is used in an extensive, integrated and optimised manner to automate the workflow and provide tools to improve quality and effectiveness. The risks and returns of the IT processes are defined, balanced and communicated across the enterprise. External experts are leveraged and benchmarks are used for guidance. Monitoring, self-assessment and communication about governance expectations are pervasive within the organisation and there is optimal use of technology to support measurement, analysis, communication and training. Enterprise governance and IT governance are strategically linked, leveraging technology and human and financial resources to increase the competitive advantage of the enterprise.

COBIT 4.0 Executive Summary

Includes excerpts from the COBIT 4.0 Executive Summary.
Source: © 1996, 1998, 2000, 2005 IT Governance Institute (ITGI).
All rights reserved. Used by permission.

EXECUTIVE OVERVIEW

For many enterprises, information and the technology that supports it represent their most valuable, but often least understood, assets. Successful enterprises recognise the benefits of information technology and use it to drive their stakeholders' value. These enterprises also understand and manage the associated risks, such as increasing regulatory compliance and critical dependence of many business processes on IT.

The need for assurance about the value of IT, the management of IT-related risks and increased requirements for control over information are now understood as key elements of enterprise governance. Value, risk and control constitute the core of IT governance.

IT governance is the responsibility of executives and the board of directors, and consists of the leadership, organisational structures and processes that ensure that the enterprise's IT sustains and extends the organisation's strategies and objectives.

Furthermore, IT governance integrates and institutionalises good practices to ensure that the enterprise's IT supports the business objectives. IT governance thus enables the enterprise to take full advantage of its information, thereby maximising benefits, capitalising on opportunities and gaining competitive advantage. These outcomes require a framework for control over IT that fits with and supports the Committee of Sponsoring Organisations of the Treadway Commission (COSO) *Internal Control—Integrated Framework*, the widely accepted control framework for enterprise governance and risk management, and similar compliant frameworks.

Organisations should satisfy the quality, fiduciary and security requirements for their information, as for all assets. Management should also optimise the use of available IT resources, including applications, information, infrastructure and people. To discharge these responsibilities, as well as to achieve its objectives, management should understand the status of its enterprise architecture for IT and decide what governance and control it should provide.

Control Objectives for Information and related Technology (COBIT®) provides good practices across a domain and process framework and presents activities in a manageable and logical structure. COBIT's good practices represent the consensus of experts. They are strongly focused on control and less on execution. These practices will help optimise IT-enabled investments, ensure service delivery and provide a measure against which to judge when things do go wrong.

For IT to be successful in delivering against business requirements, management should put an internal control system or framework in place. The COBIT control framework contributes to these needs by:
• Making a link to the business requirements
• Organising IT activities into a generally accepted process model
• Identifying the major IT resources to be leveraged
• Defining the management control objectives to be considered

The business orientation of COBIT consists of linking business goals to IT goals, providing metrics and maturity models to measure their achievement, and identifying the associated responsibilities of business and IT process owners.

The process focus of COBIT is illustrated by a process model, which subdivides IT into 34 processes in line with the responsibility areas of plan, build, run and monitor, providing an end-to-end view of IT. Enterprise architecture concepts help identify those resources essential for process success, i.e., applications, information, infrastructure and people.

In summary, to provide the information that the enterprise needs to achieve its objectives, IT resources need to be managed by a set of naturally grouped processes.

But how does the enterprise get IT under control such that it delivers the information the enterprise needs? How does it manage the risks and secure the IT resources on which it is so dependent? How does the enterprise ensure that IT achieves its objectives and supports the business?

First, management needs control objectives that define the ultimate goal of implementing policies, procedures, practices and organisational structures designed to provide reasonable assurance that:
• Business objectives are achieved.
• Undesired events are prevented or detected and corrected.

Second, in today's complex environments, management is continuously searching for condensed and timely information to make difficult decisions on risk and control quickly and successfully. What should be measured, and how? Enterprises need an objective measure of where they are and where improvement is required, and they need to implement a management tool kit to monitor this improvement. **Figure 1** shows some traditional questions and the management information tools used to find the responses, but these dashboards need indicators, scorecards need measures and benchmarking needs a scale for comparison.

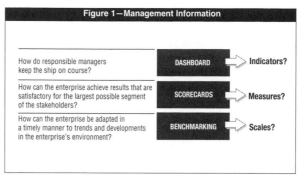

Figure 1—Management Information

How do responsible managers keep the ship on course?	DASHBOARD	Indicators?
How can the enterprise achieve results that are satisfactory for the largest possible segment of the stakeholders?	SCORECARDS	Measures?
How can the enterprise be adapted in a timely manner to trends and developments in the enterprise's environment?	BENCHMARKING	Scales?

An answer to these requirements of determining and monitoring the appropriate IT control and performance level is CobiT's definition of specific:
• **Benchmarking** of IT process capability expressed as maturity models, derived from the Software Engineering Institute's Capability Maturity Model
• **Goals and metrics** of the IT processes to define and measure their outcome and performance based on the principles of Robert Kaplan and David Norton's balanced business scorecard
• **Activity goals** for getting these processes under control, based on CobiT's detailed control objectives

The assessment of process capability based on the CobiT maturity models is a key part of IT governance implementation. After identifying critical IT processes and controls, maturity modelling enables gaps in capability to be identified and demonstrated to management. Action plans can then be developed to bring these processes up to the desired capability target level.

CobiT thus supports IT governance (**figure 2**) by providing a framework to ensure that:
• IT is aligned with the business
• IT enables the business and maximises benefits
• IT resources are used responsibly
• IT risks are managed appropriately

Performance measurement is essential for IT governance. It is supported by CobiT and includes setting and monitoring measurable objectives of what the IT processes need to deliver (process outcome) and how they deliver it (process capability and performance). Many surveys have identified that the lack of transparency of IT's cost, value and risks is one of the most important drivers for IT governance. While the other focus areas contribute, transparency is primarily achieved through performance measurement.

Figure 2—IT Governance Focus Areas

• **Strategic alignment** focuses on ensuring the linkage of business and IT plans; on defining, maintaining and validating the IT value proposition; and on aligning IT operations with enterprise operations.
• **Value delivery** is about executing the value proposition throughout the delivery cycle, ensuring that IT delivers the promised benefits against the strategy, concentrating on optimising costs and proving the intrinsic value of IT.
• **Resource management** is about the optimal investment in, and the proper management of, critical IT resources: applications, information, infrastructure and people. Key issues relate to the optimisation of knowledge and infrastructure.
• **Risk management** requires risk awareness by senior corporate officers, a clear understanding of the enterprise's appetite for risk, understanding of compliance requirements, transparency about the significant risks to the enterprise, and embedding of risk management responsibilities into the organisation.
• **Performance measurement** tracks and monitors strategy implementation, project completion, resource usage, process performance and service delivery, using, for example, balanced scorecards that translate strategy into action to achieve goals measurable beyond conventional accounting.

These IT governance focus areas describe the topics that executive management needs to address to govern IT within their enterprises. Operational management uses processes to organise and manage ongoing IT activities. COBIT provides a generic process model that represents all the processes normally found in IT functions, providing a common reference model understandable to operational IT and business managers. The COBIT process model has been mapped to the IT governance focus areas (see appendix II), providing a bridge between what operational managers need to execute and what executives wish to govern.

To achieve effective governance, executives expect controls to be implemented by operational managers within a defined control framework for all IT processes. COBIT's IT control objectives are organised by IT process; therefore, the framework provides a clear link among IT governance requirements, IT processes and IT controls.

COBIT is focused on what is required to achieve adequate management and control of IT, and is positioned at a high level. COBIT has been aligned and harmonised with other, more detailed, IT standards and best practices (see appendix IV). COBIT acts as an integrator of these different guidance materials, summarising key objectives under one umbrella framework that also links to governance and business requirements.

COSO (and similar compliant frameworks) is generally accepted as the internal control framework for enterprises. COBIT is the generally accepted internal control framework for IT.

The COBIT products have been organised into three levels (**figure 3**) designed to support:
- Executive management and boards
- Business and IT management
- Governance, assurance, control and security professionals

Primarily of interest to executives is:
- *Board Briefing on IT Governance, 2nd Edition*—Designed to help executives understand why IT governance is important, what its issues are and what their responsibility is for managing it

Primarily of interest to business and technology management is:
- *Management Guidelines*—Tools to help assign responsibility, measure performance, and benchmark and address gaps in capability. The guidelines help provide answers to typical management questions: How far should we go in controlling IT, and is the cost justified by the benefit? What are the indicators of good performance? What are the key management practices to apply? What do others do? How do we measure and compare?

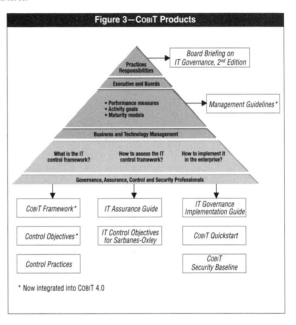

Figure 3—COBIT Products

Board Briefing on IT Governance, 2nd Edition

Management Guidelines*

* Now integrated into COBIT 4.0

Primarily of interest to governance, assurance, control and security professionals are:
- *Framework*—Explaining how COBIT organises IT governance objectives and best practices by IT domains and processes, and links them to business requirements
- *Control objectives*—Providing generic best practice management objectives for all IT activities
- *Control Practices*—Providing guidance on why controls are worth implementing and how to implement them
- *IT Assurance Guide*—Providing a generic audit approach and supporting guidance for audits of all COBIT's IT processes
- *IT Control Objectives for Sarbanes-Oxley*—Providing guidance on how to ensure compliance for the IT environment based on the COBIT control objectives
- *IT Governance Implementation Guide*—Providing a generic road map for implementing IT governance using the COBIT resources and a supporting tool kit
- COBIT *Quickstart*™—Providing a baseline of control for the smaller organisation and a possible first step for the larger enterprise
- COBIT *Security Baseline*™—Focusing the organisation on essential steps for implementing information security within the enterprise

All of these COBIT components interrelate, providing support for the governance, management, control and audit needs of the different audiences, as shown in **figure 4**.

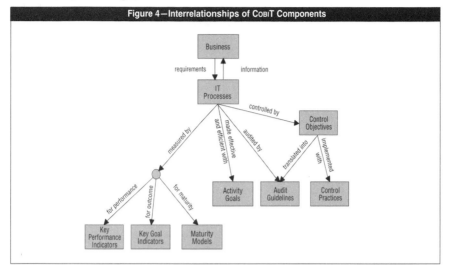

Figure 4—Interrelationships of COBIT Components

COBIT is a framework and supporting toolset that allow managers to bridge the gap with respect to control requirements, technical issues and business risks, and communicate that level of control to stakeholders. COBIT enables the development of clear policy and good practice for IT control throughout enterprises. COBIT is continuously kept up to date and harmonised with other standards. Hence, COBIT has become the integrator for IT best practices and the umbrella framework for IT governance that helps in understanding and managing the risks and benefits associated with IT. The process structure of COBIT and its high-level business-oriented approach provide an end-to-end view of IT and the decisions to be made about IT.

The benefits of implementing COBIT as a governance framework over IT include:
• Better alignment, based on a business focus
• A view, understandable to management, of what IT does
• Clear ownership and responsibilities, based on process orientation
• General acceptability with third parties and regulators
• Shared understanding amongst all stakeholders, based on a common language
• Fulfillment of the COSO requirements for the IT control environment

The rest of this document provides a description of the COBIT framework, and all of the core COBIT components organised by COBIT's IT domains and 34 IT processes. This provides a handy reference book for all of the main COBIT guidance. Several appendices are also provided as useful references.

Implementation is supported by a number of ISACA/ITGI products including online tools, implementation guides, reference guides and educational materials. The latest information on these products can be found at *www.isaca.org/cobit*.

Source: © 1996, 1998, 2000, 2005 IT Governance Institute (ITGI). All rights reserved. Used by permission.

FRAMEWORK

COBIT FRAMEWORK

THE NEED FOR A CONTROL FRAMEWORK FOR IT GOVERNANCE

Why

Increasingly, top management is realising the significant impact that information can have on the success of the enterprise. Management expects heightened understanding of the way information technology (IT) is operated and the likelihood of its being leveraged successfully for competitive advantage. In particular, top management needs to know if information is being managed by the enterprise so that it is:
• Likely to achieve its objectives
• Resilient enough to learn and adapt
• Judiciously managing the risks it faces
• Appropriately recognising opportunities and acting upon them

Successful enterprises understand the risks and exploit the benefits of IT, and find ways to deal with:
• Aligning IT strategy with the business strategy
• Cascading IT strategy and goals down into the enterprise
• Providing organisational structures that facilitate the implementation of strategy and goals
• Creating constructive relationships and effective communications between the business and IT, and with external partners
• Measuring IT's performance

Enterprises cannot deliver effectively against these business and governance requirements without adopting and implementing a governance and control framework for IT to:
• Make a link to the business requirements
• Make performance against these requirements transparent
• Organise its activities into a generally accepted process model
• Identify the major resources to be leveraged
• Define the management control objectives to be considered

Furthermore, governance and control frameworks are becoming a part of IT management best practice and are an enabler for establishing IT governance and complying with continually increasing regulatory requirements.

IT best practices have become significant due to a number of factors:
• Business managers and boards demanding a better return from IT investments, i.e., that IT delivers what the business needs to enhance stakeholder value
• Concern over the generally increasing level of IT expenditure
• The need to meet regulatory requirements for IT controls in areas such as privacy and financial reporting (e.g., the Sarbanes-Oxley Act, Basel II) and in specific sectors such as finance, pharmaceutical and healthcare
• The selection of service providers and the management of service outsourcing and acquisition
• Increasingly complex IT-related risks such as network security
• IT governance initiatives that include adoption of control frameworks and best practices to help monitor and improve critical IT activities to increase business value and reduce business risk
• The need to optimise costs by following, where possible, standardised rather than specially developed approaches
• The growing maturity and consequent acceptance of well-regarded frameworks such as COBIT, ITIL, ISO 17799, ISO 9001, CMM and PRINCE2
• The need for enterprises to assess how they are performing against generally accepted standards and against their peers (benchmarking)

Who

A governance and control framework needs to serve a variety of internal and external stakeholders each of whom has specific needs:
- Stakeholders within the enterprise who have an interest in generating value from IT investments:
  - Those who make investment decisions
  - Those who decide about requirements
  - Those who use the IT services
- Internal and external stakeholders who provide the IT services:
  - Those who manage the IT organisation and processes
  - Those who develop capabilities
  - Those who operate the services
- Internal and external stakeholders who have a control/risk responsibility:
  - Those with security, privacy and/or risk responsibilities
  - Those performing compliance functions
  - Those requiring or providing assurance services

What

To meet the previous requirements, a framework for IT governance and control should meet the following general specifications:
- Provide a business focus to enable alignment between business and IT objectives.
- Establish a process orientation to define the scope and extent of coverage, with a defined structure enabling easy navigation of content.
- Be generally acceptable by being consistent with accepted IT best practices and standards and independent of specific technologies.
- Supply a common language with a set of terms and definitions that are generally understandable by all stakeholders.
- Help meet regulatory requirements by being consistent with generally accepted corporate governance standards (e.g., COSO) and IT controls expected by regulators and external auditors.

HOW Cobit MEETS THE NEED

In response to the needs described in the previous section, the Cobit framework was created with the main characteristics of being business-focused, process-oriented, controls-based and measurement-driven.

Business-focused

Business orientation is the main theme of Cobit. It is designed to be employed not only by IT service providers, users and auditors, but also, and more important, as comprehensive guidance for management and business process owners.

The Cobit framework is based on the following principle (**figure 5**): to provide the information that the enterprise requires to achieve its objectives, the enterprise needs to manage and control IT resources using a structured set of processes to deliver the required information services.

The Cobit framework provides tools to help ensure alignment to business requirements.

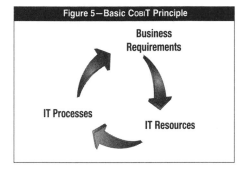

Figure 5—Basic Cobit Principle

Business Requirements

IT Processes

IT Resources

Cobit'S INFORMATION CRITERIA

To satisfy business objectives, information needs to conform to certain control criteria, which Cobit refers to as business requirements for information. Based on the broader quality, fiduciary and security requirements, seven distinct, certainly overlapping, information criteria are defined as follows:
- Effectiveness deals with information being relevant and pertinent to the business process as well as being delivered in a timely, correct, consistent and usable manner.
- Efficiency concerns the provision of information through the optimal (most productive and economical) use of resources.
- Confidentiality concerns the protection of sensitive information from unauthorised disclosure.
- Integrity relates to the accuracy and completeness of information as well as to its validity in accordance with business values and expectations.
- Availability relates to information being available when required by the business process now and in the future. It also concerns the safeguarding of necessary resources and associated capabilities.
- Compliance deals with complying with those laws, regulations and contractual arrangements to which the business process is subject, i.e., externally imposed business criteria, as well as internal policies.
- Reliability relates to the provision of appropriate information for management to operate the entity and exercise its fiduciary and governance responsibilities.

BUSINESS GOALS AND IT GOALS

While information criteria provide a generic method for defining the business requirements, defining a set of generic business and IT goals provides a business-related and more refined basis for establishing business requirements and developing the metrics that allow measurement against these goals. Every enterprise uses IT to enable business initiatives and these can be represented as business goals for IT. Appendix I provides a matrix of generic business goals and IT goals and how they map to the information criteria. These generic examples can be used as a guide to determine the specific business requirements, goals and metrics for the enterprise.

If IT is to successfully deliver services to support the enterprise's strategy, there should be a clear ownership and direction of the requirements by the business (the customer) and a clear understanding of what needs to be delivered and how by IT (the provider). **Figure 6** illustrates how the enterprise strategy should be translated by the business into objectives for its use of IT-enabled initiatives (the business goals for IT). These objectives in turn should lead to a clear definition of IT's own objectives (the IT goals), and then these in turn define the IT resources and capabilities (the enterprise architecture for IT) required to successfully execute IT's part of the enterprise's strategy. All of these objectives should be expressed in business terms meaningful to the customer, and this, combined with an effective alignment of the hierarchy of objectives, will ensure that the business can confirm that IT is likely to support the enterprise's goals.

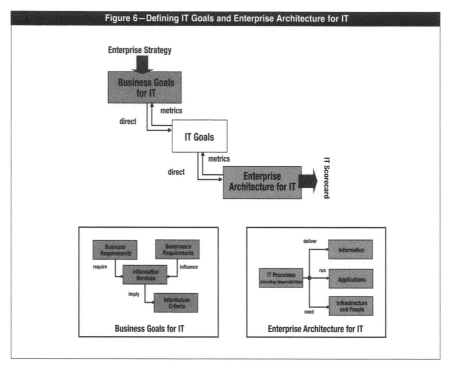

Figure 6—Defining IT Goals and Enterprise Architecture for IT

Once the aligned goals have been defined, they need to be monitored to ensure that actual delivery matches expectations. This is achieved by metrics derived from the goals and captured in an IT scorecard that the customer can understand and follow and that enables the provider to focus on its own internal objectives.

Appendix I provides a global view of how generic business goals relate to IT goals, IT processes and information criteria. The tables help demonstrate the scope of COBIT and the overall business relationship between COBIT and business drivers.

IT RESOURCES
The IT organisation delivers against these goals by a clearly defined set of processes that use people skills and technology infrastructure to run automated business applications while leveraging business information. These resources, together with the processes, constitute an enterprise architecture for IT, as shown in **figure 6**.

To respond to the business requirements for IT, the enterprise needs to invest in the resources required to create an adequate technical capability (e.g., an enterprise resource planning system) to support a business capability (e.g., implementing a supply chain) resulting in the desired outcome (e.g., increased sales and financial benefits).

The IT resources identified in COBIT can be defined as follows:
• Applications are the automated user systems and manual procedures that process the information.
• Information is the data in all their forms input, processed and output by the information systems, in whatever form is used by the business.
• Infrastructure is the technology and facilities (hardware, operating systems, database management systems, networking, multimedia, etc., and the environment that houses and supports them) that enable the processing of the applications.
• People are the personnel required to plan, organise, acquire, implement, deliver, support, monitor and evaluate the information systems and services. They may be internal, outsourced or contracted as required.

Figure 7 summarises how the business goals for IT influence how the IT resources need to be managed by the IT processes to deliver IT's goals.

Figure 7—Managing IT Resources to Deliver IT Goals

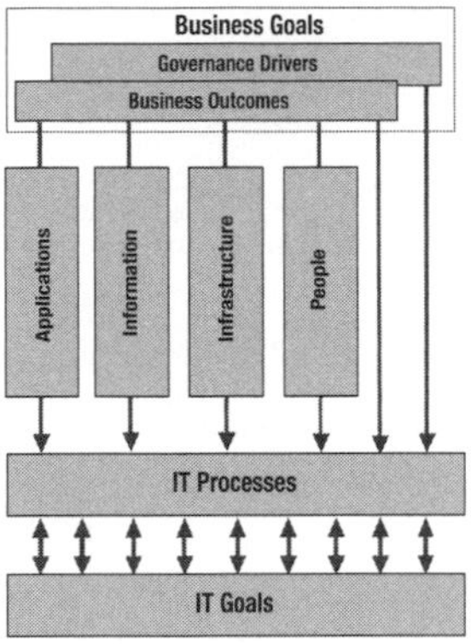

Process-oriented

COBIT defines IT activities in a generic process model within four domains. These domains are Plan and Organise, Acquire and Implement, Deliver and Support, and Monitor and Evaluate. The domains map to IT's traditional responsibility areas of plan, build, run and monitor.

The COBIT framework provides a reference process model and common language for everyone in an enterprise to view and manage IT activities. Incorporating an operational model and a common language for all parts of the business involved in IT is one of the most important and initial steps toward good governance. It also provides a framework for measuring and monitoring IT performance, communicating with service providers and integrating best management practices. A process model encourages process ownership, enabling responsibilities and accountability to be defined.

To govern IT effectively, it is important to appreciate the activities and risks within IT that need to be managed. These can be summarised as follows.

PLAN AND ORGANISE (PO)
This domain covers strategy and tactics, and concerns the identification of the way IT can best contribute to the achievement of the business objectives. Furthermore, the realisation of the strategic vision needs to be planned, communicated and managed for different perspectives. Finally, a proper organisation as well as technological infrastructure should be put in place. This domain typically addresses the following management questions:
• Are IT and the business strategy aligned?
• Is the enterprise achieving optimum use of its resources?
• Does everyone in the organisation understand the IT objectives?
• Are IT risks understood and being managed?
• Is the quality of IT systems appropriate for business needs?

ACQUIRE AND IMPLEMENT (AI)
To realise the IT strategy, IT solutions need to be identified, developed or acquired, as well as implemented and integrated into the business process. In addition, changes in and maintenance of existing systems are covered by this domain to make sure the solutions continue to meet business objectives. This domain typically addresses the following management questions:
• Are new projects likely to deliver solutions that meet business needs?
• Are new projects likely to be delivered on time and within budget?
• Will the new systems work properly when implemented?
• Will changes be made without upsetting current business operations?

DELIVER AND SUPPORT (DS)
This domain is concerned with the actual delivery of required services, which includes service delivery, management of security and continuity, service support for users, and management of data and the operational facilities. It typically addresses the following management questions:
• Are IT services being delivered in line with business priorities?
• Are IT costs optimised?
• Is the workforce able to use the IT systems productively and safely?
• Are adequate confidentiality, integrity and availability in place?

MONITOR AND EVALUATE (ME)
All IT processes need to be regularly assessed over time for their quality and compliance with control requirements. This domain addresses performance management, monitoring of internal control, regulatory compliance and providing governance. It typically addresses the following management questions:
• Is IT's performance measured to detect problems before it is too late?
• Does management ensure that internal controls are effective and efficient?
• Can IT performance be linked back to business goals?
• Are risk, control, compliance and performance measured and reported?

Controls-based

PROCESSES NEED CONTROLS
Control is defined as the policies, procedures, practices and organisational structures designed to provide reasonable assurance that business objectives will be achieved and undesired events will be prevented or detected and corrected.

An IT control objective is a statement of the desired result or purpose to be achieved by implementing control procedures in a particular IT activity. CoBiT's control objectives are the minimum requirements for effective control of each IT process.

Guidance can be obtained from the standard control model shown in **figure 8**. It follows the principles evident in this analogy: when the room temperature (standard) for the heating system (process) is set, the system will constantly check (compare) ambient room temperature (control information) and will signal (act) the heating system to provide more or less heat.

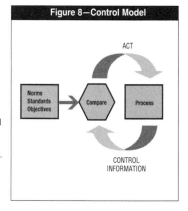

Figure 8—Control Model

Operational management uses processes to organise and manage ongoing IT activities. CoBiT provides a generic process model that represents all the processes normally found in IT functions, providing a common reference model understandable to operational IT and business managers. To achieve effective governance, controls need to be implemented by operational managers within a defined control framework for all IT processes. Since CoBiT's IT control objectives are organised by IT process, the framework provides clear links among IT governance requirements, IT processes and IT controls.

Each of CoBiT's IT processes has a high-level control objective and a number of detailed control objectives. As a whole, they are the characteristics of a well-managed process.

The detailed control objectives are identified by a two-character domain reference plus a process number and a control objective number. In addition to the detailed control objectives, each CoBiT process has generic control requirements that are identified by PCn, for Process Control number. They should be considered together with the detailed process control objectives to have a complete view of control requirements.

PC1 Process Owner
Assign an owner for each CoBiT process such that responsibility is clear.

PC2 Repeatability
Define each CoBiT process such that it is repeatable.

PC3 Goals and Objectives
Establish clear goals and objectives for each CoBiT process for effective execution.

PC4 Roles and Responsibilities
Define unambiguous roles, activities and responsibilities for each COBIT process for efficient execution.

PC5 Process Performance
Measure the performance of each COBIT process against its goals.

PC6 Policy, Plans and Procedures
Document, review, keep up to date, sign off on and communicate to all involved parties any policy, plan or procedure that drives a COBIT process.

Effective controls reduce risk, increase the likelihood of value delivery and improve efficiency because there will be fewer errors and a more consistent management approach.

In addition, COBIT provides examples for each process that are illustrative, but not prescriptive or exhaustive, of:
• Generic inputs and outputs
• Activities and guidance on roles and responsibilities in a RACI chart
• Key activity goals (the most important things to do)
• Metrics

In addition to appreciating what controls are required, process owners need to understand what inputs they require from others and what others require from their process. COBIT provides generic examples of the key inputs and outputs for each process including external IT requirements. There are some outputs that are input to all other processes, marked as 'ALL' in the output tables, but they are not mentioned as inputs in all processes, and typically include quality standards and metrics requirements, the IT process framework, documented roles and responsibilities, the enterprise IT control framework, IT policies, and personnel roles and responsibilities.

Understanding the roles and responsibilities for each process is key to effective governance. COBIT provides a RACI chart (who is Responsible, Accountable, Consulted and Informed) for each process. Accountable means 'the buck stops here'—this is the person who provides direction and authorises an activity. Responsibility means the person who gets the task done. The other two roles (consulted and informed) ensure that everyone who needs to be is involved and supports the process.

BUSINESS CONTROLS AND IT CONTROLS
The enterprise's system of internal controls impacts IT at three levels:
• At the executive management level, business objectives are set, policies are established and decisions are made on how to deploy and manage the resources of the enterprise to execute the enterprise strategy. The overall approach to governance and control is established by the board and communicated throughout the enterprise. The IT control environment is directed by this top-level set of objectives and policies.
• At the business process level, controls are applied to specific business activities. Most business processes are automated and integrated with IT application systems, resulting in many of the controls at this level being automated as well. These controls are known as application controls. However, some controls within the business process remain as manual procedures, such as authorisation for transactions, separation of duties and manual reconciliations. Controls at the business process level are, therefore, a combination of manual controls operated by the business, business controls and automated application controls. Both are the responsibility of the business to define and manage although the application controls require the IT function to support their design and development.
• To support the business processes, IT provides IT services, usually in a shared service to many business processes, as many of the development and operational IT processes are provided to the whole enterprise, and much of the IT infrastructure is provided as a common service (e.g., networks, databases, operating systems and storage). The controls applied to all IT service activities are known as IT general controls. The reliable operation of these general controls is necessary for reliance to be placed on application controls. For example, poor change management could jeopardise (by accident or deliberate act) the reliability of automated integrity checks.

IT GENERAL CONTROLS AND APPLICATION CONTROLS
General controls are those controls embedded in IT processes and services. Examples include:
• Systems development
• Change management
• Security
• Computer operations

Controls embedded in business process applications are commonly referred to as application controls. Examples include:
- Completeness
- Accuracy
- Validity
- Authorisation
- Segregation of duties

COBIT assumes the design and implementation of automated application controls to be the responsibility of IT, covered in the Acquire and Implement domain, based on business requirements defined using COBIT's information criteria. The operational management and control responsibility for application controls is not with IT, but with the business process owner.

IT delivers and supports the applications services and the supporting information databases and infrastructures.

Therefore, the COBIT IT processes cover general IT controls, but not application controls, because these are the responsibility of business process owners and, as described previously, are integrated into business processes.

The following list provides a recommended set of application control objectives identified by ACn, for Application Control number.

Data Origination/Authorisation Controls
AC1 Data Preparation Procedures
Data preparation procedures are in place and followed by user departments. In this context, input form design helps ensure that errors and omissions are minimised. Error-handling procedures during data origination reasonably ensure that errors and irregularities are detected, reported and corrected.

AC2 Source Document Authorisation Procedures
Authorised personnel who are acting within their authority properly prepare source documents and an adequate segregation of duties is in place regarding the origination and approval of source documents.

AC3 Source Document Data Collection
Procedures ensure that all authorised source documents are complete and accurate, properly accounted for and transmitted in a timely manner for entry.

AC4 Source Document Error Handling
Error-handling procedures during data origination reasonably ensure detection, reporting and correction of errors and irregularities.

AC5 Source Document Retention
Procedures are in place to ensure original source documents are retained or are reproducible by the organisation for an adequate amount of time to facilitate retrieval or reconstruction of data as well as to satisfy legal requirements.

Data Input Controls
AC6 Data Input Authorisation Procedures
Procedures ensure that only authorised staff members perform data input.

AC7 Accuracy, Completeness and Authorisation Checks
Transaction data entered for processing (people-generated, system-generated or interfaced inputs) are subject to a variety of controls to check for accuracy, completeness and validity. Procedures also assure that input data are validated and edited as close to the point of origination as possible.

AC8 Data Input Error Handling
Procedures for the correction and resubmission of data that were erroneously input are in place and followed.

Data Processing Controls
AC9 Data Processing Integrity
Procedures for processing data ensure that separation of duties is maintained and work performed is routinely verified. The procedures ensure that adequate update controls such as run-to-run control totals and master file update controls are in place.

AC10 Data Processing Validation and Editing
Procedures ensure that data processing validation, authentication and editing are performed as close to the point of origination as possible. Individuals approve vital decisions that are based on artificial intelligence systems.

AC11 Data Processing Error Handling
Data processing error-handling procedures enable erroneous transactions to be identified without being processed and without undue disruption of the processing of other valid transactions.

Data Output Controls
AC12 Output Handling and Retention
Handling and retention of output from IT applications follow defined procedures and consider privacy and security requirements.

AC13 Output Distribution
Procedures for the distribution of IT output are defined, communicated and followed.

AC14 Output Balancing and Reconciliation
Output is routinely balanced to the relevant control totals. Audit trails facilitate the tracing of transaction processing and the reconciliation of disrupted data.

AC15 Output Review and Error Handling
Procedures assure that the provider and relevant users review the accuracy of output reports. Procedures are also in place for identification and handling of errors contained in the output.

AC16 Security Provision for Output Reports
Procedures are in place to assure that the security of output reports is maintained for those awaiting distribution as well as those already distributed to users.

Boundary Controls
AC17 Authenticity and Integrity
The authenticity and integrity of information originated outside the organisation, whether received by telephone, voice mail, paper document, fax or e-mail, are appropriately checked before potentially critical action is taken.

AC18 Protection of Sensitive Information During Transmission and Transport
Adequate protection against unauthorised access, modification and misaddressing of sensitive information is provided during transmission and transport.

Measurement-driven

A basic need for every enterprise is to understand the status of its own IT systems and to decide what level of management and control the enterprise should provide.

Obtaining an objective view of an enterprise's own performance level is not easy. What should be measured and how? Enterprises need to measure where they are and where improvement is required, and implement a management tool kit to monitor this improvement.

To decide on what is the right level, management should ask itself: How far should we go and is the cost justified by the benefit?

COBIT deals with these issues by providing:
• Maturity models to enable benchmarking and identification of necessary capability improvements
• Performance goals and metrics for the IT processes, demonstrating how processes meet business and IT goals and are used for measuring internal process performance based on balanced scorecard principles
• Activity goals for enabling effective process performance

MATURITY MODELS

Senior managers in corporate and public enterprises are increasingly asked to consider how well IT is being managed. In response to this, business cases require development for improvement and reaching the appropriate level of management and control over the information infrastructure. While few would argue that this is not a good thing, they need to consider the cost-benefit balance and these related questions:
• What are our industry peers doing, and how are we placed in relation to them?
• What is acceptable industry best practice, and how are we placed with regard to these practices?
• Based upon these comparisons, can we be said to be doing enough?
• How do we identify what is required to be done to reach an adequate level of management and control over our IT processes?

It can be difficult to supply meaningful answers to these questions. IT management is constantly on the lookout for benchmarking and self-assessment tools in response to the need to know what to do in an efficient manner. Starting from COBIT's processes and high-level control objectives, the process owner should be able to incrementally benchmark against that control objective. This responds to three needs:
1. A relative measure of where the enterprise is
2. A manner to efficiently decide where to go
3. A tool for measuring progress against the goal

Maturity modelling for management and control over IT processes is based on a method of evaluating the organisation, so it can evaluate itself from a level of non-existent (0) to optimised (5). This approach is derived from the maturity model that the Software Engineering Institute defined for the maturity of software development capability. Whatever the model, the scales should not be too granular, as that would render the system difficult to use and suggest a precision that is not justifiable because, in general, the purpose is to identify where issues are and how to set priorities for improvements. The purpose is not to assess the level of adherence to the control objectives.

The maturity levels are designed as profiles of IT processes that an enterprise would recognise as descriptions of possible current and future states. They are not designed for use as a threshold model, where one cannot move to the next higher level without having fulfilled all conditions of the lower level. Using the maturity models developed for each of COBIT's 34 IT processes, management can identify:
• The actual performance of the enterprise—Where the enterprise is today
• The current status of the industry—The comparison
• The enterprise's target for improvement—Where the enterprise wants to be

To make the results easily usable in management briefings, where they will be presented as a means to support the business case for future plans, a graphical presentation method needs to be provided (**figure 9**).

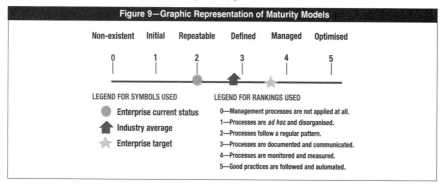

A maturity model has been defined for each of the 34 IT processes, providing an incremental measurement scale from 0, non-existent, through 5, optimised. The development was based on the generic maturity model descriptions shown in **figure 10**.

COBIT is a framework developed for IT process management with a strong focus on control. These scales need to be practical to apply and reasonably easy to understand. The topic of IT process management is inherently complex and subjective and is, therefore, best approached through facilitated assessments that raise awareness, capture broad consensus and motivate improvement. These assessments can be performed either against the maturity level descriptions as a whole or with more rigour against each of the individual statements of the descriptions. Either way, expertise in the enterprise's process under review is required.

Figure 10—Generic Maturity Model

0 Non-existent. Complete lack of any recognisable processes. The enterprise has not even recognised that there is an issue to be addressed.

1 Initial. There is evidence that the enterprise has recognised that the issues exist and need to be addressed. There are, however, no standardised processes; instead there are *ad hoc* approaches that tend to be applied on an individual or case-by-case basis. The overall approach to management is disorganised.

2 Repeatable. Processes have developed to the stage where similar procedures are followed by different people undertaking the same task. There is no formal training or communication of standard procedures, and responsibility is left to the individual. There is a high degree of reliance on the knowledge of individuals and, therefore, errors are likely.

3 Defined. Procedures have been standardised and documented, and communicated through training. It is, however, left to the individual to follow these processes, and it is unlikely that deviations will be detected. The procedures themselves are not sophisticated but are the formalisation of existing practices.

4 Managed. It is possible to monitor and measure compliance with procedures and to take action where processes appear not to be working effectively. Processes are under constant improvement and provide good practice. Automation and tools are used in a limited or fragmented way.

5 Optimised. Processes have been refined to a level of best practice, based on the results of continuous improvement and maturity modelling with other enterprises. IT is used in an integrated way to automate the workflow, providing tools to improve quality and effectiveness, making the enterprise quick to adapt.

The advantage of a maturity model approach is that it is relatively easy for management to place itself on the scale and appreciate what is involved if improved performance is needed. The scale includes 0 because it is quite possible that no process exists at all. The 0-5 scale is based on a simple maturity scale showing how a process evolves from a non-existent capability to an optimised capability.

However, process management capability is not the same as process performance. The required capability, as determined by business and IT goals, may not need to be applied to the same level across the entire IT environment, e.g., not consistently or to only a limited number of systems or units. Performance measurement, as covered in the next paragraphs, is essential in determining what the enterprise's actual performance is for its IT processes.

While a properly applied capability already reduces risks, an enterprise still needs to analyse the controls necessary to ensure risk is mitigated and value is obtained in line with the risk appetite and business objectives. These controls are guided by CobiT's control objectives. Appendix III provides a maturity model on internal control that illustrates the maturity of an enterprise relative to establishment and performance of internal control. Often this analysis is initiated in response to external drivers, but ideally it should be institutionalised as documented by CobiT processes PO6 *Communicate management aims and directions* and ME2 *Monitor and evaluate internal control.*

Capability, performance and control are all dimensions of process maturity as illustrated in **figure 11**.

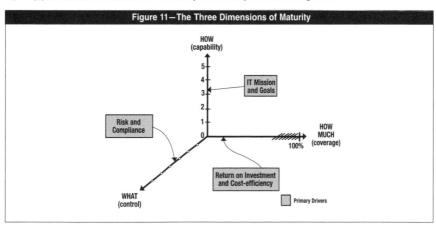

Figure 11—The Three Dimensions of Maturity

The maturity model is a way of measuring how well developed management processes are, i.e., how capable they actually are. How well developed or capable they should be primarily depends on the IT goals and the underlying business needs they support. How much of that capability is actually deployed largely depends on the return an enterprise wants from the investment. For example, there will be critical processes and systems that need more and tighter security management than others that are less critical. On the other hand, the degree and sophistication of controls that need to be applied in a process are more driven by the enterprise's risk appetite and applicable compliance requirements.

The maturity model scales will help professionals explain to managers where IT process management shortcomings exist and set targets for where they need to be. The right maturity level will be influenced by the enterprise's business objectives, the operating environment and industry practices. Specifically, the level of management maturity will depend on the enterprise's dependence on IT, its technology sophistication and, most important, the value of its information.

A strategic reference point for an enterprise to improve management and control of IT processes can be found by looking at emerging international standards and best-in-class practices. The emerging practices of today may become the expected level of performance of tomorrow and are therefore useful for planning where an enterprise wants to be over time.

The maturity models are built up starting from the generic qualitative model (see **figure 10**) to which principles from the following attributes are added in an increasing manner through the levels:
• Awareness and communication
• Policies, standards and procedures
• Tools and automation
• Skills and expertise
• Responsibility and accountability
• Goal setting and measurement

The maturity attribute table shown in **figure 12** lists the characteristics of how IT processes are managed and describes how they evolve from a non-existent to an optimised process. These attributes can be used for more comprehensive assessment, gap analysis and improvement planning.

In summary, maturity models provide a generic profile of the stages through which enterprises evolve for management and control of IT processes, and are:
• A set of requirements and the enabling aspects at the different maturity levels
• A scale where the difference can be made measurable in an easy manner
• A scale that lends itself to pragmatic comparison
• The basis for setting as-is and to-be positions
• Support for gap analysis to determine what needs to be done to achieve a chosen level
• Taken together, a view of how IT is managed in the enterprise

The COBIT maturity models focus on capability, but not necessarily on performance. They are not a number for which to strive, nor are they designed to be a formal basis for certification with discrete levels that create thresholds that are difficult to cross. However, they have been designed to be always applicable, with levels that provide a description an enterprise can recognise as best fitting its processes. The right level is determined by the enterprise type, its environment and strategy.

Performance, or how the capability is used and deployed, is a cost-benefit decision. For example, a high level of security management may have to be focused only on the most critical enterprise systems.

Finally, while higher levels of maturity increase control over the process, the enterprise still needs to analyse, based on risk and value drivers, which control mechanisms it should apply. The generic business and IT goals as defined in this framework will help with this analysis. The control mechanisms are guided by COBIT's control objectives and focus on what is done in the process; the maturity models primarily focus on how well a process is managed. Appendix III provides a generic maturity model showing the status of the internal control environment and the establishment of internal controls in an enterprise.

A properly implemented control environment is attained when all three aspects of maturity (capability, performance and control) have been addressed. Improving maturity reduces risk and improves efficiency, leading to fewer errors, more predictable processes and a cost-efficient use of resources.

Figure 12—Maturity Attribute Table

	Awareness and Communication	Policies, Standards and Procedures	Tools and Automation	Skills and Expertise	Responsibility and Accountability	Goal Setting and Measurement
1	Recognition of the need for the process is emerging. There is sporadic communication of the issues.	There are *ad hoc* approaches to process and practices. The process and policies are undefined.	Some tools may exist; usage is based on standard desktop tools. There is no planned approach to the tool usage.	Skills required for the process are not identified. A training plan does not exist and no formal training occurs.	There is no definition of accountability and responsibility. People take ownership of issues based on their own initiative on a reactive basis.	Goals are not clear and no measurement takes place.
2	There is awareness of the need to act. Management communicates the overall issues.	Similar and common processes emerge, but are largely intuitive because of individual expertise. Some aspects of the process are repeatable because of individual expertise, and some documentation and informal understanding of policy and procedures may exist.	Common approaches to use of tools exist but are based on solutions developed by key individuals. Vendor tools may have been acquired, but are probably not applied correctly, and may even be shelfware.	Minimum skill requirements are identified for critical areas. Training is provided in response to needs, rather than on the basis of an agreed plan, and informal training on the job occurs.	An individual assumes his/her responsibility, and is usually held accountable, even if this is not formally agreed. There is confusion about responsibility when problems occur and a culture of blame tends to exist.	Some goal setting occurs; some financial measures are established but are known only by senior management. There is inconsistent monitoring in isolated areas.
3	There is understanding of the need to act. Management is more formal and structured in its communication.	Usage of good practices emerges. The process, policies and procedures are defined and documented for all key activities.	A plan has been defined for use and standardisation of tools to automate the process. Tools are being used for their basic purposes, but may not all be in accordance with the agreed plan, and may not be integrated with one another.	Skill requirements are defined and documented for all areas. A formal training plan has been developed, but formal training is still based on individual initiatives.	Process responsibility and accountability are defined and process owners have been identified. The process owner is unlikely to have the full authority to exercise the responsibilities.	Some effectiveness goals and measures are set, but are not communicated, and there is a clear link to business goals. Measurement processes emerge, but are not consistently applied. IT balanced scorecard ideas are being adopted, as is occasional intuitive application of root cause analysis.
4	There is understanding of the full requirements. Mature communication techniques are applied and standard communication tools are in use.	Process is sound and complete; internal best practices are applied. All aspects of the process are documented and repeatable. Policies have been approved and signed off on by management. Standards for developing and maintaining the processes and procedures are adopted and followed.	Tools are implemented according to a standardised plan and some have been integrated with other related tools. Tools are being used in main areas to automate management of the process and monitor critical activities and controls.	Skill requirements are routinely updated for all areas, proficiency is ensured for all critical areas and certification is encouraged. Mature training techniques are applied according to the training plan and knowledge sharing is encouraged. All internal domain experts are involved and the effectiveness of the training plan is assessed.	Process responsibility and accountability are accepted and working in a way that enables a process owner to fully discharge his/her responsibilities. A reward culture is in place that motivates positive action.	Efficiency and effectiveness are measured and communicated and linked to business goals and the IT strategic plan. The IT balanced scorecard is implemented in some areas with exceptions noted by management and root cause analysis is being standardised. Continuous improvement is emerging.
5	There is advanced, forward-looking understanding of requirements. Proactive communication of issues based on trends exists, mature communication techniques are applied and integrated communication tools are in use.	External best practices and standards are applied. Process documentation is evolved to automated workflows. Processes, policies and procedures are standardised and integrated to enable end-to-end management and improvement.	Standardised toolsets are used across the enterprise. Tools are fully integrated with other related tools to enable end-to-end support of the processes. Tools are being used to support improvement of the process and automatically detect control exceptions.	The organisation formally encourages continuous improvement of skills, based on clearly defined personal and organisational goals. Training and education support external best practices and use of leading-edge concepts and techniques. Knowledge sharing is an enterprise culture and knowledge-based systems are being deployed. External experts and industry leaders are used for guidance.	Process owners are empowered to make decisions and take action. The acceptance of responsibility has been cascaded down throughout the organisation in a consistent fashion.	There is an integrated performance measurement system linking IT performance to business goals by global application of the IT balanced scorecard. Exceptions are globally and consistently noted by management and root cause analysis is applied. Continuous improvement is a way of life.

PERFORMANCE MEASUREMENT

Goals and metrics are defined in COBIT at three levels:
- IT goals and metrics that define what the business expects from IT (what the business would use to measure IT)
- Process goals and metrics that define what the IT process must deliver to support IT's objectives (how the IT process owner would be measured)
- Process performance metrics (to measure how well the process is performing to indicate if the goals are likely to be met)

COBIT uses two types of metrics: goal indicators and performance indicators. The goal indicators of the lower level become performance indicators for the higher level.

Key goal indicators (KGI) define measures that tell management—after the fact—whether an IT process has achieved its business requirements, usually expressed in terms of information criteria:
- Availability of information needed to support the business needs
- Absence of integrity and confidentiality risks
- Cost-efficiency of processes and operations
- Confirmation of reliability, effectiveness and compliance

Key performance indicators (KPI) define measures that determine how well the IT process is performing in enabling the goal to be reached. They are lead indicators of whether a goal will likely be reached or not, and are good indicators of capabilities, practices and skills. They measure the activity goals, which are the actions the process owner must take to achieve effective process performance.

Effective metrics should meet the following characteristics:
- A high insight-to-effort ratio (i.e., insight into performance and the achievement of goals as compared to effort to capture them)
- Be comparable internally (e.g., percent against a base or numbers over time)
- Be comparable externally irrespective of enterprise size or industry
- Better to have a few good metrics (may even be one very good one that could be influenced by different means) than a longer list of lower quality
- Should be easy to measure and should not be confused with targets

Figure 13 illustrates the relationship among process, IT and business goals, and among the different metrics, with examples from DS5 *Ensure systems security*.

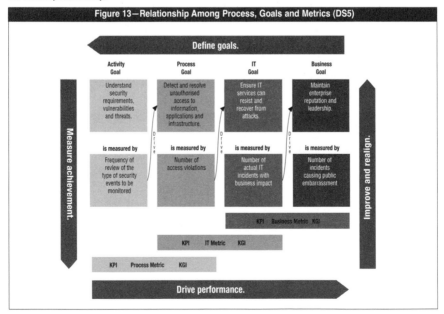

Figure 13—Relationship Among Process, Goals and Metrics (DS5)

Goals are defined top-down in that business goals will determine a number of IT goals to support them, IT goals will decide the different process goals needed, and each process goal will establish the activity goals. The achievement of goals is measured by outcome metrics (called key goal indicators, or KGIs) and drives the higher-level goal. For example, the metric that measured the achievement of the activity goal is a performance driver (called key performance indicator, or KPI) for the process goal. Metrics allow management to correct performance and realign with the goals.

The CobiT Framework Model

The CobiT framework, therefore, ties the businesses requirements for information and governance to the objectives of the IT services function. The CobiT process model enables IT activities and the resources that support them to be properly managed and controlled based on CobiT's control objectives, and aligned and monitored using CobiT's KGI and KPI metrics, as illustrated in **figure 14**.

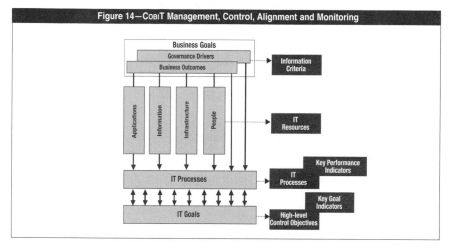

Figure 14—CobiT Management, Control, Alignment and Monitoring

To summarise, IT resources are managed by IT processes to achieve IT goals that respond to the business requirements. This is the basic principle of the CobiT framework, as illustrated by the CobiT cube (**figure 15**).

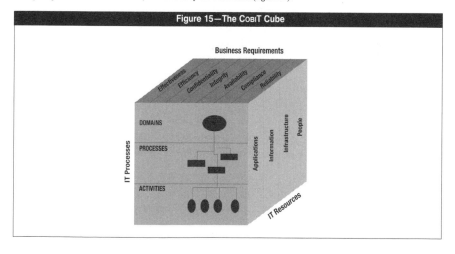

Figure 15—The CobiT Cube

In more detail, the overall CoBiT framework can be shown graphically as in **figure 16**, with CoBiT's process model of four domains containing 34 generic processes, managing the IT resources to deliver information to the business according to business and governance requirements.

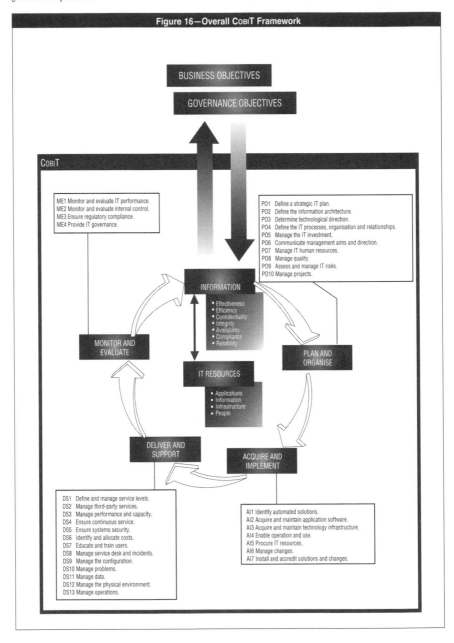

Figure 16—Overall CoBiT Framework

BUSINESS OBJECTIVES

GOVERNANCE OBJECTIVES

CoBiT

ME1 Monitor and evaluate IT performance.
ME2 Monitor and evaluate internal control.
ME3 Ensure regulatory compliance.
ME4 Provide IT governance.

PO1 Define a strategic IT plan.
PO2 Define the information architecture.
PO3 Determine technological direction.
PO4 Define the IT processes, organisation and relationships.
PO5 Manage the IT investment.
PO6 Communicate management aims and direction.
PO7 Manage IT human resources.
PO8 Manage quality.
PO9 Assess and manage IT risks.
PO10 Manage projects.

INFORMATION
• Effectiveness
• Efficiency
• Confidentiality
• Integrity
• Availability
• Compliance
• Reliability

MONITOR AND EVALUATE

PLAN AND ORGANISE

IT RESOURCES
• Applications
• Information
• Infrastructure
• People

DELIVER AND SUPPORT

ACQUIRE AND IMPLEMENT

DS1 Define and manage service levels.
DS2 Manage third-party services.
DS3 Manage performance and capacity.
DS4 Ensure continuous service.
DS5 Ensure systems security.
DS6 Identify and allocate costs.
DS7 Educate and train users.
DS8 Manage service desk and incidents.
DS9 Manage the configuration.
DS10 Manage problems.
DS11 Manage data.
DS12 Manage the physical environment.
DS13 Manage operations.

AI1 Identify automated solutions.
AI2 Acquire and maintain application software.
AI3 Acquire and maintain technology infrastructure.
AI4 Enable operation and use.
AI5 Procure IT resources.
AI6 Manage changes.
AI7 Install and accredit solutions and changes.

CobiT's General Acceptability

COBIT is based on the analysis and harmonisation of existing IT standards and best practices and conforms to generally accepted governance principles. It is positioned at a high level, driven by business requirements, covering the full range of IT activities, and concentrating on what should be achieved rather than how to achieve effective governance, management and control. Therefore, it acts as an integrator of IT governance practices and appeals to executive management; business and IT management; governance, assurance and security professionals; as well as IT audit and control professionals. It is designed to be complementary to, and used together with, other standards and best practices.

Implementation of best practices should be consistent with the enterprise's governance and control framework, be appropriate for the organisation, and be integrated with other methods and practices that are being used. Standards and best practices are not a panacea and their effectiveness depends on how they have been actually implemented and kept up to date. They are most useful when applied as a set of principles and as a starting point for tailoring specific procedures. To avoid practices becoming shelfware, management and staff should understand what to do, how to do it and why it is important.

To achieve alignment of best practice to business requirements, it is recommended that COBIT be used at the highest level, providing an overall control framework based on an IT process model that should generically suit every enterprise. Specific practices and standards covering discrete areas can be mapped up to the COBIT framework, thus providing a hierarchy of guidance materials.

COBIT appeals to different users:
• Executive management—To obtain value from IT investments and balance risk and control investment in an often unpredictable IT environment
• Business management—To obtain assurance on the management and control of IT services provided by internal or third parties
• IT management—To provide the IT services that the business requires to support the business strategy in a controlled and managed way
• Auditors—To substantiate their opinions and/or provide advice to management on internal controls

COBIT has been developed and is maintained by an independent, not-for-profit research institute, drawing on the expertise of its affiliated association's members, industry experts, and control and security professionals. Its content is based on continuous research into IT best practice and is continuously maintained, providing an objective and practical resource for all types of users.

COBIT is oriented toward the objectives and scope of IT governance, ensuring that its control framework is comprehensive, in alignment with enterprise governance principles and, therefore, acceptable to boards, executive management, auditors and regulators. In Appendix II, a mapping is provided showing how COBIT's detailed control objectives map onto the five focus areas of IT governance and the COSO control activities.

Figure 17 summarises how the various elements of the COBIT framework map onto the IT governance focus areas.

Figure 17—CobiT Framework and IT Governance Focus Areas				
	Goals	Metrics	Practices	Maturity Models
Strategic alignment	P	P		
Value delivery		P	S	P
Risk management		S	P	S
Resource management		S	P	P
Performance measurement	P	P		S

P=Primary enabler S=Secondary enabler

CobiT Framework Navigation

For each of the CobiT IT processes, a high-level control objective statement is provided, together with key goals and metrics in the form of a waterfall (**figure 18**).

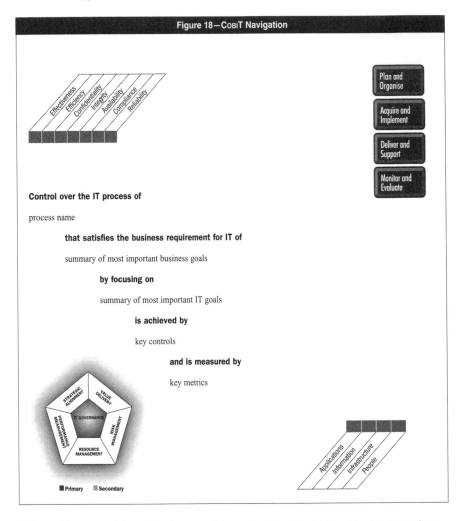

Figure 18—CobiT Navigation

Within each IT process, detailed control objectives are provided as generic action statements of the minimum management best practices to ensure the process is kept under control.

Index

sox institute
From the Sarbanes-Oxley Group

The only global provider of Sarbanes-Oxley professional certifications

Established just months after the passing of the SOX Act, the Institute is committed to establishing and encouraging best practices for Sarbanes-Oxley compliance, professionalism, knowledge, expertise and ethics.

With thousands of subscribers on all five continents, representing such diverse backgrounds as finance, accounting, IT, law, ethics and audit, the Institute is one of the largest and most active SOX communities.

TRAINING PROGRAMS

Guided Self-Study Programs

Compilation of the
Sarbanes-Oxley Body of Knowledge
(SOXBoK®)

Earn up to 48 CPE and PDU credits

Seminars and Workshops

- From Fundamentals to Advanced Topics
- With Practical Hands-On Case Studies
- Experienced Instructors and Trainers
- Job Placement Assistance Included

INDUSTRY ACCREDITATION

Earn Valuable CPE and PDU Credits from:

NASBA.ORG   PMIREP.ORG

CERTIFICATION PROGRAMS

SOXBase-level (CSOX®)

Exam based on the
Sarbanes-Oxley Body of Knowledge
(SOXBoK®)

Earn the "Certified in SOX" credential

SOXPro-level (CSOXP®)

- Sarbanes-Oxley Experience Evaluation
- Demonstrate Highest Level of Expertise
- Set Yourself Apart from the Crowd
- Become a "Certified SOX Professional"

INSTITUTE MEMBERSHIP

Become a Member Today and Receive …

- Free and discounted seminars, newsletters
- Discounts on Sarbanes-Oxley certifications
- Discounts on workshops/training programs
- Discounted entry to conferences and more
- Access to a global professional community